Input Devices

COMPUTER GRAPHICS—
TECHNOLOGY AND APPLICATIONS

Input Devices

Edited by

SOL SHERR

Westland Electronics Ltd.
Old Chatham, New York

ACADEMIC PRESS, INC.
Harcourt Brace Jovanovich, Publishers

Boston   San Diego   New York
Berkeley   London   Sydney
Tokyo   Toronto

ACADEMIC PRESS, INC.
1250 Sixth Avenue, San Diego, CA 92101

United Kingdom Edition published by
ACADEMIC PRESS, INC. (LONDON) LTD.
24–28 Oval Road, London NW1 7DX

Library of Congress Cataloging in Publication Data

Input devices.

  (Computer graphics—technology and applications ; 1)
  Bibliography: p.
  Includes index.
  Contents: Human factors considerations in the design and selection of computer input devices/Lynn Y. Arnaut and Joel S. Greenstein—Keyboards/Joel S. Greenstein and William H. Muto—Digitizers and input tables/Thomas E. Davies, H. Gerard Matthews, and Paul D. Smith—[etc.]
  1. Computer input-output equipment. I. Sherr, Sol. II. Series.

TK7887.5.I55   1987   004.7′6   87-12956
ISBN 0-12-639970-0

88 89 90 91   9 8 7 6 5 4 3 2 1
Printed in the United States of America

Contents

Contributors

Numbers in parentheses indicate the pages on which the author's contributions begin.

Lynn Y. Arnaut (71), Hewlett-Packard, Personal Office Computer Division, 974 E. Arques Avenue, Sunnyvale, CA 94086

N. S. Caswell (1), IBM T. J. Watson Research Center, Box 207, Yorktown Heights, NY 10598

Thomas E. Davies (179), Summagraphics Corporation, 777 State Street Extension, Fairfield, CT 06430

David Doran (251), Weston Controls, Archbald, PA 18403

Carl Goy (219), MSC Technologies, Inc., 2600 San Tomas Expressway, Santa Clara, CA 95051

Joel S. Greenstein (71, 123), Department of Industrial Engineering, Clemson University, Clemson, SC 29634-0920

H. Gerard Matthews (179), Summagraphics Corporation, 777 State Street Extension, Fairfield, CT 06430

William H. Muto (123), Texas Instruments, Inc., PO Box 225474, MS 8223, Dallas, TX 75265

Paul D. Smith (179), Summagraphics Corporation, 777 State Street Extension, Fairfield, CT 06430

Sam S. Viglione (271), Interstate Voice Products, 1849 West Sequoia Street, Orange, CA 92668

Preface

This is the first volume of the new series, "Computer Graphics — Technology and Applications," specifically concerned with the technologies used in equipment and systems for computer graphics and the applications for which computer graphics is intended. Although there are a number of volumes that deal with various aspects of computer graphics, none, to the editor's knowledge, concentrates on the actual equipment and the many technologies that are employed in the design of this equipment and the systems that result from the combinations of hardware and software that make up the operating systems. Thus, this series embodies a novel approach to the subject, and this volume, as well as the others planned and in preparation, provides information not readily available from any other sources. Therefore, this series should be of unique value as reference material to both designers and users of computer graphics equipment and systems.

This volume bears the general title of "Input Devices" and covers in considerable detail all of the popular examples of this type of device that are used in computer graphics systems. These range from the tried and true typewriter keyboard to the latest means for achieving data input as represented by such diverse units as the Mouse and Voice Input. The other types included in separate chapters are Data Input Panels in their various forms, such as Graphic Panels, Digitzers, and Touch Input Panels, and the combination of Joy Sticks and Track Balls has its own chapter as well. In addition, in the interest of a broad treatment of the general subject, an introductory chapter is provided that discusses and analyses the overall problems associated with the inputting of data, followed by another chapter on the human factors or ergonomic considerations involved. The Light Pen does not have a chapter of its own, but is discussed to a limited extent in the introductory chapter and elsewhere. Thus, all except perhaps the most specialized types are covered somewhere in the seven chapters contained in this volume.

Reviewing the chapter titles and sequence, Chapter 1 is termed "Introduction" and is written by N. S. Caswell, but it should be noted that I. F.

Chang was involved in the original planning and made significant contributions at that time, although he was unable to continue in a sufficiently active role to warrant inclusion as a co-author. As noted previously, this chapter is concerned with the general requirements for input devices and both analyzes and discusses the problems that must be surmounted.

Next comes the chapter devoted to the factors involved in selecting the best techniques for attaining acceptable input means by humans, appropriately titled "Human Factors Considerations" and written by L. T. Arnaut and J. S. Greenstein. This chapter provides extensive data on relative performance for the various devices and lists the advantages and disadvantages of each for this type of usage.

The third chapter, entitled "Keyboards," has as co-authors J. S. Greenstein and W. Muto. It deals with what is probably still the most ubiquitous of the input devices, and is the first chapter devoted exclusively to one specific class of device. It contains descriptions of hardware and discussions of various human factors considerations not covered in the previous chapter.

Chapter 4, authored by T. Davies, H. Matthews, and P. Smith, covers the different panel input devices that have become a popular means of allowing the user to interface with the computer graphics system. The major example of this type is the digitizer, and it is treated in considerable depth, but the graphics and touch panel types are not neglected. Design and performance considerations as well as representative operating parameters for the various types are presented here.

Chapter 5 by C. Goy is devoted to another popular input device, the mouse, which was first invented at Xerox and which has become widely accepted after it was adopted by Apple as the preferred unit for its highly successful Macintosh. Subsequent developments such as the optical version are covered in this chapter as well as the electrical characteristics and output formats.

Chapter 6 by D. Doran is about track balls and joy sticks, two types of input devices that have a long history of usage, but have not managed to attain a prominent position except in their low cost versions intended primarily for video games. It should be noted, however, that the mouse is essentially an upside down track ball, and the track ball should be credited as being the progenitor of that device.

Finally, Chapter 7 by S. S. Viglione is about voice input systems, a technique that has not fully achieved its potential as yet but shows considerable promise of doing so in the near future. Several different approaches to achieving the desired results of increases in vocabulary size and recognition of connected speech are described in this chapter and illustrated by specific instrumentations.

The net result of combining all of these chapters in a single volume is an up-to-date compendium of essentially all of the current types of input devices used in computer graphics systems, made available in a single publication that can be used for both education and reference. Subsequent volumes in this series will follow the same approach, with the second volume devoted to Output Hardcopy Devices, the third to Monitors, Projectors, and Work Stations, and later ones to Applications and Graphics Software. Other topics will be included in later volumes as they become relevant and the earlier volumes will be revised and reissued whenever sufficient new developments occur to make such action desirable.

Sol Sherr

1 Introduction to Input Devices

N. S. CASWELL

IBM T. J. Watson Research Center
Yorktown Heights, New York

1.1 Introduction

A data input system is the demarcation line between the real world of
objects and forces and the computer world of symbolic representations of
information. This chapter reviews the fundamental principles of interactive input systems, the components used in input systems, and the systems
themselves. The three major elements in any such discussion are:

- the user, a human being who wishes to accomplish some useful work on
  the computer system,
- the application program (referred to here simply as the application),
  which runs on the computer system to perform the work for the user,
  and
- the input system, which with the output system mediates the interaction
  between user and application.

Since the input systems are such an integral part of the information
processors they serve, and since the information is generally more important than the method by which it was obtained, the role of the input system
has often gone unnoticed and unexamined. This is changing as the computer moves out of the glass house and onto the desk top and factory floor.
For a glass house computer, another human being, the operator, programmer, or key punch specialist performs the primary interface function for
the principal user of an application. There is no intermediate between the

1

user and the system on the desk, so the system must enable the user to communicate effectively with the application.

Modern computers input information in two distinct ways. The first is interactive input obtained from a user. Such input consists of commands directing the flow of information and processing power and data on which to operate. Interactive input will be the focus of this book. The second type of input is direct input, where the user is dispensed with, and the processor senses and acts on the state of the physical world without human intervention. While the devices appropriate for the second type of input have much in common with interactive input devices, they will not be discussed explicitly here. The emphasis is solely on the methods of interaction between a human user and the machine.

The description and discussion of input systems to be covered here are at once very complex and very simple topics. Individual devices and systems are deceptively simple when considered in isolation. However, comparison of devices that accomplish the same end through widely different technical means requires a very broad consideration of the technical and engineering merits of the devices, the user interaction with the device, and the interaction both of the device and the user with the application. Furthermore, input systems are only a part of a larger system consisting of the real world, the user, the processor, and the output systems of the processor. While this is obvious, it causes a great deal of confusion. How much of the system is included in the discussion of input and which interaction (user/device, user/application, device/application) drives the discussion is a matter of purpose and taste.

One resolution to this confusion is a hierarchy of descriptions of the input system. The descriptive categories and design concerns useful at each hierarchical level fuse and transform at the next, allowing a coherent view of widely divergent viewpoints. The hierarchy to be used here is based on the sequence of quantities and operations that connect the user to the application. These are:

- the mechanical motion by the user,
- the electromechanical transducer imbedded in the input device, which converts the motion into an electrical signal,
- the converter, which converts the transducer signal to a digital form, and
- the processing performed on the digital data to transform the raw data into the digital codes used by the application.

The elements of this chain can be grouped together to form the transducer, device, and system views of the input system.

Focusing on the user-transducer interaction leads to consideration of the forces and motions required on the part of the user and the physics of the system (transducer) response. This viewpoint finds its best application in ergonomic studies, which also derive from viewing the input system as a whole.

Considering the transducer and converter as a unit leads to consideration of the input device. Categorization at this level depends on the mode of user interaction (pointing, pushing, or rotating, for example) and the digital result this produces but not necessarily on how it produces the result. Devices with essentially identical transducers (such as the trackball and rollerball mouse) can be very different from the device viewpoint, while devices with radically different transducers (such as the mechanical and optical mouse) are functionally identical. Categorization by device is by far the most common in the review literature (Parker, 1982; Kley, 1983; Vees, 1985; Potts, 1985; Nobbe, 1985) and, of course, has the advantage that the unit of discussion is the unit that can be purchased. It is important to realize, however, that it is a limited viewpoint that ignores the delicacies of the transducer implementation on one side and the requirements of the application on the other.

Inclusion of processing leads in two different directions. The first is a global view of the entire input system, discussed below. The second, which has a more direct relation to processing, is the notion of simple and complex devices.

The simple or complex distinction is based on the quantity of processing required to extract the desired information from the raw input data provided by a device. It is crudely quantified by the ratio of raw data bits collected to data bits delivered to the application. Simple devices have a low ratio, while complex devices have a high ratio. A keyboard is a simple device where each keystroke is delivered essentially unmodified to the application for a ratio of collected to delivered data very close to one.

In a vision or voice system, on the other hand, the situation is not as clear. These input devices typically collect large quantities of raw data. Data rates from video devices range from 10 million bytes per second to several hundred million bytes per second. (A typical image requires 10^6 bytes, give or take a factor of 10.) Digitization of a spoken word requires around a second of data collection at 20k/s (kilobytes per second). Simply recording, storing, and recalling these quantities of information requires a substantial amount of processor power. Input systems such as digital voice message forwarding, which do just this, have a low ratio, however, since what is collected is what is delivered. To perform the next step, extraction of information content, the processing requirement jumps considerably, as does the collected to delivered ratio. A voice recognition system reduces roughly 20k to something less than 2 bytes, for a ratio of 20,000 to 1. This is what is meant by a complex device.

The most global view groups everything between the user and the application into a single unit, the input system. Categorizations based on the intent of the system and cognitive content emerge from this view. Some very general observations can also be made from this vantage point, first, that there are a relatively few truly fundamental operations, pointing being one small but arguably complete set.

The second conclusion one immediately draws from this view is that the output channel is a very important component of the input channel, since effective input will depend on feedback of the results of that input. From the global conclusion, one quickly backtracks to realize that feedback occurs at every level in an input system. Many transducers incorporate mechanical feedback, such as the click of a keyboard switch or stylus pen down switch. Some devices provide feedback, such as an audible click, light flash, or other visible indication, as part of the device and independent of any processing. At the processing level, what is referred to as the input varies but normally breaks into two parts: feedback for every user operation as part of the input system and feedback for logical units of several user operations as feedback from the application.

Consider the two examples of inputting a command line with a keyboard and selecting a menu item with a mouse. The keyboard line entry consists of many individual input operations (key presses) that are individually fed back to the user by an immediate echo on the display. This echo is part of the input system processing, rather than part of the application. From the application point of view, the input does not occur with each key press operation but occurs when an entire line is available and the "ENTER" key is pressed. Similarly, the pointing selection by a mouse consists of many "Move One Step" inputs generated by the mouse motion and reflected in the cursor motion, while the application input is a code indicating which item was pointed to when a select button is pressed.

Even when the hierarchical level of discourse is agreed on, difficulties remain. Input systems are a prime example of a multidisciplinary field. Each section of this chapter reviews contributions from a specific field of inquiry, each with its own structuring of problems and view of what the problems are. The language (in the extreme case, jargon) used in one field may not coincide or may actively collide with the language used in another. This is perhaps the largest barrier to the effective description of input devices. The transducer maven must have an appreciation of the application philosophy and direction, while the application programmer must have a solid understanding of how devices operate and to what lengths they can be driven. One objective of this chapter is to collect some of the disparate elements of input device technology into one place to encourage this breadth of viewpoint.

This chapter is divided into five sections, three on individual elements of input systems and two on groupings of these elements. Note that the material in these sections is mutually interdependent, making a linear arrangement of sections problematic. Each depends on and supports the other sections:

Transducers. A transducer transforms information in one form into information in another form. The particularly interesting types of transducers are those that transform a mechanical motion into an electrical signal. Several forms of transducers appropriate to interactive computer input, the physics of their operations, their advantages and disadvantages, and some discussion of how they are applied are reviewed.

Converters. Data from transducers tend to be in inconvenient forms. The computer, for reasons of noise immunity and convenient, reproducible circuit operation, uses discrete, digital voltage levels to represent information, the most common method using one of two states, or binary digits. Information requiring more than two states to define is constructed by multiple occurrences of the two states either as a time sequence or by physically parallel wires. Transducers tend to produce (apparently) continuously variable analog outputs with distinct states represented by a voltage or current level, so translation of the voltage or current output of the transducer to digital form is required.

Processing. Processing converts the device output into a form convenient to the application. The boundaries of the input system are fuzzy, occurring somewhere between the input device and the application that uses the input. The flexible element in the boundary is the processing power required to extract the desired information from the raw data produced by the real device. The real device may produce a value in angle instead of directly in linear coordinates, as in the case of a triangulation device, or may produce a large bit map instead of a series of character codes.

Real Devices. The real device is what is most often thought of as the input device. These are the combinations of transducer and converter such as the light pen, tablet, touch screen, mouse, trackball, and joystick, along with their variants and permutations. Widely available devices are discussed, as well as some novel schemes that have not seen commercial application. The emphasis throughout is on the general principles on which such devices operate and that are applicable to classes of devices.

Man–Machine Interactions/Ergonomics. Ultimately, the user is not aware (or should not have to be aware) of the steps intermediate between his or her intents, and actions, and the input to the application. The input system, the application, and the output system should fade into the background as the interactive user pursues the problem at hand rather than the problem in his or her hand. There are two aspects to the question of man–machine interactions. The first takes a general view of input, considering the whole interface structure and its relation to human cognitive capabilities. The second explores interactions between users and particular devices, typically asking whether device A or device B requires less time to perform some task.

1.2 Man–Machine Interface

The logical structure, content, and implications of a general theory for user interfaces draws heavily on the fields of cognitive psychology and machine ergonomics. It is a lively, controversial field with varying opinions on every topic. This section will provide some definitions and a porthole into the literature rather than a complete description and review. The review by Foley et al. (1984) provides an excellent introduction.

In every application, alternatives are possible, some with philosophical advantages, some with elegant hardware, from among which the designer must choose. The critical factor, often overlooked in scholarly reviews and partisan promotion alike, is that input devices are not works of art, beautiful in their own right. They are practical gizmos whose form must follow their function. The commonsense questions, "Does it work?" and "Can the same function be obtained for less cost?" are of overriding concern, far exceeding the appropriateness of the device to a particular theory or marketing plan. The marketing plan does have the advantage that its success is in some measure dependent on the effective functioning of the device. One consequence of this fact is that much state-of-the-art information on user interface systems can be gleaned from the back pages of popular magazines and the user manuals of actual systems rather than from scholarly journals.

1.2.1 Empirical Characteristics of Input Systems

The design of the lexical level, the input device and its characteristics, is a cornerstone in the design of a successful application. It must smoothly link the goals or intentions of the user with the capabilities of the machine. There are several general considerations, independent of particular technologies, that go into the selection and design of an input system. These are empirical in nature and depend on functional utility rather than on theoretical elegance for justification.

A very useful concept of this type is the "imperative." The "ENTER" lexical element represents a class of elements with the special characteristics of causing something to happen at the application level. Single lexical elements with this characteristic will be referred to as "imperative elements." Typically, keyboards have a variety of imperative keys, often called function keys, in addition to the "ENTER" key. At least an "ENTER" key is required, however. The enter imperative is the punctuation that allows separation of strings of lexical elements into syntactical strings. Provision of such a lexical element becomes a concern with pointing devices such as a light pen or tablet where the interpretation of the lexical elements as data (positions) seems more natural than their interpretation as imperative elements. Furthermore, the lexical elements may be connected to each other in such a way that reaching the arbitrarily selected imperative element requires generating more data than the syntactical string requires. The straightforward resolution is to provide multiple devices, each with a particular function. In a light pen, for example, it is common to include a button, or other pen down detection, in an input channel distinct from the position data generated by the pen as an imperative element.

The operations that an input system needs to accomplish fall into well-defined categories. Bases on experience with graphics systems, Foley et al. (1984) have defined six things (interaction tasks) the input system may do:

- selection, of menu items or command lists by typing text or a label, using a direct stylus pick, a cursor match, or an on- or off-screen pushbutton;
- positioning, of a cursor using a continuous positioning device such as a tablet, mouse, joystick, trackball, light pen, or cursor keys;
- orienting, of an object in the display space;
- path, or describing a sequence of positions and orientations;
- quantification, of a variable, by physical devices such as dials or scales, simulated stopwatch, a variety of on-screen cursor controlled techniques, or direct type in; and
- text input.

While these were originated for graphics applications, they are appropriate for many text applications also. The one item that should be added to this list is

- association, of groups of display data, as in blocking areas of text for move or copy operations, or associating vectors (lines on a graphics display) into a higher level object.

In the sense that some of the items on this list can be accomplished by repeated application of others, pathing as a series of positions, for example, they are not primitive. However, because they are conceptually distinct, they do form a good basic set for designing an input system.

These interaction tasks allow interpretation of the semantic, syntactic, and lexical elements that accomplish them. The details of the mapping of this interpretation vary widely according to the taste of the designer and the technology available. Discussion of such mappings occurs (implicitly at times) in the section on real devices.

There are a few other general empirical observations that have become sufficiently ingrained and appear obvious. Chief among these is that there is a distinction between casual or naive users and continuous "power" users. Extensive use of menus, icons, help screens, and generally simple interactions are appropriate for the less experienced user while they impede the productivity of the more experienced user. Confusion about the intended user population for an application is the root of many debates over the slippery notion of "user friendliness." The conclusion is simply that the intended user must be kept in mind when designing the input system. There is no such thing as the typical user continually delighted by the one-size-fits-all, good-for-everything, interface. Delicate devices and complicated interfaces are not for public access terminals, while three-item menus and limited numbers of buttons (either as buttons or on touch screens) will soon drive the professional programmer to another system.

A closely related and widely held notion is that complicated applications, capable of a wide variety of operations, can be serviced by a simple, transparent, trivial-to-learn interface. This is, of course, false. Use of menus, single keystroke power commands, or speaker independent continuous speech recognition does not automatically help the user understand the intent and consequences of the commands or data issued to the application. The best an interface system can do is not make the application more subtle or complicated. Dangers lurk in forcing an interface structure based on a model of how interfaces should operate on an application unsuitable for it. The counterargument, that what is required is a sufficiently well developed theory of interfaces that can account for all existing applications reduces to triviality, since if one separately designs and optimizes an interface for each application, the union of all these interfaces becomes a description of the presumed general theory.

Mapping operations onto real devices is not a straightforward task because of the wide variety of building blocks available and the number of ways of combining them. Martin (1973) argues that there are three dangers to a good design of an input system represented by three advocates:

- The natural language advocate, who argues that every interaction with the computer must take place as between two old friends on the street corner. This is a very processing-intensive task, leaving the designer in the position of designing the application to fit the requirements of the input system rather than the other way around.

- The software advocate, who argues that the physical interface doesn't matter—the software can do it all. Like the natural language advocate, software requires processor resource. Advantages of a clean, obvious physical relation between action and data are lost by forcing whatever device is on hand into an inappropriate role.
- The hardware advocate, who goes to great lengths to engineer elegant but overdone devices. This is the opposite of the software advocate. Overspecialization of the hardware increases the cost and decreases the utility of a device.

1.2.2 Descriptive Language for User Interfaces

The purpose of any input system is to control an application, so it is useful to ask what the structure of an application is and how it can be controlled. The purpose of a theory of user interfaces is to describe how this is done and to provide a conceptual framework that makes existing devices and techniques comprehensible while providing the raw material for inventing new devices and techniques.

Algebraic Formalism for User Interfaces. This description of user interfaces draws on the terminology of abstract algebra (hence the heading) and formal logic theory to separate and define the parts of an application. It is also a base for more elaborate models of user interfaces, so will be described at length.

There are four levels of description:

- Interpretation
- Semantic
- Syntax
- Lexical.

The most general statement about a processing system is that it accepts input data, performs operations on that data, and produces output data. The user has an "interpretation" of these events in terms of mental constructs. For example, the hand calculator adds numbers to produce a sum. The notion of moving data from one location to another, as in a file copy operation, has a significance to the user independent of its implementation in an application. The interpretation is a human function by which meaning is attached to the various symbols and operations.

The collection of objects, relations between objects, and operations that can be performed on objects are collectively referred to as the semantics of the application. These are the primitive elements that are subject to interpretation. Typically, semantic elements can be broken up into data and operations (commands), although this is not a rigorous distinction (operations may in general operate on other operations). In most applications it is useful, however, particularly if the devices for command and data entry can be separated. The semantic elements of a four-function calculator are the digits 0 to 9 and the operations add, subtract, multiply, and divide. Note that at the semantic level these are symbols. The meaning is supplied by the interpretation. One common operation in both graphical and text processing systems is moving an object (a block of vectors or a portion of bit map) or text block from one place to another. The operation (MOVE) and the data (BLOCK) are semantic constructs of the language. They are words that may be combined to form complicated operations.

The syntax of an operation is the rules used to string semantic elements together. While the semantics of an algebraic and a reverse polish notation (RPN) calculator may be almost identical (the difference is in the (EQUAL) and (ENTER) elements), the syntax is very different. In the algebraic calculator two numbers are added by the sequence of semantic elements '2','+', '2','=' while in the RPN syntax this reads '2','Enter', '2','+'. If a text editing system has the semantic elements (BLOCK) to select a block, (LOCATION) for the location to move the block to, and (MOVE) for the command to move the block, then clearly these three can be issued in any order. It is often convenient to consider the input operation as consisting of entering a complete (and correct) syntactic expression, such as a line of text or command complete with parameters. While exercising this convenience in the discussion of input systems, it is important to bear in mind the distinction between the syntactical level and the lexical level.

The final level, the lexical level, is where the actual input device shows up (although each level is present in the input system). The lexical elements are the letters of the alphabet or the primitive physical operations available. At this level, the semantic elements and their syntactic structure are tied to particular operations on real devices. The semantic element '1' is normally produced on the calculator by pushing a button. It could also be selected by appropriate transducers by saying the word "one" or by orienting one's body to 15° east of north. Similarly, in the block move example, the block position, destination position, and move command could be typed at a keyboard, pointed to on a screen, selected from dedicated keys, or interpreted from sketching hand motions by the user.

All four levels are required to describe and evaluate the function of an input system. As pointed out above, it may be better to consider the input as a string of lexical elements followed by a command. The lexical string is considered as data at the semantic level and a special lexical element (the enter key on a keyboard or button on a mouse) is interpreted as a command to interpret the previous data as either a command or data. This has been discussed in the previous section in the context of the relationship between input devices and input systems. The device may be thought of as a producer of lexical elements. The processing adds the possibility of interpreting these in a variety of ways.

1.2.3 Interaction Models

There are a variety of attempts to describe theoretically what occurs during the user/application interaction. Two examples will be described here, one relying on a constructive formalism and the other on psychological description.

GOMS Rule Formalism.   Card et al. (1983) describe a constructive view of the user/machine interaction in terms of GOMS:

- goals,
- operations,
- methods, and
- selection rules.

Goals, like intentions, are what the user wishes to accomplish with the machine. The cyclical notion is not present, however, leading to a notion of goal structures for the goals and subgoals required to achieve the main goal. Operations are mental representations of the various functions an application is capable of. Methods are the device-specific information required to accomplish goals and subgoals. Selection rules are context-sensitive rules that allow picking the appropriate method when several are available. Kieras and Polson (1985) have presented a study of user interactions based on this formalism, with the added feature of formal analysis of the task to be performed using production rules. Production rules are statements of the form

IF (condition) THEN (action).

The result is a description of the goals and methods of the user, as conveyed by manuals, training, and untutored expectation, which can be compared to a formal description of the machine. As shown by Kieras and

Polson (1985), this detailed method can lead directly to inconsistencies in the interaction and less complex user interactions.

Cognitive Formalism. Norman (1984) describes the interaction between user and application from a cognitive point of view as involving four stages:

- intention,
- selection,
- execution, and
- evaluation.

The intention stage involves the user setting the goal of the interaction. It is a mental process that corresponds well with the interpretation level of the algebraic formalism. The user desires to move a thing from one place to another, for example. At this stage the user must know or be made aware of the possible types of operations the application is capable of, that is, it is a text editor, graphics drafting system, or compiler capable of certain types of operations.

The intention drives a selection. In one way or another the user must select the operation and data to operate on. In this formalism this is still a user function and does not imply typing the command. The user must know or be shown the possible operations and the possible data from which a selection is made. This corresponds in a rough sense to the transition from interpretation to semantics.

The user selection leads to execution, informing the application what to do by inputting a syntactically complete and correct statement. Execution could be typing in a command or positioning a cursor; the stage at which the actual input operation to the application takes place. At this stage the user must know or be informed of the details of how to manipulate the input devices (lexical elements).

Finally the result of the execution is evaluated to judge if the intended action took place. Evaluation closes the loop in that it allows the formation of new intentions based on the results of previous intentions.

This interaction model has a certain intuitive appeal in that it described the cyclical operation from the user point of view. In detailed application, it also becomes recursive. The intention of changing the order of paragraphs in a document involves selecting invocation of an editor, executing the command to start the editor, forming the intention to move a block of text, selecting how to move the block (if the syntax allows a choice about this), executing the command, and evaluating the result. It also provides the framework for stating that there are different types of information the user requires during the different stages.

1.2.4 Ergonomics

Ergonomics, often loosely referred to as human factors, describes on a mechanistic level the interaction between the human machine and processing machine. It can be thought of as optimizing the impedance match across the interface. Ideally, to achieve this match the human side must be specified and quantified to a degree comparable to the specification of the processor. The complexity of human beings makes this a difficult task. Ergonomics succeeds best in strictly mechanistic areas, such as matching the return force and travel of keyboard switches to the muscle characteristics of the human finger or stylus motion ranges to the range of motion at the elbow.

The most stringent limitation on input systems is the human user controlling them. There are two major bandwidth limitations of the human system, the amount of short-term memory available for recalling the state of the system and the rate at which physical motions can be executed. The amount of short-term storage seems to center on the magic number seven. While the differential sensitivity to changes in pitch, loudness, and illumination is high (on the order of 1 percent), only about seven levels of these quantities can be remembered for later comparison. Similarly, the number of names or random digits that can be remembered also is around seven. Interestingly, the size of each of the seven pieces of information can be large. Seven telephone numbers can be learned quickly if they are learned as patterns rather than strings of digits. The pattern is then decoded to obtain the number. (For an exposition of this and references to the original literature, see Martin (1973).) There are also limitations on how fast muscle motions can occur. The information content (from a measure too detailed to review here) in human motion ranges from four to seven bits per second (Knight and Dagnall, 1967). One way to view this number is that it will take at least a second for a random relocation of a finger on a 12×12 ($2^{3.5} \times 2^{3.5}$) array at a seven bit per second bandwidth. These limitations add up to what has been described as the input bandwidth diode (Thornburg, 1983), since information can be received from an application at rates far exceeding the input rate.

Most experimental ergonomic studies of input devices focus on the speed and accuracy of an individual device and tend to show that devices with comparable numbers of primitive input operations perform about the same function when compared using the criteria of speed and accuracy. It is tempting to conclude that the user can do whatever is (reasonably) required to operate a device and a simple measure distinguishing devices is how much motion is required, consistent with the bandwidth limitation on motion plus an overhead for multiple operations such as would be encountered in repeatedly pressing a key. One example of this is the comparison of light pens and keyboard cursor keys for cursor positioning tasks by Goodwin (1975). It was shown that the single operation of positioning the light pen was between two and five times faster (depending on the degree of correlation between adjacent selection points, which means the distance traveled to the next point) than the keyboard. The keyboard is operated by using several key presses (i.e., several primitive operations) to move the cursor.

Since the late 1970s, it has been recognized that the keyboard is not the best device for cursor positioning, based partly on the work of Card et al. (1978), who found the mouse to be the preferred device. Because of this, keyboards and positioning devices are not often directly compared in later references. One exception is the work by Karat et al. (1984), which actually finds the keyboard faster than the mouse for a mix of tasks. However, for cursor positioning tasks, positioning devices are comparable, while voice and keyboard seem comparable for those tasks assigned to them. A study by Haller et al. (1984) on devices for correction of typing errors exemplifies this statement. After comparing five locators (light pen, tablet, mouse, trackball, and voice recognition) and two correctors (keyboard and voice), the locator devices were ranked but closely grouped while the correctors were very similar. Other comparisons of voice and touch screen input (Crane, 1984) show little difference. On-screen and off-screen touch input does not significantly affect the speed and accuracy of the results (Whitfield et al., 1983), as would be expected by considering the similar motions involved and assuming that the motion was bandwidth limited by the human output rather than human input. (In other words, the user knows where to move faster than the move can be made.)

The notion of a simple measure of devices holds in several comparisons of keyboards. The long debate about the advantages of the Dvorak versus QWERTY keyboard layout leads to the conclusion that the keyboard layout makes little difference except in special cases where an arguable but small (up to 10 percent claimed) improvement in raw entry speed is significant. This is also true for the novice user where a random arrangement of keys works as well as any other. The effort measure works here, as ordered (alphabetic) layouts actually slow response time, since the user seems to perform two operations to find the key, first ascertaining its alphabetic order, then performing the same hunt and peck required for a random layout. Comparisons of various numeric pad layouts (calculator, telephone, cash register) also show small differences (Conrad and Hull, 1968; Seibel, 1972; Long, 1984; Goodman et al., 1985).

Voice also seems to be limited by human bandwidth. In a series of reports on voice for aircraft control applications (a complex, heavily loaded multifunction control environment), Curry et al. (1985) conclude that previously reported performance advantages for voice (Aretz, 1983; Curry, 1984) were the result of implementation factors. With suitable logic for controlling a manual system, "performance for both systems was essentially equal." This should be contrasted with claims of up to 50 percent improvements in "productivity" (Rabin, 1985). If further studies confirm the theme of minor performance differences between voice and manual input methods, it would suggest that the human bandwidth limitation is not in muscle flexing rates but in the cognitive processing required to decide what action is required.

One area where consistent distinctions between devices seem to emerge is in the high resolution positioning of a cursor. Epps and Snyder (1986) compare a trackball, optical mouse, absolute touch pad, relative touch pad, force joystick, and displacement joystick in a target acquisition task as a function of target size. There are modest differences in acquisition time for targets greater than 1 cm, ranging from 1.5 to 2.5 seconds. For 0.13 cm targets, this range expands to 2.5 to 6.0 seconds, with the mouse and trackball fastest, the absolute touch pad second (around 3.5 s), and the joysticks slowest. It is interesting to note that the times for acquisition of a 2 cm target were around 1 s. The data were taken on a 33 cm diagonal screen, which corresponds roughly to the 12 × 12 array mentioned earlier. Clearly, details intrude at the higher resolutions, since the scaling is not as one would naively predict. The bandwidth argument suggests the times should increase exponentially with decreasing target size. An alternate mechanism of sequential motions on finer scales (coming close with a large motion, then homing in with smaller motions) would predict a slower increase in time (as is observed) with decreasing target size. The distance dependence of the acquisition time was not strong, but again the mouse, trackball, and absolute touch pad were significantly faster at all distances. It has also been recognized that high speed, accurate entry of high resolution data may require the personalization of touch pads for the individual user (Beringer and Peterson, 1983).

Difficulties occur in application of these measurements to more general interaction questions like the relative utility of devices. The question changes from "Would the device work better if the user moved more or less?" to "Which device is a more efficient communication channel between the mind of the user and the application?" Real interaction situations are messy and hard to quantify. For one thing, the results of the second question are extremely dependent on the results of the first. The converse of this is that it is hard to apply the results of controlled limited variable experiments to the real situation. The result of experiments may be an apples-to-apples comparison of steaks. Often, too, the experiment may have a purpose other than to ask a question. As an example, consider the statement:

> These results must be viewed with the understanding that the subjects were novices with respect to voice input but were very experienced with keyboard input. In this light it can be seen that voice holds much promise as a mode of input for computer programming (Leggett and Williams, 1984)

that occurs in the abstract of a paper giving quantitative evidence that keyboard input was superior in speed for the defined task. The conclusion seems to be that a complicated, expensive system that is almost as good as the keyboard has a bright future. One wonders what could be achieved with a keyboard if the processing power required for voice recognition were harnessed.

While it is an abomination to discourage the collection of accurate, objective data, it is commensurately important that in complex interactive situations the data be carefully used. In the example given above, the point is not that voice does not have a future (which it does when it ceases to penalize the user who is "a novice with respect to voice input") but that care must be exercised in drawing conclusions from carefully objective data. It should also be remembered that the measurable quantities such as speed of accuracy of entry may not be the relevant criteria. This occurs on two levels. First, if the device is used with another device, a mouse with a keyboard, for example, the performance penalty involved in switching devices for parts of the task may outweigh the advantage of the faster device. Secondly, the interaction speed available may exceed the rate the user can generate data. This applies particularly well to keyboard entry other than retyping. The speed advantages of alternative layouts may be swamped by the time spent thinking what word to type next. These effects may be quantified, although the complexity involved in reaching generalized conclusions becomes formidable.

Perhaps the best strategy for such complex problems is that taken by Stammers and Bird (1980), who performed an "indelicate experiment" to judge the performance of a touch input system for air traffic control. The term was used since

> . . . the evaluation fell into the middle ground of system design, between "expert knowledge" and "controlled and lengthy experimentation." The major objective was to judge the opinions and attitudes of the controllers (Stammers and Bird, 1980).

Without drawing conclusions applicable to input systems everywhere, they established the efficacy of the test system for the intended application, along with areas for improvement. Currently this, along with some comments about time scales and bandwidths at which human users operate, is perhaps the best that can be achieved.

1.3 Transducers

Transducers convert the mechanical motion of the user into a usable form by measuring that motion. For some "computer" systems, the physical quantities may carry information directly, as in a mechanical analog computer. The position of the slide in a slide rule carries the information of one term in multiplication or division. While it is tempting to view this example as overly simple, the slide rule slide represents an excellent example of an input device. The state of the input device determines the state of the slide rule system and, in conjunction with the input for the other operand (the hairline cursor), completely determines the output state. Generally, however, the computer of interest is an electronic one that requires that the physical quantity measured be represented as a voltage, current, or resistance produced at the output of an electromechanical transducer. Electromechanical transducers are available to produce a wide variety of electrical outputs from an equally wide variety of mechanical inputs.

Given the variety of input devices and transducers applicable to those devices, the number of physical quantities that can be measured is astonishingly small. Recall that physics only requires units of length, mass, time, and the coupling strengths of the basic forces, of which only electric and magnetic fields are important for input applications.

The complexity derives from the multitude of methods for measuring these few quantities. Mechanical measurements rely on measurements of length and time, the desired quantity is usually some nonunique combination of these. Velocity, how fast the user moves a stylus, for example, is measured by the time derivative of position, dx/dt, where x is a measure of length, and t is the time. It can be obtained by measuring the time required to traverse a fixed distance or the distance traveled in a fixed time. Force, or how hard the user is pressing a touch screen, can be measured dynamically by Newton's law, $F = ma$, where m is a mass and a is an acceleration, the time derivative of velocity or measured statically by a displacement, which for an elastic material (such as a spring), is given by Hooke's law, $F = kx$, where k is a constant of the elastic material. The choice of measurement method determines a subset of possible transducers, and the choice of transducer determines many characteristics of the input device.

Note that while many transducers produce analog values where the transducer output is continuously related to the mechanical input, direct production of a digital value is also possible. Converters to transform the transducer output into a digital signal will be discussed in the next section, but the distinction between transducer and converter can be blurred. The fundamental operation in digitizing a measured quantity is threshold detection, which means determining whether the measured quantity is greater or less than some reference value. This function may be an intrinsic part of the transducer, as in the case of a switch or easily integrated with the transducer, as in the case of solid state transducers. A switch measures displacement and makes a contact if the displacement exceeds a threshold value. Another example is optical source detector pairs, where light from the source generates an electrical signal in the detector whose presence or absence may directly represents a digital signal.

The review presented here divides all transducers into three kinds:

- contact transducers, which rely on the mechanical contact between electrical elements,
- electromagnetic transducers, which rely on the modification of electric, magnetic, or optical fields, and
- solid state transducers, which rely on variations in the electrical properties of materials by mechanical means.

1.3.1 Contact Transducers

Switches. The simplest transducer is the switch, a transducer for the conversion of mechanical motion into a two-state electrical signal. The simplicity of its function contrasts dramatically with its usefulness and potential complexity of operation. While this section will focus on contact switches, many other types of transducers can be configured as switches including hall effect, optical, capacitive, and inductive devices.

Complex switch devices can be arranged in several ways. One of the simplest is a series of contacts around a shaft that contains a sliding contact, yielding a rotary switch. One common lead connects to one of N contacts as the shaft is rotated, resulting in a one of N selection. Multiple switches can be stacked on the same shaft so that entire code words are output at each switch position. Although seldom used as computer input devices, they provide a straightforward method of selecting from a small set of alternatives and have the distinct advantage of plainly displaying their position. An extension of the rotary switch, the position encoder, is discussed as a converter (of angular input to digital values) below.

A second arrangement is an array of switches. For small arrays each switch can be connected individually, but for larger arrays of switches, crosspoint arrays are typically used. These consist of a grid of conductors and a mechanical means of making a connection at the crosspoints of the

X and Y lines in the grid. Such arrays are the basis of many input devices, notably the keyboard and several types of position-sensitive devices. (These are discussed in Section 1.6 on real devices.)

The most serious problem common to all mechanical switches is contact bounce. When the two contacts are pressed together there will be a rebound, causing the switch to connect then disconnect several times. The cure is to use a redundant code. The switch has three states: connected in the off-state, connected in the on-state, and not connected. This is accomplished by a double-throw, single-pole switch and a RS latch with the set line connected to one side of the switch and the reset line connected to the other. When the on contact is closed, the latch sets. Setting it several times due to the contact bounce causes no harm; it is still set. The same operation takes place to reset the latch with the other set of contacts. A second alternative requiring only a single-pole, single-throw switch is to use the switch input to trigger a retriggerable single shot multivibrator. The first bounce triggers the multivibrator, which has a pulse length longer than the bounce period. Each bounce retriggers the multivibrator, keeping its output constant. If the multivibrator output is *or' ed* with the switch output, a debounced output is obtained. The typical bounce periods for small mechanical switches are in the 0.1 ms to 5 ms range. While adequately fast for single switch applications, the bouncing time may require extra precautions for switch arrays in which the state of each switch must be detected within a short time.

Resistive Transducers. The potentiometer or variable resistor is another very simple transducer. The primary advantages of variable resistance transducers are cost, ease of use, and wide availability in a multitude of forms. The essential mechanism is a mechanically positioned wiper, which is moved along a resistive medium. Commonly available devices have circular resistive elements with radial wipers on a rotary shaft, linear resistive elements with linear motion wipers, or linear resistive elements with rotary input driving wipers on a screw shaft. The quantity measured may be either a distance or an angle. For rotary devices the distance is the arc length and related to the angle by $d = r\theta$, where r is the radius of the circular resistive element. For a full circle, $\theta = 2\pi$, the distance is $d = 2\pi r$, which is the circumference. By using other mechanical arrangements various mappings of external onto internal motion can be obtained.

The primary constraint on allowable mechanisms is that the electrical connections to the wiper and resistive element must be insulated from each other, and preferably also from the mechanical mechanism. There are two methods of solving the wiper insulation issue. First, there can be in effect two wipers with one contacting the resistive element and another contacting a low-resistance conductor. Second, there can be a flexible connection between the wiper and the external connection. The first suffers from having two mechanical connections to degrade and the second from possible failure of the flexible lead.

While the linear variable resistors clearly come to a limit of travel, in the rotary case it is possible to rotate indefinitely in one direction. Ideally, a sharp transition from the maximum to the minimum resistance would occur once per revolution. However, the width of the wiper and the necessity of making contacts limits the active region to $\sim 355°$, so rotations of greater than 2π are better measured by multiple turn linear resistors. Exceptions to this occur when the desired quantity is not the total rotation but the angle within a single rotation.

By variation of the resistivity, ρ, of the resistive element as a function of distance, almost arbitrary mappings between input position and output resistance can be obtained. The resistance at the wiper is the integral resistance between its position and an end contact,

$$R(d) = \int_0^d \rho(x)dx \cdot$$ (1.1)

the distance dependence of the resistance is the derivative of the desired mapping,

$$\rho(d) = \frac{dR(x)}{dx}|_d \cdot$$ (1.2)

For example, a log taper pot has a resistance that varies like $1/d$. Variations in ρ as a function of distance can be achieved by varying the winding pitch for a wire wound resistor or varying the width or thickness of the resistive film. An example of the utility of a resistance mapping would be a rotary input device whose resistance was proportional to the sine of the angle rather than the angle, thus simplifying the processing required in a triangulation system.

1.3.2 Electrostatic and Electromagnetic Transducers

Capacitive (Electrostatic) Transducers. Capacitive or electrostatic transducers rely on flow of charges in conductors when the electric fields in their environment are changed. They have the distinct advantage that no electrical contact is required. Thus, problems of contamination and corrosion are avoided. Furthermore, in many applications to input devices, there are no moving parts to cause mechanical wear. The capacitance can be modulated by moving the conductors that make up the capacitor or moving the dielectric. The moving dielectric arrangement has an advantage over the moving conductor arrangement in that all the conductors are fixed so there are no sliding or flexing connections to wear or break.

The moving conductor variable capacitor varies either the area or separation between capacitor plates. For two parallel plates (disregarding edge effects), the capacitance is given by

$$C = \frac{\varepsilon A}{d} \tag{1.3}$$

where A is the area of the plate, ε is the dielectric constant of the space between the plates, and d is the separation between them. The area arrangement, as found in the rotating half plates of radio tuning input devices, is rare in input devices. Most moving conductor capacitive input devices modulate the separation of two plates. A (conceptually) simple example is the capacitive microphone, where the spacing between plates varies with the applied acoustic pressure. Very similar to the microphone is a type of capacitive touch panel where finger pressure deflects one electrode. Since the capacitance varies as $1/d$, sharp changes in capacitance can be obtained for small displacements. Note that the mobile conductor need not be mechanically attached to the other conductor. For example, it could be contained in a user-held stylus, which is used to select among several fixed electrodes. In such a transducer, both d and A, where A is understood as the overlap of the electrodes, would vary.

Modulating capacitance with a moving dielectric not only has the mechanical advantage of no sliding or flexing contacts, it has the distinct advantage that it may require no special stylus. The human body is over 70 percent water, which has a large dielectric constant, $\varepsilon = 78$, and inserting a water dielectric into a capacitor results in a factor of 78 increase in the capacitance. This is, however, better news for water level detectors than for input devices since the mechanics of inserting a finger as the only dielectric in a capacitor are formidable.

In real systems, a change in capacitance by a factor of two to ten is achievable using a finger as a dielectric. The reason for the factor smaller than 78 is straightforward. If the dielectric medium does not completely fill the space enclosed by a capacitor, the resultant combination may be viewed as two capacitors in series. For a parallel plate capacitor half filled with water, the capacitance is $C = 1.975 C_0$, where C_0 is the capacitance of the empty capacitor. The effect is very nearly that of moving one plate to the top of the high dielectric region and considering only the empty region. Because of the inconvenience of placing fingers inside a capacitor, capacitors whose fields extend outside the capacitor to a region accessible by fingers are used.

Two possibilities are a lateral capacitor and one where the top plate is smaller than the bottom plate so the fringing field extends above the plane. The latter case is difficult analytically although attractive practically. The capacitance of two parallel lines (a lateral capacitor) is (Smythe, 1968)

$$C = \frac{2\varepsilon K(k)}{K((1 - k^2)^{1/2})}, \; k = (ab)^{1/2}(a + c)^{-1/2}(b + c)^{-1/2} \qquad (1.4)$$

where $K(k)$ is a complete elliptic integral of modulus k, a and b are the widths of the strips, and c is the gap between them. Such devices tend to have very small capacitances (in the picoFarad range), so the spacings are made small to maximize the capacitance. This also means that the finger must be very close (on the order of the spacing) to effect a significant change in capacitance. Since spacings of thousandths of an inch are not in the control range of the unaided finger, these devices are only effective as switches that detect some threshold level, rather than as analog devices that produce multiple output states.

Capacitance changes can be converted into a usable signal in three basic ways: 1) by using the capacitance as a timing element in an oscillator or single shot multivibrator and detecting the output frequency or pulse width; 2) through the impedance modulation using a fixed frequency excitation; or 3) by detecting an injected signal.

Detection by changing the frequency of an oscillator requires the use of a notch (or spike) filter. When the frequency is pulled from the center value, output signal disappears (or appears). Such a circuit would suffer from alignment and drift problems, so a phase locked loop (PLL) detector would be a better solution. The detector produces an output voltage, which varies with the input frequency so the alignment problem reduces to setting threshold values.

In an impedance modulation scheme, the capacitor is placed in a voltage divider arrangement and the amplitude of the signal across one element is measured. Typically 10kHz to 100kHz excitation is used. The output is low pass filtered, so the response time is determined by the filter time constant, which should be 10 to 100 times the excitation frequency. This results in a typical response time from 1 to 10 ms, which is fast enough for a multiplexed array where multiple elements are connected to a single detector in turn.

The injection detection scheme relies on one electrode being mobile. If the two electrodes of a capacitor are remote, their capacitance will be very small. Thus, the current due to the injected signal will be very small. When the mobile electrode is close, the signal appears. The advantage of this scheme is that no frequency sensitive detection is required and the on/off ratio can be large. Notice that it does not matter which electrode, the mobile or the fixed, is excited.

A very useful implementation of the injection scheme is to detect the 60 Hz (or 50 Hz) noise signal coupled by the proximity of a finger. The fields due to the power distribution system generate a polarization charge that can, in turn, induce a charge on a probe plate. The effect is familiar to anyone who has touched an otherwise unconnected oscilloscope probe. Typically, a high input impedance CMOS gate is connected directly to a probe plate, such as the metal body of a lamp. Once each cycle, the gate output will change.

A continuous output can be obtained by exciting the trigger input of a retriggerable single shot multivibrator such as the HEF4528. If the timing components are chosen to be larger than one frequency period, the output will remain stable while the finger is in place. By making it longer than several periods, the bounce possible when the finger is placed and removed can be eliminated. A disadvantage of this scheme is that it relies on a low excitation frequency, making multiplexed sensing of several electrodes unacceptably slow (Phillips, 1979).

The relatively slow speed can be turned into a feature by connecting the probe to a counter circuit so that each cycle of the input increments the counter. By connecting two electrodes to an up/down counter, a combination equivalent to a variable resistor and analog to digital converter is formed (Istvan, 1980). If a short counter (say, three bits) is used, the eye cannot follow the output, and an effective random number generator (electronic dice) is formed (Heap, 1981).

Inductive (Magnetic) Transducers. Inductive or magnetic transducers rely on flow of charges in conductors induced by changes in the magnetic field in their environment. Like capacitive transducers, they have the advantage that no electrical contact is required, so problems of contact wear and corrosion are avoided. Unlike capacitive transducers, however, there are moving parts in most applications to input devices.

Several possible transducer configurations are possible. With a single inductor, the self inductance can be modulated, as capacitance is modulated, either by changing the geometry of the coil or inserting a permeable core. For single inductor transducers, the detection mechanisms mentioned for capacitive transducers can be used. In addition, systems with mutual inductance can be modulated by moving one coil relative to another or by modulating the permeability of the region between the coils. Unfortunately, while the finger has a very large dielectric constant, its permeability is indistinguishable from free space so inductive transducers must either use a movable permeable member or rely on relative motion of the coils. Permanent magnets also can be used, but this reduces to the mutual inductance case where a constant excitation current is placed on one coil.

Most inductive transducers used in practice are of the mutual inductance type. These amount to variable transformers where the coupling is typically measured by injecting an AC signal into one coil while measuring the response in the other. Details of the coupling become mathematically complex even for rather simple geometries. (Extensive tables for calculation of mutual inductances are given by Grover (1962).)

One geometry of particular interest is the mutual inductance between a long straight wire and a small loop (MKS units). From Grover (1962) we obtain

$$L_{1,2} = 4\pi(c\sec\alpha - (c^2\sec^2\alpha - \alpha^2)^{1/2}) \times 10^{-7}, c > a$$

$$L_{1,2} = 4\pi c \tan\left(\frac{\pi}{4} - \frac{\alpha}{2}\right) \times 10^{-7}, c < a \qquad (1.5)$$

where a is the loop radius, c is the normal distance from the loop center to the wire, and α is the acute angle between the plane of the loop and the plane defined by its center and the wire. (If the wire was imbedded in a planar tablet and the loop wound around the circumference of a stylus, α would be $\pi/4$ (90°) for the pen normal to the surface. In this case, $L_{1,2} = 4\pi c \times 10^{-7}$ for $c < a$). The most useful feature of this system is that the sign of $L_{1,2}$ changes sign as the coil moves from one side of the straight wire to the other, with the coupling going to zero when the loop is centered over the wire. Because the zero crossing allows for some degree of signal independence in detecting when a probe coil is over a wire, this is a very attractive transducer for position input tablets. By sensing the coupling between two wires a known distance apart, less than the loop diameter, the coupling constant can be eliminated and the loop position between the wires obtained independent of signal level. Furthermore, while the coil is over the wire, the mutual inductance varies linearly with the distance c. This is only approximated in practical situations though, since if the loop is contained in a stylus held at a constant angle to a tablet surface (rather than relative to the plane formed by the wire and the center of the loop), the angle α will be a function of c.

Optical Transducers. Optical transducers consist of a source of light, a transmission path through which the light travels, and a detector that measures the quantity of light that reaches it. The detector in an optical transducer may measure a change in light from the source or a change in light due to modulation in the transmission path. The simplest form of this is the source/detector pair, which yields one state if the transmission path from source to detector is unbroken and another if it is. Box counters on an assembly line or intruder detectors in security systems are devices of this type. It gives relatively crude position information; something blocks the beam or it does not. The same source detector pair is useful in a reflective mode also, where it measures the amount of light reflected from an object. The single bit of information obtained from a source/detector pair can be parlayed into complex multiple bit devices by scanning, multiplexing, and modulating.

Like inductive and capacitive transducers, optical transducers have no mechanical contacts to corrode or wear. However, while inductive and capacitive types are susceptible to electromagnetic interference, optical transducers are not. This can be a significant advantage in high noise environments. The electrical generation and detection circuits are, of course, still susceptible, but since these need not be accessible by the user they can be shielded. One environment where this is a great benefit is close to cathode ray tubes (CRTs). In a high resolution CRT, high field, high frequency sources abound in the deflection circuits, in the dynamic focus circuits, and in some cases in the beam energy itself. The chief disadvantage of optical transducers is contamination of the optical path by environmental contaminants such as dust and spilled coffee. A particularly bad environment for this is the CRT, where the high electrostatic potential of the faceplate charges, attracts, and collects dust.

Detectors.   While there are a wide variety of light sources applicable to input devices, the almost universal choice for detector is the silicon photodiode or phototransistor. When photons of sufficient energy (in the visible or near infrared spectral range) impinge on a semiconductor, they generate electron-hole pairs. These electrons and holes appear in the external circuit as a current. The normal way to utilize these photo-induced charges is by measuring the induced current in a photodiode or using the charge injected into the base of a phototransistor to control the device. There are two ways to bias photodiodes to detect the photocurrent. One method is to reverse bias the diode and amplify the generated photocurrent with a low input impedance amplifier. In this configuration, the photodiode is effectively short-circuited and the amplifier output is linear in the optical flux. The second alternative, useful when a large range of input intensities is expected, is to operate the diode open circuit with no bias. The voltage measured with a high input impedance amplifier depends on the logarithm of the optical flux.

The silicon photodetector comes in a variety of shapes and sizes. There are two basic diode electrical configurations, the PN junction diode and the PIN diode in which an intrinsic layer is included between the P and N layers. The effect of the undoped intrinsic layer is to reduce the leakage current and junction capacitance resulting in a very low noise, very high speed detector. Typical sensitivities are in the range 0.1 to $0.5\mu A/\mu W$

(microamps per microwatt) at a wavelength of 770 nm. This corresponds to a quantum efficiency of around 0.7 electrons per incident photon. Leakage current determines the minimum detectable signal, and these range from several μA for large area PN junction diodes to as little as $0.15nA$ for small PIN diodes. Device speed depends strongly on the junction capacitance and can range from 100kHz for large area devices to 1GHz. For most input applications, neither the speed nor the sensitivity are limiting factors. Since few input systems operate in the dark, the significant limitation is resolving the desired signal from stray room light.

Multiple photodiodes can be fabricated in linear or square arrays to obtain spatial information (images) from the incident flux. Such circuits contain analog shift registers (the CCD, or charge coupled device) that allow collection and readout of the photoinduced charge. Arrays of up to 2048 elements are commercially available, with arrays of fewer elements available in quantity at low cost.

For input applications, one very interesting variant of the photodiode is the position sensitive photodiode based on the lateral photoeffect. In this device, contacts are placed at either end of a long junction region and the relative current flowing to each contact due to a point illumination measured to determine the position of the incident flux. Both linear and angular position sensitive devices have been reported (Xing and Boeder, 1985). Unlike the diode array, which measures the optical flux simultaneously at each spatial position, the lateral photoeffect diode requires a single source of light. The light source is small compared to the device dimensions. For systems that only require the location of a single point, however, it has the advantage of being a significantly simpler device with comparable or higher resolution.

Sources. Sources of light for optical detectors are characterized by several numbers:

- the spectral distribution (fraction of total power in a wavelength range $\delta\lambda$),
- the emitted energy density, in photons per second, or energy per second per unit area (Watts/meter^2),
- the angular distribution of the emitted light, and
- the energy conversion efficiency or ratio of electrical power into optical power out.

There are two basic kinds of spectral distributions, thermal and nonthermal. In the thermal case, the emission parameters are determined from Planck's law of black-body radiation. The peak emission wavelengths

(λ_{max}) for a body at a temperature T are given by

$$\lambda_{max}T = 0.2898 \; cm \; K. \tag{1.6}$$

For temperatures around 2500 K, tungsten emits roughly 5 percent of its radiation in the visible region, with a peak wavelength in the micrometer (near infrared) region. Since the electrical power in must be balanced by the radiated power out (if the hot filament is well insulated, as it is in a typical vacuum light bulb), a 10 W light bulb produces roughly 0.5 W of optical power.

For nonthermal emitters, the spectral range is a function of the atomic processes producing the radiation and the method used to excite them. They range from $< 1 \; nm$ bandwidth for lasers and some line emission phosphors to several hundred nm. Nonthermal emitters include:

- CRT phosphors excited by the CRT electron beam,
- fluorescent lamp phosphors excited by ultraviolet radiation from a gas discharge in the lamp,
- light emitting diodes (LEDs) excited by the current density in the active region, and
- lasers with a variety of excitation mechanisms.

Energy conversion efficiencies for nonthermal emitters of 10 percent (from electrical energy input to optical energy output) are good but may be as low as a few hundredths of a percent.

1.3.3 Solid State Transducers

This class of transducers relies on the coupling of properties of solid state materials with external forces and fields in some user controllable manner. There are two basic types, those that depend on external electromagnetic fields, Hall effect, and magneto resistive elements, for example, and those that depend on coupling of the electromagnetic field with the elastic properties of the material. Piezoelectric (electrostrictive), magnetostrictive, and piezoresistive (strain gauge) transducers are of this type. The physics by which these devices operate will not be described here. For further information and applications to input devices, see Norton (1969), Cooper and Brignell (1985), Lian and Middlehoek (1986).

1.4 Converters

Information from the transducer often is represented as a voltage or current level that must be converted into a digital value for further processing. This section reviews circuits used for this purpose.

1.4.1 Timing/Counters

The measurement of time, either as the probing independent variable or the resulting dependent variable, lies at the heart of many input systems. The distinction between independent and dependent time measurements can be shown by considering a velocity measurement. With time as the independent variable, velocity is calculated from the ratio of the distance traveled to a fixed time. With time as the dependent variable, it is calculated as the ratio of a fixed distance to the time required to traverse that distance. The former requires a source of constant time and a method to measure a variable distance, while the latter requires a constant distance and a method to measure a variable time. As this example shows, it is often easier to fix the mechanical parameters of a system and rely on a measurement of time. Note that generation of a fixed interval is also a measurement of time that has much in common with the measurement of a variable interval.

Irrespective of the source of time unit information, counting the number of units in an interval is the basic method of measuring time. The wheel and escapement clock can be thought of as a counter counting the number of pendulum swings. In digital systems, the transitions of an oscillator (clock) are counted. The clock signal need not be a known frequency or even regular. Frequency meters operate by computing the ratio of the counts in two counters, one clocked at a constant rate and the other at the unknown frequency to be measured. Typically, the known frequency is allowed to accumulate to a value that makes calculation of the ratio particularly simple, such as 1 second. One-thousand counts in the variable counter would then indicate a frequency of 1 kHz.

Counters are intrinsically digital devices, so the number of available states, their precision and accuracy are easily obtainable. The number of states for a binary counter is 2^N, where N is the number of bits. In one sense, the accuracy is absolute. If the counter reads 7356, then there were 7356 clock pulses during the counting interval. However, the counting accuracy must really be considered to be $\pm\frac{1}{2}$ count since there is an unknown phase between the measured signal and the reference clock. Since the accuracy is in counts, the fractional error is $1/N$, which is large for small numbers of counts. As an example, consider measuring low frequencies by counting for 1 second. The frequency resolution will be 1 Hz, meaning that distinguishing between an 11.5 Hz signal and an 11.75 Hz signal is impossible with a single measurement.

The converter function in a timing based input system lies in determining when an interval starts or stops, or when an event to count has taken place. This is done by generating a digital signal from a comparator when the analog input passes a reference threshold value. The bandwidth required in the analog system is commonly misunderstood to be related to the timing resolution obtainable. This is only indirectly true. The analog bandwidth determines the rate at which transitions can take place, but does not affect the relative timing of those transitions. The accuracy with which the time at which a transition takes place can be measured is limited only by the noise in the input signal. For noisy signals, limiting the input bandwidth can actually increase the available resolution. To illustrate this, consider the case of distinguishing an 11.50 Hz and an 11.75 Hz signal. The analog input bandwidth need only be sufficient to pass the two signals, while the two frequencies can be clearly distinguished with a high accuracy measurement of the time between zero crossings.

1.4.2 Analog to Digital Conversion

Several types of analog to digital converters (ADCs) are in common use and will be reviewed. ADCs operate by comparing the input signal with a reference signal and obtaining a binary digit indicating which is larger. Several schemes are available for combining many such comparisons into a digital representation of the input signal, four of which will be discussed here. Viewing the conversion process as a digital search procedure matching the input signal with a reference signal allows convenient classification of converters according to the type of search performed.

An ADC produces a digital integer output that represents the input voltage (or current) in units of the voltage represented by the least significant bit (LSB), V_{LSB}. Any voltage within a range $\pm V_{LSB}/2$ will be represented by the same output code. (Note that an important specification is the set of voltages at which the output code changes.)

A few other parameters are used to characterize ADCs. These are precision (the number of bits produced per conversion), monotonicity, and linearity. Typically, linearity is specified to be 1/2 LSB, which means that the transition between one state and the next occurs with $V_{LSB}/2$ of where it should. A converter is monotonic if an increase in voltage will never result in a decrease in the output code. Almost all converters are specified to be monotonic with no missing codes. "No missing codes" indicates that not only will the output code increase when the input signal increases, it will also only increase by 0 or 1 for a voltage increase of less than 1 LSB.

There are four general kinds of analog to digital converters (in order of practical importance):

- active feedback,
- timing,
- flash, and
- stochastic.

These will be discussed in an order based on the electrical complexity of the converter.

Stochastic Converter.   A very simple converter consists of a comparator with a noise source connected to one input and the signal to be converted to the other. It then simply averages the one bit conversions

$$N_v = \frac{1}{n} \sum_1^n (V_{noise} < V_{in}) \tag{1.7}$$

resulting in a number N_v, which is the number of times out of n trials that $V_{noise} < V_{in}$. The ratio N/n is the probability that $V_{noise} < V_{in}$. As is apparent, the converter depends on the probability distribution of the noise source biased by the input voltage. If $P(V)$ is the probability that V_{noise} has the value V, then

$$P(V_{noise} < V_{in}) = \int_{-\infty}^{V_{in}} P(V) dV. \tag{1.8}$$

For an amplitude limited white noise source in which any voltage in the interval $V_{min} \ldots V_{max}$ is equally probable, this is straightforward. Band-limiting the noise results in a Gaussian distribution characterized by a variance σ^2. In this case $P(V_{noise} < V_{in})$ is given by the normal probability function

$$P(V_{noise} < V_{in}) = \frac{1}{\sigma\sqrt{2\pi}} \int_{-\infty}^{V} e^{-\frac{V^2}{\sigma^2}}. \tag{1.9}$$

Notice that the nonlinearity is significant. In application, this can be handled either by computation (solving Equation 9) or by a table lookup procedure.

By adding some logic to the converter, a clock and counter for example, and ensuring that the noise is uniformly distributed, a useful converter can be constructed. At every clock transition, the counter is either incremented or not, depending on the output of the comparator. The only possible values of the terms in Equation (7) are 1 or 0, so this performs the addition required for the average.

One area where stochastic converters may be viable is in integrated detectors with low level transducers. Lian and Middlehoek (1986) have described a circuit in which the comparator function is performed by a metastable flip-flop. When power is applied to a flip-flop circuit, the state depends on the balance between the two legs. In the absence of asymmetry, it is determined by the noise and the probability of the flip-flop state being 1 or 0 is 0.5, while an asymmetry will push the circuit towards 1 or 0. A transducer is constructed by placing a circuit element sensitive to the quantity measured in one leg. This circuit can be extremely sensitive, with changes on the order of 1 ppm in circuit parameters detectable. Lian and Middlehoek (1986) showed a silicon piezoresistive stress transducer with a resolution of $8kPa$ ($1Pa = 1N/m^2$) and a range in the relative change in resistance of ± 35 *ppm*.

Timing Converters.   Since obtaining a white noise source is difficult, an obvious modification of the stochastic converter is to use a periodic reference input, such as a linear ramp (or sawtooth wave). If the counter is allowed to count for exactly one period of the ramp, then each possible input state will have been sampled exactly once, and the counter will contain a number of counts proportional to V_{in}. A variant of this scheme, the dual slope converter, finds wide application in digital volt meters (DVMs). The input voltage drives a ramp at a rate determined by the voltage for a fixed time. Then the input is disconnected and the time to ramp back to zero volts at a constant rate measured.

Another timing scheme is used in the game port on popular personal computers where the input device is a resistive joystick. The converter consists of a single shot multivibrator, which is simply a RC network, and comparator with the length of an output pulse determined by the resistance. By requiring that the pulse length be determined in software, a very cheap converter can be constructed.

Active Feedback Converters.   This type of converter determines the input voltage by actively controlling the reference voltage. A digital to analog converter (DAC) produces V_{ref} for comparison with the input V_{in}. The accuracy of these devices is controlled by the accuracy of the DAC. Actively controlling V_{ref} allows application of standard search algorithms to the conversion. The variety of active feedback converters corresponds to the variety of state space search algorithms.

A straightforward search through the state space by incrementing the DAC results in a converter very similar to the ramp timing converter discussed earlier. A closely related converter is the tracking converter. It uses an up/down counter, which is incremented when $V_{in} < V_{ref}$ and decremented when $V_{in} > V_{ref}$. If the signal changes slowly compared to the clock period of the counter, the value in the counter represents the current value of V_{in}. For a full-scale jump in the input voltage, the time to recover the signal will be the same as in the linear comparison converter. This converter, while inexpensive and very simple to construct, suffers from the disadvantage that the last bit dithers since the counter counts either up or down on each clock pulse and from the fact that it requires only marginally less logic than the successive approximation converter.

By far the most common search algorithm, because it is the fastest, is the binary search. Converters using this algorithm are called successive approximation converters. They operate by first comparing V_{in} to half the maximum voltage, $V_{max}/2$. This determines the most significant bit of the result by determining if the result is greater or less than $V_{max}/2$. In the next cycle, the same procedure is applied within the subrange determined by the previous cycle and so on until the resolution of the DAC is reached. If an N bit result is desired, N cycles are required for conversion. This number is fixed. Converters of this type are commercially available with resolutions varying from 8 to 16 bits and conversion times of from 1 to 100 microseconds. The most common variety is the 12 bit converter with a 10 to 20 microsecond conversion time.

Flash Converters. In video applications, it is necessary to digitize the incoming data stream at rates above 20MHz to capture frequencies in the 10MHz range. The successive approximation converter would have to operate at internal frequencies approaching 1 GHz to produce data at this rate. The solution is to provide one comparator for each input state and generate a separate reference voltage for each. A digital decoder detects the highest voltage comparator that is true and produces a parallel digital output. Flash converters with 4, 5, 6, and 8 bit outputs are available. Some high speed designs use a combination of successive approximation and flash conversion; at each time step, 4 bits are determined by flash conversion, the gain of the converter increased by a factor of 16, and the next 4 bits determined. Since the reference voltages in a flash converter are generally derived from a resistance divider chain, monotonic output is easy to guarantee. It is also possible to tailor the voltage range represented by each output state by making nonuniform jumps in the reference voltages. The disadvantage also comes from the divider chain, as it contains up to 256 resistors that must be accurately matched if a linear device is desired.

1.4.3 Voltage to Frequency Conversion

As transducers become integrated with signal processing, conversion of an analog signal to a frequency becomes an attractive option. It operates by modulating the frequency of an oscillator with the signal from the transducer or by including the transducer as an element of the oscillator. Note that in the latter case, the notion of a definable transducer signal is lost, and the oscillator output becomes the transducer signal. The advantages of the VtoF approach are:

- Easy signal transmission over a single channel, since the information is carried in frequency, not in amplitude.

• Intrinsically digital transmission since if each cycle is considered one count the value is the number of counts in a fixed time.
• Simple electronics.

The primary drawback is in the time required to acquire a high precision signal. There are two frequency measurement schemes: counting cycles for a fixed time or timing the length of one cycle.

1.4.4 Phase Sensitive Detectors

The phase sensitive detector and phase locked loop find application in input devices that rely on frequency or phase detection. In principle, the phase sensitive detector is an electrical device for performing the Fourier integral

$$V_{psd} = V_0 \int_{-\infty}^{\infty} e^{j(\omega_1 t + \phi_1)} e^{j(\omega_2 t + \phi_2)} dt \qquad (1.10)$$

where ω_1, ω_2, ϕ_1, ϕ_2, are the frequencies and phases of the two inputs to the phase sensitive detector. If $\omega_1 \neq \omega_2$, the output will be zero. If the inputs have the same frequency, the output will vary like

$$V_{psd} = V_0 \cos(\phi_1 - \phi_2) \qquad (1.11)$$

being at maximum when the phases are identical or 180° apart, and zero when they are 90° apart. The phase locked loop is the combination of a phase sensitive detector with a voltage controlled oscillator (VCO). The circuit is arranged so the output of the phase sensitive detector drives the VCO in such a way that its output matches the input in frequency and phase. By adding frequency dividers to the loop, accurate submultiples of a reference frequency can be generated.

The implementation of Equation 1.10 is very difficult as written since it requires integration over an infinite time in the past and in the future. The first approximation in a real device is to perform the integral

$$V_{psd} = V_0 \int_{-\infty}^{t} e^{j(\omega_1 t + \phi_1)} e^{j(\omega_2 t + \phi_2)} e^{\alpha t} dt \qquad (1.12)$$

which involves only past times and has the exponential decay strongly damping the effect of times much larger than $1/\alpha$. The effect of the exponential term is to smear the frequency resolution so that the output will be nonzero for some range ($\sim \alpha$) of difference frequencies between ω_1 and ω_2. There is a trade-off between frequency resolution and measurement time. The time for a measurement or, stated another way, the time required for the output to settle for a change in input, is $\sim \frac{1}{\alpha}$, while the resolution is $\sim \alpha$.

The second approximation is in the multiplication operation. For many applications, adequate function is obtained by approximating the inputs as square waves and performing a digital *and, or,* or *exclusive or* function. This decreases the resolution and requires consideration of higher harmonics for an analytical analysis. In practice, this approximation works well for applications such as frequency synthesis, time base synthesis, or tone recognition.

1.4.5 Rotary Encoders/Position Encoders

The encoder is a device for the direct conversion of rotational or translation position into a digital code. It consists of a series of switches that are connected to form a position-dependent output code. Although any switch type can be used, optical switches using source/detector pairs (S/Ds) are the most common. Devices using Hall effect sensors with a magnetized track are also employed (Jones and Zia, 1981). In an optical absolute encoder, a series of S/Ds are arranged radially along a glass disk, which has transparent and opaque regions arranged such that the pattern under the pairs represents the angular position of the disk. The number of bits available in such an encoder is ultimately limited by the resolving power of the light. In practice, it is limited by the angular alignment of the series of S/Ds, since each S/D must be looking at a bit from the same word. For an encoder that uses a straight binary plate, the situation is even worse, since the alignment of the edges is critical. If one S/D is slightly out of position, it will read a bit from an adjacent word rather than the correct one, resulting in a glitch as the encoder rotates past that position.

This condition can be helped by using Gray codes in which only one bit changes between adjacent words. There is, in fact, an entire class of codes in which only one bit changes between adjacent states. Sporton (1982) shows codes of this type in which error correction is possible without redundant bits. The significant characteristic of these codes is that they maximize the distance in code space between successive transitions of the same bit allowing the detection and correction of errors.

Another technique for improving resolution is to increase the radius of the disk. This approach works because the resolution limiting elements depend on linear distances and not intrinsically on the angles. There is a limit to acceptable size for input devices, however. The practical resolution limit for absolute encoders is around 12 bits, or $360°/4096 = 0.088°$.

A rotary encoder that avoids many of the problems of the absolute encoder is the incremental encoder. In its simplest form, this encoder is the least significant bit of an absolute encoder; the output changes state once per resolution element. The effective result is a tachometer with multiple pulses per revolution useful for speed measurement and control. Reverse motion can be accounted for by utilizing a second S/D positioned so its output is 90° out of phase with the first. The direction of motion is determined by whether one signal leads or lags the other. If one position is known, the absolute position of the encoder is determined by counting the number of pulses forward or in reverse in an up/down counter. The resolution of incremental encoders is limited by the same factors as absolute encoders, with the major improvement that only two S/Ds must be aligned rather than many.

For long travel translation devices, it is practical to determine the position by placing a single track of pseudorandom bits along with a clock track along the travel path. Measurement of an absolute position requires knowing the bit pattern for several bit positions around the current position and matching this to an expected code. (The value of "several" is determined by the number of bits needed to describe the position.) This is midway between an incremental device, which must travel to a single reference position and maintain a count to determine an absolute position, and an absolute encoder in which the position is encoded at each location.

1.5 Processing Primitives

It is the intent of this section to review concepts useful in the reduction of raw data from input devices to codes representing states useful to an application. The first involves a discussion of states, information content, and information bandwidth that are the basic concepts required to describe the transition from raw data to coded data suitable for an application. The general characteristics of interactive input systems are reflected in the computational requirements of this transition. These characteristics and two computational techniques, table lookup and polynomial approximation, will be discussed. Finally, coordinate transformations will be discussed. Since triangulation is a fundamental operation of many position input systems, a section will be devoted to solutions to this problem.

1.5.1 Information

The field of information theory, along with the use of the term *bit,* originated with Shannon and Weaver (1949). A comprehensive and readable review can be found in Godman (1953).

State Space.   The information content of an input system is measured by the number of distinct states the system can represent, N_s, where a state is an abstract description of a unique configuration of the system. Room lights may be on or off, for example, forming a two state system. "Walking forward" and "walking backward" are two states appropriate to a walking robot. While it might be desirable to add a third state, such as "standing still," if backward and forward are the only two states available to the robot, then an input device with two states such as an on/off switch can be mapped onto the states of the robot to control its actions. This illustrates an important point—that the description of a state does not measure anything internal to the state. Walking is a very difficult and complex task but this complexity is lost in the forward/backward state description. The definition of a state requires only that it distinguish the state from other states of the system.

The number of binary digits (bits) required to represent all the states of the system is conventionally used to measure the quantity of information. Since each bit has two states, a total of n_b bits can represent

$$N_s = 2^{n_b} \tag{1.13}$$

distinct states. It is often convenient to think in terms of the number of bits rather than the number of states, so the relation is rewritten as

$$n_b = \log_2(N_s). \tag{1.14}$$

There is no mathematical constraint that n_b be an integer. A system with six states contains 2.585 bits of information. Since binary representations do have integral numbers of bits, the code may be structured so there are fewer valid code points than the number of bits might suggest.

The discussion above covers states appropriate for manipulation by an application. The same description is appropriate for the information content of transducers and conversers.

For an intrinsically digital device such as a switch, the meaning of N_s or n_b is obvious; the single-pole, single-throw (SPST) switch has $N_s = 2$ and $n_b = 1$. The switch can be expanded in two directions. First, if several switches are placed in parallel they can represent 2^N states, where N is the number of switches. Note that these must be independently controllable switches. A multipole switch has the same information content as the single-pole switch, since it can only be in two states as pointed out above for the walking robot. The second expansion direction is the multiposition switch, which has N positions, and therefore can represent N states. A multiplexed keyboard represents a modified form of an N-position switch. The information from the multiposition switch can be carried in a variety of ways. Two possibilities are a wire per switch contact or a single wire with distinct voltages present at each contact. In the limit of large N, the latter type of device is the potentiometer. It is enticing to think of the limit as meaning that an arbitrary number of voltages can be obtained, but this is not true.

As an example of the information content of a simple input device consider the keyboard. In a typical keyboard with 96 keys, there are in principle $2^{96} = 7.923 \times 10^{28}$ configurations of the keys (states). This is a large number.

Obviously, this number of states is not usable, so it is desirable to select a smaller number, say 256. Such a subset can be generated by one key press with a possible second key press from a much smaller set (shift, control, or alternate on many keyboards). The drastic reduction in the quantity of data desired leads to the use of a matrix selection scheme that allows only a few pressed combinations of keys. Selection of the subset of states can occur because the normal application of a keyboard is generation of alphanumeric data, which has relatively few states.

Other keyboard applications are not so simple. Input keys for musical note selection requires that arbitrary (or perhaps selectively arbitrary, depending on your taste) combinations of keys be pressed and recognized simultaneously. In this case, even though vast numbers of the possible combinations are disallowed or unaesthetic, it is a much simpler engineering solution to carry them along rather than selecting for the allowable combinations.

The unimaginable numbers of possible inputs from a set of 96 switches results from very reliable determination of the state of a particular switch and the presence of multiple parallel switches. For a device with an analog output, a variable voltage, current or resistance, the meaning of N_s is not as obvious. Clearly, it cannot represent an arbitrarily large number of states. Limiting factors include the number of states possible in the converter and the intrinsic characteristics of the device. In a wire wound potentiometer, for example, the resistance will be determined by the first wire contacted. One limit on N_s is the number of wires the wiper can contact since there will be a discrete change in resistance in moving the wiper from one wire to the next.

Ultimately, the electrical noise in the system will limit N_s. This noise may come from external sources, which can in principle be shielded, or internal sources related to the atomic structure and thermal vibrations of that structure. The noise means that if a given voltage is measured, it may be from one of a range of transducer positions. Typically, six to ten bits of information can be obtained from analog input transducers.

Information Bandwidth. A fundamental property of any input device closely related to N_s is its information bandwidth. This number quantifies the amount of information obtainable from a device per unit time, written as a number of bits per second

$$\omega = \log_2(N_s)/t_s \tag{1.15}$$

where N_s is the number of states the device can be in and t_s is the time required to establish that state (so $1/t_s$ is the frequency at which random states are produced). The quantity ω should be matched to the application requirements. Note that information may be transmitted either in parallel, as with keyboard keys, or serially in a time sequence. The information bandwidth refers to the total bandwidth of the system.

As an example of top-down application of this formula, consider a handwriting input device. If the required resolution for the input is 100 lines per inch over an 8.5×11 sheet of paper, then there are

$$n_s = (100 \times 8.5) \times (100 \times 11) = 9.35 \times 10^5 \qquad (1.16)$$

possible states of the pen position. For good fidelity, pen positions must be collected over 100 times per second, resulting in $\omega > 100 \times \log_2(9.35 \times 10^5) = 1983$ bits per second. Nothing has been said about how these bits are organized; only that at least this many must be produced by the device to meet the resolution and fidelity assumptions. Most coding schemes will require considerably more bandwidth than this, but with no increase in accuracy.

It is interesting to note that in a case such as handwriting where there are constraints on the distance between consecutive code points, the actual precision of the measurement may be less than the accuracy. In other words, since the hand moves only so fast, the system need not allow for arbitrarily large changes in the measured pen position between measurements. The system may measure the change in position instead of the position itself with a saving in the number of bits produced.

Analyzing a device instead of the application means knowing how many distinct states the device is capable of and how fast it can produce them. If it can be switched in 200 ms, or five times/second, then it has an information bandwidth of five bits/second ($=\log_2(2)/0.2$). The same bandwidth can be obtained with five devices that can be switched in 1 second, $\omega = \log_2(2^5)/1$ where there are 2^5 states generated by five binary switches.

Real analog devices will require translation into digital form in most applications. The methods for doing this are discussed in the section titled Converters, but we will make some comments relating to the device information bandwidth here. Converters are characterized by the number of bits used to represent the input and the time it takes to perform the conversion. A 12 bit converter that converts in 10^{-5} s has an information bandwidth, ω, of 1.2×10^6 bits/s. Since this is readily calculable, it is seductive to think it is the information bandwidth of the device. It is not. Intrinsic limitations, device bandwidth, electrical noise, and mechanical precision are limiting factors. It is very easy to use a 16 bit converter performing a conversion once every microsecond to detect the state of a switch. Even if the transducer, converter, and system software are capable of handling a high precision, there is no assurance that the accuracy is matched to this precision.

Accuracy and Precision.   Accuracy and precision are concepts vital to the effective design of input systems. Accuracy is a measure of how close the value that results from an input operation corresponds to the true value. It is affected by noise, systematic errors, nonlinearities (in systems presumed to be linear), and operator capabilities. Precision is the number of digits used to describe the numerical result of the input operation.

Unfortunately, the distinction between them is not always recognized. In a well-designed system, the accuracy and precision will be roughly the same. Rarely does a system have less precision than its intrinsic accuracy. In the more common occurrence, a high precision masks a low accuracy. The mismatch may occur at any point in the logical chain from measurement to interpreted code. The quantity measured may be a function of uncontrolled variables such as temperature, humidity, local mechanical vibration, or user instability. Transducers are subject to drift, nonlinear behavior, or any of several other accuracy-limiting effects. At the code level, there is generally little choice in the size of the code word used to represent the measurement. It then becomes important for the system implementers to recognize that the number available to them with 24 or 32 bits of precision may represent a quantity with 7 bits of accuracy.

A closely related concept is *resolution.* Resolution is a measure of the number of states representable by a system. (An alternative definition of resolution is as a measure of the phase space volume of the enclosing state space that a particular state occupies.) It can be confusing, since it can mean either precision or accuracy. This actually is interesting since it points directly to the major difficulty in distinguishing accuracy and precision. When the term resolution is applied to a transducer, it typically refers to the accuracy of the transducer. When applied to a converter, it applies to the precision of the converter (which is presumed to also be a good measure of its accuracy). Both are valid applications of the term. What then is the resolution of the system? The accuracy will be determined by the lowest accuracy component while the precision will have been determined by the highest precision component.

1.5.2 Approximation of Functions

Computation of nonlinear functions is often a necessity in input systems. Two types of situations occur, one when transformation of the raw data involves a nonlinear function, such as triangulation problems involving the calculation of trigonometric functions, and the second when the transducer signal is nonlinear. The latter case can be either a matter of correction for small nonlinearities or linearization of a manifestly nonlinear transducer.

Two basic techniques are used for processing in nonlinear input systems, lookup and computation, along with combinations of these. One important characteristic of input systems is that time, rather than precision, is the important factor in performing the computation. The precision of input systems falls in the 8 to 12 bit range, which is more than adequately handled (except in very special cases) by 16 bit integer operations. The time required for the computation must certainly be less than the response time of the user. Performing the computation on the same processor that the application uses makes it equally important that the input system not require large quantities of the processor resource.

Lookup Method. The condition of low resolution and requirement of low overhead combine to make lookup calculations a viable alternative. In a straight lookup operation, the appropriate output code for each input obtained from the converter is either calculated or determined empirically and stored in processor memory (typically in read only memory (ROM) but possibly in writable storage or on a secondary medium such as disk). The input code is then used as an index into the table of output codes.

The number of input states determines the number of memory locations required for the table. An input converter having ten bit precision would require 1024 words of storage for the table. Note that a low-resolution requirement is a great advantage here, since the number of words required goes as 2^N where N is the number of bits in the input code. The output code can contain as many bits as required, although the system will only be capable of generating as many or fewer states than in the input code. In general, the output should be wider than the input, since one way to view the objective of the computation is to divide the spacing between the input states into several states. It is, of course, possible that several input states produce the same output state.

Lookup methods can be combined with the polynomial approximations discussed next. The simplest example of this is to store the actual output values of a small set of input states and linearly interpolate between them for the others. This technique is used extensively in computing the temperature from the nonlinear voltage produced by a thermocouple, for example. Note that in this case it may be better to store the coefficients of the polynomial expansion used for the interpolation rather than the output values themselves.

Polynomial Approximations. The objective of computations in interactive inputs systems is to obtain adequate precision in minimum time. One straightforward way to approximate nonlinear functions is as power series of the form

$$f(x) = a_0 + a_1 x + a_2 x^2 + \cdots + a_n x^n \tag{1.17}$$

where the coefficients a_i are to be determined and n is the order of the polynomial. The objective can be satisfied by optimizing the a_i for a minimum n. For some functions, a better approximation (in the sense of smaller number of operations for a given precision) can be obtained by using ratios of polynomials. But because of the low precision requirements of interactive input systems, second- or third-order polynomials generally are sufficient. The more sophisticated techniques will not be discussed here.

The straightforward method of obtaining a power series is by the Taylor expansion around a point x_0

$$f(x) = f(x_0) + \frac{df(x)}{dx}\bigg|_{x_0} (x_0 - x) + \frac{d^2 f(x)}{dx^2}\bigg|_{x_0} \frac{(x_0 - x)^2}{2!}$$
$$+ \frac{d^3 f(x)}{dx^3}\bigg|_{x_0} \frac{(x_0 - x)^3}{3!} \cdots \tag{1.18}$$

where the coefficients of the $(x_0 - x)^i$ are taken as the a_i. While straightforward, this method does not result in the optimum accuracy for a given-order polynomial and has the further disadvantage that the actual error may be large for some values of the argument.

Optimization of the coefficients can be performed empirically by adjusting them until the best fit is obtained. This method has the advantage that if the empirical fit is performed and stored for each device, variations among devices can be minimized. The device can also be recalibrated during its life to account for aging.

From a theoretical point of view, the appropriate method is to approximate the nonlinear function using orthogonal polynomials. Orthogonal polynomials are sets of polynomials of order n that satisfy the equation

$$\int_a^b w(x) f_n(x) f_m(x) dx = \begin{bmatrix} 0, & n \neq m \\ h_n, & n = m \end{bmatrix} \tag{1.19}$$

where $f_n(x)$ is an orthogonal polynomial or order n evaluated at x, $a < x < b$, and $w(x)$ is a function called the weighting function. The interval (a, b) over which the orthogonal polynomial is defined and the weighting function are properties of the particular orthogonal polynomials. The utility of such functions comes from the fact that any function over the interval may be written as a sum of the orthogonal functions

$$g(x) = \sum_{n=0}^{N} a_n f_n(x) \tag{1.20}$$

where the coefficients can be calculated from the orthogonality relation

$$a_n = \frac{1}{h_n} \int_a^b w(x) f_n(x) g(x) dx. \tag{1.21}$$

This can be verified by substitution back into the previous equation. Note that a particular set of orthogonal polynomials is defined only over a particular interval and that a change of variables will map any other interval into the required one.

The orthogonal polynomials of particular interest are the Chebyshev polynomials $T_n(x)$, which are defined over the interval $-1 < x < 1$ by the relations

$$w(x) = (1 + x^2)^{-\frac{1}{2}}$$

$$h_n = \pi, \left(\frac{\pi}{2} \text{ for } n = 0 \right)$$

$$T_0(x) = 1 \tag{1.22}$$

$$T_1(x) = x$$

$$T_{n+1}(x) = 2x T_n(x) - T_{n-1}(x).$$

The critically important feature of Chebyshev polynomials, aside from their orthogonality, is the fact that they are bounded such that

$$|T_n(x)| \leq 1 \tag{1.23}$$

for any n and x. This allows computation of polynomial approximations of functions with an accuracy known to be better than a defined value.

To see how this is accomplished, consider the function $g(x)$, which may be expanded exactly in terms of Chebyshev polynomials

$$g(x) = \sum_{n=0}^{N} a_n T_n(x) \tag{1.24}$$

where N may be finite or infinite. A polynomial approximation to $g(x)$, $g_{apx}(x)$ would have the form

$$g_{apx}(x) = \sum_{n=0}^{m} a_n T_n(x) \tag{1.25}$$

where $m < N$. The error, δ, is the difference between the exact function and the approximation

$$\delta = \sum_{n=m+1}^{N} a_n T_n(x). \tag{1.26}$$

But since $|T_n(x)| \leq 1$, it is true that

$$|\delta| \leq \sum_{n=m=1}^{N} a_n \qquad (1.27)$$

independent of x. This is an important result, since it guarantees the accuracy for every x. Once the Chebyshev polynomial approximation is obtained, it is a simple matter to collect terms and write a polynomial approximation of the form

$$g_{apx}(x) - \sum_{n=0}^{m} b_n x^n. \qquad (1.28)$$

1.5.3 Coordinate Transformation

Coordinate transformations are the most common form of processing applied to the raw data from input devices. The purpose of transformations is to enable the input system to use units in a coordinate system convenient for the operations required at each stage of the input system. They come in many forms, some almost transparent. A simple linear transducer and amplifier is a coordinate transformation system, determined by the gain and offset of the amplifier. Within constraints set by signal to noise and dynamic range considerations, it does not matter what the signal levels of the transducer are or what the offset is (where the zero of the coordinate system is) since these are taken care of in the amplifier. The same transformation could take place digitally in the computer. A detailed exposition of linear algebra and coordinate transformations can be found in almost any elementary engineering or mathematical physics text (Sokolnikoff and Redheffer (1966), for example).

Linear Transformations. The information content of an input system may be most naturally expressed as sequences of numbers rather than as a single number. Most commonly, this appears as a two-dimensional coordinate system, such as the row and column character position on a display and the (x, y) pair input from a tablet. The method of indicating a point in an N-dimensional space is as a vector, written

$$\vec{x} \equiv (x_1, x_2, \ldots, x_N). \qquad (1.29)$$

Each x_i is the length to the point along the ith dimension (or axis). Special vectors are often used to represent a unit distance along one axis. They are denoted with a caret. Any vector can be written as a sum of unit vectors multiplied by a scalar length along that axis. For two dimensions, this would be

$$\vec{x} = x\hat{\mathbf{a}} + y\hat{\mathbf{b}}, \ \hat{\mathbf{a}} = (1,0), \ \hat{\mathbf{b}} = (0,1). \tag{1.30}$$

The set of unit vectors is referred to as the *basis set* for the N-dimensional space. The $\hat{\mathbf{a}}$ and $\hat{\mathbf{b}}$ that immediately spring to mind are the Cartesian coordinates x and y.

The essential and fundamental operation of almost every position input device is the linear transformation, which converts one set of coordinates into another by changing the basis set. A linear transformation is an operation of the form

$$x_1 = a_{1,0} + \sum_1^n a_{1,i} x'_i$$
$$\vdots \tag{1.31}$$
$$x_n = a_{n,0} + \sum_1^n a_{n,i} x'_i.$$

For a two-dimensional system, such as the surface of a display or input tablet, the linear transformation from one set of coordinates (x', y') to another set (x, y) is

$$x = a_{1,1} x' + a_{1,2} y' + a_{x,0}$$
$$y = a_{2,1} x' + a_{2,2} y' + a_{y,0}. \tag{1.32}$$

Note that the constants $a_{i,0}$ simply move the origin. This is a very useful operation for many input applications. If the off-diagonal elements $a_{1,2}$, $a_{2,1}$ are zero, the transformation scales the axis keeping the same unit vector directions but changing their magnitude. Nonzero off-diagonal elements result in a mixing of the basis vectors.

A special kind of transformation is the *orthogonal transformation,* which simply rotates the coordinate system around the origin while preserving all relative angles and lengths. The rotation has one parameter, the rotation angle θ. The coefficients a_{ij} are given by

$$x = \cos(\theta)x' + \sin(\theta)y'$$
$$y = -\sin(\theta)x' + \cos(\theta)y'. \tag{1.33}$$

There is a useful ambiguity of viewpoint in an orthogonal transformation. It can be viewed as rotation of the coordinate system or, equivalently, as rotation of the vector from the origin to the point (x, y).

Dimensionality.   While it is convenient to think of a system in the most natural coordinates, this is not necessarily the best way to represent it in the computer. A system of any dimension described by a finite set of coordinates can be reduced to a one-dimensional system without loss of information. This criterion will be met for any system representable on the computer, since the computer representation has a finite number of values (2^N where N is the number of bits in the representation), so a single number can be used to index all the vectors in the multidimensional space. An array of points with N points in the $\hat{x}$ direction and M points in the $\hat{y}$ direction with coordinates $x = (1 \ldots N)$ and $y = (1 \ldots M)$ can be indexed by the scalar quantity

$$I = x + yN. \tag{1.34}$$

For display memory addressing purposes, it is often convenient to do this. However, few users would recognize position 168 as the eighth character on the third row of a 24×80 display without some mental gymnastics, so it is convenient and natural to retain the array coordinates for user (and programmer) interactions. In another input device application, an (x, y) position can be measured by probing each possible (x, y) sequentially and measuring either the time until the probe is sensed (for a constant probing rate) or counting the number of points the probe has passed.

Triangulation.   Many devices that produce the position of a stylus for data input rely on some form of triangulation. Because of this importance, it will be covered in substantial detail. The method for measuring the lengths of triangle sides and angles will be covered in the sections on transducers and real devices.

For reference purposes, the points, angles, and lengths of sides of triangles will be labeled as follows: the position of the points $\vec{x}_i$ are vectors in Cartesian coordinates; the angles, θ_i, are indexed so they match the side opposite, ℓ_i.

The normal situation in input applications of triangulation is to know the position of two reference points in a plane, here assumed to be $\vec{x}_1$ and $\vec{x}_3$. With these, the position of a third, $\vec{x}_2$, can be calculated from any combination of two distances or angles from the reference points. It is convenient to choose the x axis to lie on the line between the two reference points. The positions of the two reference points determine the scale and orientation of the natural coordinate system of the device, while the two variables associated with the input point determine a position in this coordinate system.

There are a few constraints on the position of the point $\vec{x}_2$ to be measured that can be combined in most cases to lead to solutions. First, specifying a length from a reference point means that $\vec{x}_2$ must lie on a circle with a radius of the specified length around the reference point and that specifying an angle from a reference point and reference line means that $\vec{x}_2$ lies on a line passing through the reference point. A less obvious geometrical constraint is that if the angle between the two reference points measured at $\vec{x}_2$ is θ_2, then $\vec{x}_2$ is constrained to lie on a circle with radius R defined by

$$\sin(\theta_2) = \frac{\ell_2}{2R} \tag{1.35}$$

where ℓ_2 is the distance between the reference points. R is the radius of the circle circumscribed around the triangle. The familiar result that any triangle inscribed in a semicircle is a right triangle is a special case of this relation where $\theta = \pi/4$ and $2R = \ell_2$ is the diameter of the semicircle.

One useful triangulation case is when the two angles θ_1 and θ_3 are known. Choosing the origin at $\vec{x}_1$ is convenient. By constructing the height y from $\vec{x}_2$ to the x axis, one obtains

$$y = x \tan(\theta_1) = (\ell_2 - x) \tan(\theta_3)$$
$$x = \frac{\ell_2 \tan(\theta_3)}{\tan(\theta_1) + \tan(\theta_3)} \tag{1.36}$$
$$y = \frac{\ell_2 t\, an(\theta_3) \tan(\theta_1)}{\tan(\theta_1) + \tan(\theta_3)}.$$

Tangents are difficult to deal with numerically, since they diverge at $\pi/4$ and accurate analytical approximations are typically defined only up to $\pi/8$. It is useful, therefore, to write the result in terms of sines and cosines. These solutions are

$$x = \frac{\ell_2 \cos(\theta_1) \sin(\theta_3)}{\sin(\theta_1 + \theta_3)}$$
$$y = \frac{\ell_2 \sin(\theta_1) \sin(\theta_3)}{\sin(\theta_1 + \theta_3)}. \tag{1.37}$$

As another example of interest for input device application, consider the jointed arm. It consists of two equal-length segments with a rotating joint connecting the two segments, a rotating joint connecting one segment and a fixed point, and the remaining end free. Any device capable of measuring an angle, such as a variable resistor or rotary encoder, can be placed at the rotating joints to make a real device. The known quantities are θ_1, θ_2, ℓ_1, and ℓ_3. The joint position is given by

$$x_j = \ell_3 \sin(\theta_1), \quad y_j = \ell_3 \cos(\theta_1) \tag{1.38}$$

while the position of the end of the second arm, taking the joint position as the origin is

$$x' = \ell_3 \sin(\pi - \theta_1 - \theta_3), \quad y' = \ell_3 \cos(\pi - \theta_1 - \theta_3). \tag{1.39}$$

Conversion to a system with the origin at the reference point is done by adding the offset of the joint

$$x = x_j + x', \quad y = y_j + y'. \tag{1.40}$$

Notice that it is useful that the lengths of the two arms are equal. If they were not, it would be impossible to reach a point in a circle around the fixed reference point of radius $\ell_3 - \ell_1$. Since the device relies on fixed-length elements, its total reach is limited to a circle of radius $\ell_3 + \ell_1$. Also note that for each point, with the exception of the origin, where any θ_1 is allowed, there are two possible arm positions. This is harmless.

1.6 Real Devices

Transducers and converters can be combined in an astonishing variety of ways to produce an input device. Even bearing in mind the hierarchical structure defined in the introduction, categorization of this diversity can be challenging, with most categorizations questionable. Real devices straddle the boundary between the user and the application system, and the criteria for categorization are different from these two viewpoints. From the user viewpoint, there are generic types of devices described by the activity required of the user: what muscle groups are involved and how they interact to perform the desired task. From the application system point of view, the distinctions are based on the kinds of information obtainable. The categorization selected here is to first organize sections based on the information system function the real device performs, then on the kind of device (joystick, tablet), and finally on the transducers and converters usable for that device.

Broad categories of real devices from the application's viewpoint are:

- Coded point input devices. These are devices in which a single user action is interpreted by the computer as selecting one code point. Each code point has a particular significance in the code used.
- Position input devices. These devices present the computer with the current position of a stylus, where stylus is liberally interpreted.

In dividing devices into these categories, it is useful to recall that a single device can be used in a variety of ways. As a simple example, consider the keyboard, which is the archtypical coded input device. It can be used as a position input by mapping the key codes onto a matrix of their physical positions on the keyboard. It is also useful to recall the simple/complex categorization discussed in the introduction. By generating time sequential strings of binary digits, a two-state device can emulate the output of any other device, even a complex one. Similarly, one of the major difficulties of complex input devices is the reduction of their raw data to a code point, so they are clearly capable of emulating the operation of a simple device.

Another feature of the division into coded and position devices is that it largely ignores the processing performed on the information, particularly for position inputs. A large variety of functions can be obtained from a position device coupled with a feedback display, assigning a value to an application quantity, for example. Since this function relies on the position input device, the division remains useful for exposition at the device level.

1.6.1 Coded Inputs

Alphanumeric Keyboard. The prime example of a coded input device is the alphanumeric keyboard. Each key selects one code point, typically of an 8 bit code, which represents the letters, numbers and special characters.

Some code points may be selected as imperatives (see the discussion of imperatives in Man Machine Interface below). In particular, the *"ENTER"* or *"CARRIAGE RETURN"* keys are commonly interpreted as imperatives to act on the information contained in the finished line of text. Some keyboards include a range of function keys whose code points are interpreted as imperatives.

To limit the number of keys (switches) required, some keys perform special functions internal to the device. The shift key, shift lock, and numeric shift keys are examples of keys that remap the keys to another region of the code space (lowercase to uppercase letters for the shift key). This does not change the essential characteristic of one key per code point, however.

Since the majority of existing applications of computers involve the entry and manipulation of textual data (either alphanumeric or numeric) and discrete information, the keyboard is, and is likely to remain, the primary input device on most general-purpose computer systems.

Key Panels. The distinction between these devices and the alphanumeric keyboard is primarily in the code set to be implemented. A key panel implements a code set particular to the application. The front panels of most modern instrumentation provide an excellent example. There are a variety of keys, each of which enters a single code point, which may be either data or an imperative.

Thumbwheels. The thumbwheel switch consists of a series of dials that the user adjusts to represent the desired data. They are typically used for numeric data input. The code points are the values of each digit in the number, and the user operation to select the code point is to increment and decrement the digit shown on the device. While such devices share the characteristic of direct code generation with keyboards, they differ in one important respect. In the keyboards, one primitive mechanism (by which we really mean the switch) has only two states, output this code or inactive. In the thumbwheel, the primitive mechanism generates several code points, such as the digits 0–9.

Dials. A device common on CAD/CAM systems is a bank of knobs (six to ten devices), which may be twiddled to adjust some parameter. They are the logical extension of the thumbwheel, which typically has 2^3 to 2^5 states to upwards of 2^8 states per primitive unit. The interpretation of the code state becomes complex but retains the characteristic that a code is output. An example of a code set appropriate to this device is a set of morphologically related drawings. The codes might represent the projection angles of a 3D drawing or the major and minor axes of an ellipse. The connection to position devices can be made since an equally valid code might be the cursor position selected by using two dials. While the distinction between position as a code point and position as position may be academic, the concept of position as code point is not. The dials are not constrained to assign adjacent positions to adjacent code points, so one dial might trace circles or random jumps rather than a linear progression through adjacent positions.

Barcode Reader. The barcode reader is a fixed code input device for large numbers of possible input codes. The essential characteristic of the barcode reader is that several bytes of information can be read by a single user operation and associated with complex objects. This is particularly useful in applications that deal with large numbers of objects where accurate identification of an object is critical. Common examples are supermarket checkout and warehouse shipping and inventory control. Readers are available in combination with a variety of data logging and time stamping functions for inventory control and tracking applications. The code is physically attached to an object, so when an object is added to or removed from stock the code is scanned and an itemized inventory updated. The accuracy of barcode readers is dependent on the device rather than the operator (as it would be in the alternative keyboard approach) and so can be very good. Another potential application is symbol selection from large sets. By providing a printed sheet with the possible selections and an associated barcode, the user is able to select from a large library of symbols by a human visual search followed by a single input operation. An example is circuit elements in a schematic capture system. Note that while most existing systems have an implied enter when the code is read, the code can also be used as a command. Supermarkets could further reduce checker keying by placing an "End Of Order" code underneath an order separation bar, for example. Scanning this code triggers the "calculate total" operation.

The barcode reader operates by sensing the width of a series of printed bars detected by modulation of reflected light. There are two types of readers: a fixed scanner such as is used in supermarket checkout and warehouse systems and a hand-held scanner. The fixed scanners use either rotating mirrors or rotating diffractive elements to scan a laser beam over the potential location of the object, looking for a valid code. Hand-held scanners are moved by hand over the bars. Hand-held scanners typically contact the paper the code is on and use LED sources. Decoding the light modulation is an involved operation that is normally done in special hardware associated with the scanner. There are a variety of codes used for barcode readers, the Universal Product Code (UPC) being the most familiar since it is placed on retail products.

Magnetic Stripe Readers.   A magnetic stripe reader is a coded input device consisting of a reader and a set of cards with information coded on them. A simple system consists of a few tens of bytes of information on the magnetic stripe, although this can be extended to hundreds if the application requires it. Entry of the data is rapid ($< 1\ s$) and extremely accurate compared to keying in this quantity of data. With this much information, these cards are not useful as command entry devices. Their characteristics as an input system are very similar to the barcode reader, in that they are most useful where there are a large number of code points possible and identification of a particular code point as data input is required. They may be thought of as data storage devices although they are still clearly distinguishable from storage media such as floppy disks, which store several hundred kilobytes of information. Their applications are to input a code point for processing in a larger context.

Consumer credit cards are the premiere example of such a system. Their primary application is to provide a code long enough to identify the user of the card and some auxiliary information such as when and by what bank the card was issued. Similar cards can be used for access control where persons entering or leaving an area are identified by possession of a card. An application using dynamic information on the card is in fare collection on public transport. The paid fare is encoded on a magnetic stripe. When the user boards the transport, the origination point is encoded on the card. At the destination, the fare is calculated and deducted from the amount coded. The logical limit of such cards is in a mass storage device with thousands or millions of bytes of information. The input context of such a card becomes initialization of the user environment and more appropriate for a discussion of storage devices.

1.6.2 Position Inputs, Overview

A position is a vector selecting one point from an array of possible points. Normally, the array is two-dimensional and rectangular, such as the character positions on a display. While this position can be thought of as selection of a code point as in a coded input device, such interpretation is normally carried out at the processing level. The interpretation of the input is simply as position data. This may then be associated in a variety of ways with other information associated with that position. Position itself, without further interpretation, is the basic form of information contained in graphic systems, as the character is the basic form of information in a text system.

The notion of position implies a close connection with a display device on which the position is defined. From the user point of view, the display is an integral part of the interaction since information on it is selected and manipulated through the association of the display data with its position. The nature of the association with the display leads to a classification of device types as on-screen or off-screen, direct or indirect, and continuous or discrete.

On-screen means that the input transducer is physically associated with the display either as an overlay or by connection with an intrinsic property of the display. On-screen devices have a distinct advantage in that the user interacts directly with the displayed image. Off-screen devices use transducers not physically associated with the screen.

Continuous or discrete is a distinction based on the relative resolutions of the input device and the display screen. A continuous device is capable of addressing each primitive element on the screen; that is, its resolution is as great or greater than the screen resolution. A discrete device has resolution lower than the screen resolution, so that only a discrete subset of screen positions can be selected. Notice the seemingly awkward use of the words primitive element in this definition rather than a more common term like picture element. This allows a certain degree of flexibility since in a text system where it makes little sense to select the dot of an *i*, a continuous position device would be one capable of selecting any character. The character then is the primitive element. Defining larger primitive elements, such as a menu item, holds the potential for overgeneralizing and demolishing the utility of the distinction between continuous and discrete. Preventing this is the primitive notion of position. The position on the display is the coordinates of a point on a fixed matrix. Defining a menu item as a primitive element is valid only if the menu positions are the only positions available and would not be valid if the menu could be shifted by a character position. There is a second sense in which continuous and discrete are used with respect to tablet-type devices. There are devices that have several discrete conductors in the active area of the tablet, each to determine a single location and devices with a continuous conductor (or resistive) layer. This distinction disappears after the continuous case is converted to a digital value, however, and the distinction specified above becomes operative.

There are two ways to specify a position: relative to the current position or as an absolute position relative to a fixed point. There are two kinds of relative specification:

- Parametric specification, where a parameter describing how to transform the current position into the desired position is specified, such as selection of two axes of velocity where the rate of motion from the current position to the selected position is selected and modulated until the desired position is reached;
- Incremental specification, a special case of parametric specification where the number of unit steps from the current position to the desired position is given. Normally, the step increment is limited to one, so to reach a given position a set of connected intermediate positions must be traversed.

Note that in either of these systems a path from one position to the next is an implicit part of the new position determination. Clever applications may use this extra information. The path information is not available in many absolute positioning systems, such as a light pen, where each position entered is independent of any other (although a series of positions can, of course, be generated by continuous sampling).

For any position device, visual feedback on the display is an important component of the input system. Normally, this takes the form of a cursor, which is a special symbol placed at the current position. The term "symbol" needs to be taken in a general sense, as it may be a distinct symbol, like a tracking cross or blinking underline, or may be a modification of the visual characteristic of the display such as normal and reverse video, color, size brightness or character set. It is well to recall that the single try, dead reckoning ability of humans has an accuracy of around 15 percent. The feedback of a cursor position allows refinement of the position by subsequent motions over a smaller field. The connection of the cursor motion with the user motion has different characteristics for on- and off-screen devices.

On-screen devices are necessarily one-to-one devices where the scale of user motions is determined by the scale of the display. This close connection carries with it user expectations about where the cursor should appear for a given indicated position since that position is part of the same visual field. The primary mechanical difficulty in accomplishing this connection is parallax.

Parallax occurs when the position measurement plane is separated from the display plane. It is a result of the fact that in normal (noncomputer input) circumstances the angle of a stylus used to point at an object does not matter, as the position pointed to is determined by the tip of the stylus. (Consider the case of pointing to a projected slide image with a pointer stick where one normally stands to the side.) With a separation between the measurement plane and display, the measured position differs from the intended position by

$$\Delta x = h\tan(\theta) \tag{1.41}$$

where h is the separation of the display plane and the position measurement plane and θ is the angle the stylus makes with the normal to the display plane. There is a third plane involved, which is the plane on which a stylus rests forming the fulcrum of the parallax lever. For a CRT, a substantial fraction of an inch of glass separates the display on the interior surface of the glass from the screen front. If a light pen is used, the plane the stylus touches is the upper while the position is measured (and the display actually appears) on the lower plane. In the case of a transparent overlay, the position will be measured on the upper surface and, in the case of an optical scanner, the position will be measured above this while the stylus rests on the glass surface.

There are two solutions to parallax, the first being to make h as small as possible. The second is to ignore it. Anecdotal experience with light pen and optical scanner systems shows that with an accurate tracking cursor, the eye-hand coordination soon adjusts so that the perceptual effect of the parallax disappears. In fact, it can become a virtue by allowing small adjustments in position by tilting the stylus without moving its tip.

For off-screen devices, there is freedom in defining how motions in the device correspond to motions of a cursor on the display. Most frequently this is expressed as a control/display ratio, which represents the ratio of hand motion to cursor motion on the screen. In the simple form, real distances are used for the ratio (inches on the mouse versus inches on the screen). The corresponding quantity for a rotary positioning device would be rotations per distance on the screen. Typical ratios are between 1 to 0.3. Since displays tend to come in a variety of sizes, it would be useful to measure the screen motion by the angular displacement in the visual field at the preferred viewing distance or by hand motion per picture elements on the screen. This sophistication seems to be obscured by the general insensitivity to the C/D ratio within some range and variability of this shallow optimum among different users. The best solution is to allow user selection of this ratio. Note also that there is no reason to fix a single value of C/D. Either explicitly user selectable C/D ranges or a C/D selected implicitly by another factor (such as stylus velocity) can be used.

All position devices require some sort of stylus to control the position. While not very important in the case of parametric devices such as trackballs or joysticks where the stylus controls the parameters, it is a major distinction among absolute position devices such as tables or screen overlays. The primary distinction is between devices that require a special stylus, which may be active or passive and connected by a wire or not, and those devices that do not require a special stylus and can be operated by touch. There are benefits to both kinds (Sutton, 1984). Because the finger (a readily available, nonspecial stylus) is relatively large, devices that use it tend to have lower resolution, while devices that require a special stylus, such as most off-screen tablets, can place a sharp point on the stylus and support higher resolution.

1.6.3 Parametric Position Devices

Joystick. The joystick is an off-screen, relative, continuous motion position control device. It consists of a stick that rotates around two orthogonal axes, along with a variety of imperative key configurations either on the stick or device housing. The normal implementation of a joystick is with two variable resistors mechanically linked to the stick so that their resistance is proportional to the stick position along the two axes. The stick is typically spring-loaded so that it returns to the vertical position. The deflection is used as a velocity parameter indicating the direction and rate at which the selected position should move. The range of velocities is generally not a device function but determined by scaling the input in the application. An empirically determined useful range for velocities is full screen motion in 0.2 to 1 second with full stick deflection and single primitive element motion in 0.2 to 1 second for a small deflection. Note that the velocity need not be a linear function of joystick deflection.

An alternative use of the joystick is as an absolute positioning device. Here the vertical stick position corresponds to the center of the screen and full deflections correspond to the corners. Typical joystick systems are hard-pressed to achieve a 7 or 8 bit accuracy, and the motions of the stick are sufficiently small that it is difficult for the user to position the stick to this accuracy. As a result, absolute joystick applications are limited.

Several transducers can be applied to joysticks, although the most common one is the variable resistor. A pressure-sensitive joystick can be constructed from strain gauges, while more conventional joysticks can use rotary encoders, linear Hall effect transducers, or electromagnetic transducers. These alternatives are rarely seen for reasons of cost.

The joystick is a limited accuracy device but in the velocity mode very little accuracy is required. The user interaction is feedback driven, so only the zero need be accurate. (The position should not move when the stick is not pushed so most joysticks include trim adjustments to ensure this condition.) The low accuracy limit is the switch joystick, where the variable resistors are replaced by four or more switches. The cursor position is either moving with a predetermined velocity or not moving as selected by a switch contact.

The simple switch-only joystick is used in consumer video games with a great deal of success (where casual observation confirms that a proportional device would spend little time off the stops), while more sophisticated models are readily available at low cost. Many articles have been published detailing the interface of a joystick to every imaginable port on a computer (Asbock, 1986). The low cost, simplicity, and durability of joysticks have led to applications as proportional input devices for the handicapped (Thrope and Letechipia, 1985).

There are two joysticklike devices, the wobble plate and the puck. The wobble plate may be thought of as a joystick without the stick. It replaces the stick with a plate that is pushed on the corner corresponding to the desired direction of motion. These devices can be very compact and made to look like a single cursor control key on a keyboard. One implementation has the four cursor control keys under a single cover, so this look is appropriate. It may also be implemented with strain gauge, piezoelectric, or variable resistor transducers. One characteristic the wobble plate does not share with the joystick is the absolute position mode, since the displacements in the wobble plate are typically very small (fractions of an inch) and pressure rather than displacement sensitive.

The puck is a joystick with lateral instead of rotational motions. It can be implemented with linear variable resistors or other distance transducer. Like the wobble plate, it can be made flat and installed in the keyboard. It has the advantage that an absolute mode is possible since it involves a displacement of the puck. The return to zero must be added by centering springs in the velocity control version. (See the discussion of the *XY* recorder input device in Section 1.6.5, Absolute Position Devices.)

1.6.4 Incremental Position Devices

Cursor Control Keys. Almost universally, keyboards include position control keys for incrementally moving the position of a cursor up, down, right, and left one elemental position per key press. Not as easily recognizable are the tab, space, and backspace keys. These perform positioning functions, but are confused with data entry since space is a character like "A", "B", or "C" as far as a text editor is concerned. While often condemned, the cursor control keys have the advantages that they are close to the normal position for the user hand, require no special hardware beyond that already present in the keyboard, and need not be limited to one step per key press. Most keyboards provide an auto-type function where, if a key is pressed for longer than a certain time (200 ms to 1 s, typically), the key code is repeatedly transmitted. For cursor control keys, this is a particularly advantageous feature. It could be improved by accelerating the rate as the key is held down so the entire screen could be accessed in a reasonable amount of time, making the keys behave like a velocity control joystick where time depressed rather than displacement determines the velocity.

Trackball. The trackball is an off-screen, relative, continuous motion position control device. It consists of a freely rotating ball, normally 1 to 3 inches in diameter, on which small wheels rotate as the ball rotates. The wheels are positioned 90° from each other, so rolling the ball in the X direction will rotate one wheel while the other slips, and conversely in the Y direction. The ball and its frame assembly are mounted in a fixed position. The fixed mounting and large-size ball are the greatest drawback to this device. A 2 inch ball requires at least 2 inches of depth, and a larger ball is desirable. Typically, trackballs are found in separate hand-held boxes or in panel mount applications such as commercial video games where there is sufficient depth. Imperative keys are included close to the trackball for command and selection functions.

The relevant transducers for trackballs are those capable of encoding rotational positions and, particularly, incremental encoders, which produce pulse outputs, each pulse output corresponding to one step in the proper direction. In trackball, there is a large gain in rotational motion possible due to the relative size of the ball and the measuring wheels. For a 2 inch ball and a 0.20 inch wheel, one rotation of the ball makes 20 rotations of the wheel. As a result, if high gain is not required, rudimentary microswitch and cam shaft encoders can be used. Since bidirectional motion is required, at least two switches are required per wheel. Other implementations with switching technologies are possible, using a magnetized wheel and Hall sensors or an optical encoder (Cornwell, 1984).

The most straightforward interface is with an up/down counter for each rotation direction. The contents of this counter are sampled when the screen position is updated and an incremental movement inferred from the change since the last reading. Interfaces to analog ports (Cook, 1985) have also been reported. They have also been used as the positioning element of multiple transducer input systems (Martindale, 1984).

Mouse. The mouse is an off-screen, relative, continuous motion position control device. It consists of a hand-held device, the mouse, whose relative motion over a surface determines the relative motion of the screen position. Mice may have 1, 2, or 3 imperative keys with the particular number being a matter for philosophical disputation. These amount to a minikeyboard with $2^N - 1$ input states, where N is the number of keys. (The -1 occurs because a "do nothing" state is required.) The dominant user interaction characteristic of the mouse is that (for most implementations) the hand-held mouse is the only component of the device. While (for most implementations) it has a tail that connects it to the processor, it approximates a direct hand motion detector when placed on a surface. The mouse has become an important nonkeyboard input device in workstation applications and is included as standard equipment on some systems.

Many mouse implementations have been reported. The most common is an upside-down trackball with a ball reduced in size to fit in the hand-held device. Other examples are a strain-gauge mouse (Perlowin and Wattenbarger, 1985), a mouse with no moving parts (Lyon, 1981), a Hall effect mouse (Comerford, 1984), and a mouse with three axis input (Nomura and Saitoh, 1984). There have also been discussions of interfacing options and comparisons of the various types of mice (Lyon, 1981; Teschler, 1984; Jackson, 1982; Wilton and McLean, 1983).

1.6.5 Absolute Position Devices

Active Surface Tablets/Touch Screens.   These devices are distinguished by having elements of the device in the active area mainly in the form of conductors or resistors.

Switching Devices.   An absolute position device can be constructed from an array of switches. While this is barely distinguishable from a keyboard or keypad, there is a functional distinction when the switch array is transparent and used as an overlay on the display. In that case, the position is the relevant property of each switch. These switch arrays, like any other switch array, require no special stylus other than an object capable of exerting sufficient force to make the contact.

The earliest on-screen devices were of the switch type (Johnson, 1967), and they remain practical. A rudimentary array of this type can be produced by gluing clear plastic rectangles to switches and arranging them in an array (Cumming, 1983), but the more typical arrangement is a grid of orthogonal sets of conductors. The X wires and Y wires are placed on separate backings, one of which is flexible and mounted with spacers such that the wires can be pressed into contact. An alternative to the spacers is the use of a carbon-loaded rubber, which is normally insulating, but becomes conductive when pressure sufficient to connect the dispersed carbon particles is applied. The position is determined by monitoring (or scanning) for connections (Goldman and Wilford, 1978). The resolution of such a device can be made sufficiently high to allow for handwritten sketch input (Sato and Kishimoto, 1983). It is also possible to construct switches with tactile feed using membrane switch technology with transparent plastic and conductors (Hasegawa et al., 1982).

In transparent overlay applications, all switch implementations have the disadvantage that the structure of the crosspoint lines will be visible. When metal wires are used, they form thin opaque lines and when a transparent conductor (ITO, indium tin oxide) is used, the difference in the index of refraction between the substrate and the ITO will cause spurious reflections. These may affect the visual quality of displays to an extent that makes them unsuitable for position inputs. A more appropriate application would be as a configurable keyboard, with the key code represented in an area adjoining the key.

Resistive Panels.   One solution to the visible structure of on-screen switch arrays is to eliminate it and use a continuous resistive layer as a variable resistor with a stylus replacing the wiper. The straightforward implementation of such a device has conductive contacts on opposing edges of a rectangular resistive sheet that apply a potential across the sheet. If the resistance of the sheet is uniform, the potential measured at a stylus contacting the sheet depends linearly on the distance from the conductive edge. This requires a stylus wired to measure the potential, but an arrangement similar to the two-layer crosspoint switch having a conductive sheet spaced above the resistive sheet can be used. In this case, pressure from any stylus on the top sheet makes a contact to the resistive sheet to measure the potential and compute the position. As in the crosspoint switch case, a pressure-sensitive rubber layer can be used for the spacer (Sato et al., 1982), although this precludes use as a transparent overlay.

The variable resistor scheme results in an intrinsically one-dimensional device in which the conductive edges must be switched to obtain a two-dimensional position input device. To do this, the edge contacts must be approximated by point contacts so that the inactive edges can float. This introduces a nonuniformity in the field across the resistive sheet, but the error from this source can be kept to fractions of a percent if enough point contacts are used and a 10 percent border near the edges is excluded from the active area (Komada et al., 1985). Typically, diode isolation with appropriate biasing is used to isolate the two measurement directions (Turner and Ritchie, 1970).

The stylus may be the source of signal, in which case a current is injected by the stylus and the ratio of the currents flowing to each edge measured. Since people are good antennas for 50–60 Hz power line radiation, the finger is a suitable stylus for injecting this signal into the resistive layer by proximity coupling (Turner and Ritchie, 1973).

The disadvantage of DC devices, that they require contact between the stylus and the resistive layer, can be eliminated by using capacitive coupling of an AC signal. There are two schemes for accomplishing this. The first is similar to the DC method. An AC signal is imposed across the resistive layer with one edge grounded and a voltage V^+ detected with a capacitive pickup. Then the other edge is grounded, the signal applied in the reverse direction, and V^- measured. The coordinates are then calculated by

$$x = \frac{V^+(x) - V^-(x)}{V^+(x) + V^-(x)}. \qquad (1.42)$$

This scheme has the advantage that it is self normalizing so the absolute values of the detected potentials are not important. Schlosser and Kable (1985) have reported commercial devices with 0.63 mm accuracy, 0.025 mm resolution, and transparent tablet sizes up to 61×91 cm using this technology.

In the second scheme, reported by Komada et al. (1985), the two edges are driven by AC signals with a 90° phase shift. The potential at a point x along the resistive sheet is given by

$$V(x) = x \sin\left(\omega t + \frac{\pi}{2}\right) + (l - x) \sin\omega t = k \sin(\omega t - \theta) \qquad (1.43)$$

where the position is derived from the phase shift θ by

$$x = \frac{\tan\theta}{1 + \tan\theta}. \qquad (1.44)$$

The phase shift due to the detection electronics can be measured by periodically driving both edges in phase. A further improvement made by Komada et al. (1985) is the use of digital square waves for the drive circuitry, eliminating the need for analog switches to alternate between the X and Y measurement directions and allowing use of standard tristate output devices. Devices with 0.2 mm resolution producing 200 X, Y pairs per second have been demonstrated.

Instead of finding a way to switch an intrinsically one-dimensional device, Waaben et al. (1986) show a device that explicitly depends on the two-dimensional distribution of current injected into the resistive sheet. Four-point contact is made to the four corners, and the position determined through a nonlinear algorithm that relates position to the currents measured at the contacts. Current may be injected either with a stylus or with a cover sheet and, since an internal normalization makes the result independent of the total injected current, AC coupling could be used.

Inductive Matrix Panels. The inductive coupling between a long wire and a small loop discussed with inductive transducers earlier is an excellent method of constructing a continuous, absolute position detector. While on-screen implementations are possible, the requirement for good conductors makes opaque, off-screen implementations more practical. In a typical implementation, an array of parallel conductors with one end common and the other end provided with a sampling switch is etched from a sheet. The position in the direction perpendicular to the conductive stripes is determined by sampling the coupling between a coil in the stylus and each conductive stripe. The position can be determined to an accuracy larger than the stripe spacing either by computing the coupling to a single stripe or by comparing the coupling between two adjacent stripes. Since the coupling changes sign when the coil moves from one side of the stripe to the other, the position can be determined by the calculated position of zero coupling between two stripes on which the coupling changes sign. A second array at right angles to the first is used for position detection in the orthogonal direction. If the stripes are sampled sequentially, the effect is the same as sweeping a single stripe under the coil. Although the stripe positions are discreet, with filtering, a circuit can be constructed that approximates a continuous sweep of the stripe and the position determined by the position of the zero crossing as the stripe sweeps under the coil. (See, for example, The Wedge Operators Manual (Talos Systems Inc., 1980).)

An alternative to measuring the coupling between a coil in the stylus and the conductive stripes is to connect the conductive stripes into loops and measure the coupling between two layers when modulated by a high permeability element (ferrite) in the stylus (Suzuki et al., 1978). If the stylus is located over the intersection of two loops, the coupling between them will be enhanced and can be detected. In this scheme, the excitation loop is stepped one stripe while the detection is swept through all possible loops. In this way, the entire surface is sampled. It is possible to add a degree of intelligence to the search procedure and sample the intersections close to the previous position first, thus minimizing the time required to locate the stylus. This scheme has the advantage that there are no active elements in the stylus, which therefore has no cord. A special stylus is required, however, which may require attachment to the tablet by a cord so it is not misplaced.

A variation on the overlapping loop scheme is to use an active stylus that couples to two loops. Using this loop excitation, Nagayama et al. (1985) have constructed a tablet with 8 line/mm resolution and 180 samples per second.

A third inductive stylus measures the coupling between an active stylus and two loops placed at the edge of the active area. By comparing the rate of change in the coupling between the stylus and each loop, an accurate value for the velocity of the stylus can be obtained, although the absolute position accuracy is low. Sugimura et al. (1979) have described such a system with a 120 mm × 120 mm active area and 8 line/mm resolution for use as a handwriting input device.

Capacitive Matrix Panels. An array of conductive stripes can also be used with capacitive excitation (Walker, 1980). This method lacks the convenient zero crossing inherent in inductive excitation, but also lacks the necessity for producing small inductive coils. The simplest scheme is to provide an excitation source in the stylus, scan the array for maximum coupling, then interpolate between stripes for increased resolution. An interesting alternative to stylus excitation is use of the stylus to modulate the spacing between the two orthogonal arrays. This scheme has been applied to use the existing conductive stripes on a multiplexed liquid crystal display. Because the stiffness of the glass prevents local changes in the spacing, only limited resolution is obtainable. Furthermore, the capacitances involved are small. Tanaka and Kobayashi (1986) have reported such a device with a 4 × 4 array of 10 × 6 mm pads. The lateral resolution in their device was around 15 mm with capacitance variations of around 20 percent for 200-gram finger presses.

Light Pens. The light pen consists of a hand-held optical imaging system and a detector, which detects the time a picture element is refreshed in a refreshed serially addressed display. The light pen as an input device has a long and venerable history, having been in use since the dawn of the computer age. It is simple in concept, operation, and construction. It is also inexpensive and reliable. Do-it-yourself versions have been described (Bryson, 1983). Light pens are the input device for the Vienna air traffic control system (Hole, 1983), a high reliability application.

Light pens have significant advantages for nonkeyboard input applications. The stylus is a natural interface requiring no training, even for small children (Avons et al., 1983). The user interacts directly with the information on the screen, either to select fields or to enter information. More subtly, the stylus also interacts directly with the screen since it is detecting the screen output so there is nothing between the user and the display surface to decrease the display visual quality and increase the parallax beyond that due to the thickness of the display screen. The direct stylus interaction with the display also has the consequence that very little digital hardware is required, since most of the digital circuitry required to generate the position is already present in the video controller. Many LSI display controllers are equipped with a light pen input, making interfacing particularly simple. The direct light pen/display interaction also means that the input is independent of the screen size and requires no calibration if the size of the display image shifts or changes size with age or power fluctuations.

The most common refreshed serially addressed display is the cathode ray tube, although light pens for plasma displays have been demonstrated (Ngo, 1975; Coates et al., 1973). By generating short light pulses from "off" picture elements, dark area detection has been demonstrated for the plasma panel light pen (Ngo, 1975). However it is universally true that position detection with a light pen requires light from an "on" picture element, even if that picture element is only flashed momentarily.

The inability to detect a position in a dark area of the display can be circumvented in several ways. One straightforward solution is to use a reverse video display, so that most of the screen is illuminated. This is a particularly good solution for handwriting and sketch input applications where detecting a dark picture element would do nothing but leave it dark, so the missed data are not crucial. In menu selection applications, there must be data written on the screen to form the menu, so the light problem is nonexistent. For position input such as handwriting or graphics sketching and point selection, the solution is to use the good practice of providing visual feedback of the light pen position with a cursor. Since the cursor consists of lighted spots, it can be detected by the light pen. After initial acquisition of the light pen position either by placing the light pen over the cursor rest position or illuminating the entire screen for one refresh period, the cursor can be repositioned to track the light pen position until it is removed from the screen.

Kesselman (1973) accurately points out that the cursor position and the light pen position are not a closed loop system. It is aesthetically pleasing to place the center of the cursor under the light pen position, but this is not necessary for accurate tracking of the light pen position. It does serve the very useful purpose of indicating where the system considers the light pen to be pointing, however. In positioning applications, this is valuable information for the user.

Light pens typically consist of a lens that images the light emitting surface of the display on a photodiode or phototransistor. Position detection depends on detecting a pulse of light from a picture element being refreshed. For a raster CRT display, the time the electron beam spends at each picture element is small, 8×10^{-8} s for a display with 250,000 picture elements (roughly 500×500) refreshed 50 times per second. The energy deposited in the phosphor during this time is also small, on the order of $10^{-7} J$ for a beam current of $5 \times 10^{-5} A$ at 25 kV. For an efficient phosphor, roughly 5 percent of this energy will emerge as light, but it will be spread out over the phosphorescent decay time of the phosphor. In the case of P39, the phosphor typically used for green monochrome displays, this decay time is on the order of 10^{-2} s, which means that the peak optical power out of a single picture element when it is refreshed is around 10^{-5} W. Of this, only a small percent is collected by the lens and focused on the photodetector, so the photodetector must be capable of sensing a change in input power of 10^{-7} W in 8×10^{-7} s. This is challenging. More light is obtainable at a lower resolution (so the pen looks at the light from more area) and with a faster phosphor decay, so the peak power (as opposed to the average power, which is determined by the electron beam power and phosphor efficiency) is higher. Light pens are often not available for displays with long persistence phosphors (such as the P39 green in the example) or with high resolution.

Optical Scanners. The optical scanner is an absolute position detection device that may be off-screen but more commonly overlays a display. Since there is nothing in the active area of an optical scanner but the light traversing it, it does not interfere with the display. The optical scanner detects the presence of objects in the field of view of the scanner by detecting the presence or absence of light. There are two major types. In the first type, the scanning light beams travel normal to one axis, while in the second type a beam rotates around a point. Typically, the first type uses an array of light sources and detectors scanned in sequence to form a grid of light beams, while the second uses only one or two light sources. Since many optical scanners operate by breaking a beam of light, any object, such as a finger, may be used as a stylus.

LED Array Scanners. LED array scanners use a grid of optical source/detector pairs (a light emitting diode (LED) and photodiode) scanned in sequence to detect opaque objects in the field of view. The modern version of these devices was reported by two groups in 1972 (Richardson, 1972; Ebeling et al., 1972). The basic innovations over previous versions were the use of a detector per emitter and sequentially scanned uncollimated emitters. The light from a single emitter would be detected at several detectors without careful collimation. By pulsing the emitters so that only one (or potentially several that did not interfere with each other) was illuminated, the crosstalk problem is eliminated. Furthermore, the light intensity available from a LED is greater in the pulse mode, so a larger instantaneous signal is available at the detector. The signal to noise can be further improved by the scanning method (Tamura et al., 1980). Many variants and improvements of these devices have been described. (Ii and Malden, 1982; Shaw, 1985).

Two characteristics of the LED array scanners are that they are resolution limited by the number of source detector pairs that can be arranged around the perimeter of the display and the fact that they determine a position in a plane above the surface of the display. Existing LED array scanners have resolutions in the 0.25 inch range that represent an engineering trade-off among cost of devices, cost of collimation, signal to noise, and useful resolution on a screen. Since they typically are used in menu selection applications, this resolution is sufficient; the resolution is not adequate for graphics input, however.

Angular Beam Scanners.   In an angular scanner system the field of view is swept by a scanning mirror coupled either to a collimated source or a collimated detector, or both. (It turns out to be hard not to collimate the detector if a collimated source is used.) Key to the operation of these scanners is *retroreflective tape,* a tape coated with glass beads having the property that any light entering them is reflected along the reverse path, so collimated light from a source crosses the active area at an angle determined by the scanning mirror, encounters a retroreflective surface, and retraces the same path back to the scanning mirror. Detection of an object is either by shadowing the beam with any stylus, such as a finger, and detecting the absence of returned light, or by placing the retroreflective tape on the stylus and detecting the presence of returned light. The latter mode allows other opaque objects, such as a hand resting on the active area, to be present in the active area. For the position to be determined by triangulation, two angles are required, which means two scanners. Only one of the scanners need be real; the other can be the reflection of the first in a mirror. This does cause some problems with shadowing, though.

Optical scanners of this type can be constructed with one inexpensive laser, a scanner motor, a detector, and a pencil with retroreflective tape wrapped around it. Resolution is determined by the angle measurement accuracy. This can be done with a shaft encoder of some sort, in which case the resolution is determined by the resolution of the encoder. An alternative method is to run the scan motor open loop and use timing from a standard position to determine the angle. The resolution then depends on the stability of the scanning motor. This stability problem is similar to the scanning problem in a laser printer. Stable motors are available. Small, cheap motors easily give accuracies of a fraction of a percent and are applicable to character selection applications. By placing reference objects (dips and reflective pulses) in the field of view, the rotational speed of the motor can be measured and corrections applied to each scan. Using this scheme results in better than single pel resolution over the face of a typical PC display.

Acoustic Devices. Acoustic systems can be used in two distinct ways. The first is the obvious acoustic radar mode in which an ultrasonic pulse is emitted and the time for a reflected return pulse to arrive measured. This is related to the distance of the reflecting object. The second is to use ultra-sonic pulses in schemes similar to the optical scanners described in the previous section by detecting the attenuation of the signal due to a stylus.

Acoustic Range Finders. There are a variety of devices based on the transit time of acoustic pulses. Using two range finders, the position of an object can be determined by triangulation (Tassinari, 1973). There is no intrinsic limitation to two dimensions, so true three-dimension input systems can be constructed (Brenner and deBruyne, 1970). Such devices can be fast and accurate. deBruyne (1980) has described an acoustic range finder device using a reflective stylus capable of 0.01 percent accuracy at 900 samples per second.

An active stylus that either emits or detects the acoustic signal allows useful devices to be constructed. Two schemes are available: one in which a short pulse is transmitted and its transit time detected (Shannon, 1985), and one in which a continuous wave is transmitted and its phase detected. For distances long than a wavelength, this latter scheme has an ambiguity that can be resolved by transmitting two frequencies and measuring the relative phase. Note that the acoustic signal can be transmitted through the air or through a solid medium, such as the surface of a tablet or the face plate of a CRT. A surface wave reflected from a finger has been described by Haldy (US Pat. 3,916,099).

Attenuation. If ultrasonic surface wave pulses are transmitted through the surface of a display, they can be readily attenuated by damping the surface with a finger. A system that operates this way has been described by Adler et al. (1986). For each orthogonal axis, one transmitter and detector are placed at the edge of a plate facing a series of 45-degree reflectors. A surface acoustic pulse ($\sim 5\,\mu s$ at 5M Hz) is launched into the line of reflectors, which direct it across the plate to corresponding reflectors on the opposite side. Since various parts of the pulse travel different distances, relative timing within the $\simeq 140\ \mu s$ pulse at the detector correspond with positions on the plate. A finger placed on the plate will attenuate the signal at a particular time. Adler et al. (1986) have shown a system with $\pm\ 0.5\ \mu s$, or 1/32 inch resolution for a 320×256 grid on a 13 inch CRT monitor. Since the amount of attenuation, and therefore depth of the detected dip in acoustic signal, depends on the pressure applied by the finger, the depth of the dip can be measured to yield up to 16 steps of pressure information.

Miscellaneous. XY *Recorder Device.* A continuous, absolute position device with historical significance is the servo driven XY recorder. The pen position was maintained by balancing the pen position as measured by a translation transducer such as a linear variable resistor against the voltage input. By breaking the servo loop and manually positioning the pen, the servo feedback voltage can be used to determine the pen position. These devices have been widely used in "home brew" graphic digitizers. This feature is sufficiently useful that many modern pen plotters, whose motion is driven by stepping rather than servo motors, simulate this function by a local direction control switch and processing.

Pressure Plates. A simple, very rugged position device consists of a rigid plate mounted on force sensing elements. When the plate is pressed, the load carried by each mounting element will depend on the location of the press. The relation of position to transducer signals is not linear, so a reasonable degree of processing is required to obtain X, Y coordinates. Several variations on the scheme are possible, using either strain gauges or piezoelectric force sensing elements. Garwin and Levine (US Pat. 4,511,760) show a device with four piezoelectric transducers and a differential detection technique where the change in pressure is detected rather than the static pressure. This provides greater accuracy and stability. The device has single character resolution on an 80×24 screen. Mori et al. (1984) have implemented a four sensor system using semiconductor strain gauges. The major advantages of this type of device are that the plate can be shaped to conform to the CRT screen and that the plate can be of any material, so it can be made rugged and of high optical quality.

Tactile Sensors. A technique little used in interactive input devices but under investigation for robotics application is a frustrated total internal reflection tactile sensor. This sensor operates by injecting light into the edge of a glass plate and scattering the trapped light out by placing a diffuse scattering material in contact with the surface of the plate. The diffuse scattering material is a rubber (molded latex) sheet with small bumps on the side facing the glass. Pressing on the top of the rubber sheet deforms the bumps so that the surface area in contact with the glass increases. The pressure required to do this and the amount of extra contact area per unit pressure is a function of the shape of the bumps (spherical, conical, or irregular, for example). The scattered light is measured by an imaging system, and information about the location and pressure exerted at the contact obtained. The pressure response of such a device can be made very similar to the pressure sensitivity of human fingers (Begej, 1984; Tanie, 1984; King and White, 1985).

Eye Trackers. The operation of entering a position using a position input device typically involves looking at the desired location, then moving a stylus to that position to perform the input operation. An obvious shortcut in this procedure is to use the gaze information (where the user is looking) directly. There are two general schemes for accomplishing this.

The first is to measure the position of the specular reflection from the cornea relative to the position of the diffuse reflection from the retina viewed through the pupil. A small infrared illumination source is reflected from the eye and imaged using a video imaging system (Geffner, 1970; Cornsweet and Crane, 1973). The major disadvantage of this scheme is that with a fixed optical system, the eye must remain in the field of view of the illumination and imaging optics. Merchant (1975) discusses a system in which head motion over roughly a cubic foot is possible, and Levine (1984) has implemented such a system. The implementation by Levine (1984) provides a resolution of 18' of visual arc, which is about the angle subtended by a typical character on a typical display CRT. The sample rate of the system was determined by the frame rate of the video system to be 60 samples per second. The eye position was tracked by a gimbaled mirror, which serves to keep the reflected image centered on the video system.

The second method of determining the gaze direction is by measuring the galvanic potentials generated by the eye muscles on the surface of the face. Such a system has low resolution and is generally unsuitable since it requires the user to wear a mask containing the probe electrodes. It has been investigated as a communication device for nonverbal handicapped persons, however (Harris, 1985).

Acknowledgment

The author wishes to acknowledge several sources of support without which this chapter would not have been possible, particularly Ifay Chang for the initial suggestion and interaction during the preparation of the manuscript and Steven Depp for several useful conversations and a critical reading of the manuscript. This work was graciously supported by the IBM Corporation.

References

Adler, Robert, Desmares, Peter J., and Fitzgibbon, James J. (1986). *SID International Symposium. Digest of Technical Papers 17* 316–317.

An Optical Tactile Array Sensor, Tech Report 84-26 (Computer and Information Science Dept., U. of Mass., Amherst, MA, 1984).

Aretz, Anthony J. (1983). A Comparison of Manual and Vocal Response Modes for the Control of Aircraft Subsystems, AFWAL-TR-83-3005.

Asbock, L. (1986). *Mikro- & Kleincomput. (Switzerland) 8* 51–55.

Avons, S. E., Beveridge, M. C., Hickman, A. T., and Hitch, G. J. (1983). *Behav. Res. Methods & Instrum. 15* 75–78.

Beringer, D. B., and Peterson, J. G. (1983) in: *Proceedings of the Human Factors Society 27th Annual Meeting Norfolk, VA*, ed., L. D. Pope.

Brenner, A. E., and deBruyne, P. (1970). *IEEE Trans. Comput. C-19* 546–548.

Bryson, D. (1983). *Micro-6502/6809 J.* 82–84.

Card, S. K., English, W. K., and Burr, B. J. (1978). *Ergonomics 21* 601–613.

Card, S. K., Moran, T. P., and Newell, A. *The Psychology of Human-Computer Interaction,* (Lawrence Erlbaum Associates, Hillsdale, NJ, 1983).

Coates, William J., Johnson, Robert J., and Tucker, Paul T. (1973). *SID International Symposium. Digest of Technical Papers. 4* 12–13.

Comerford, L. D. (1984). *IBM Tech. Disclosure Bull. 27* 3783–3784.

Conrad, R., and Hull, A. J. (1968). *Ergonomics 11* 165–173.

Cook, M. (1985). *Micro User 2* 118–121.

Cooper, A. R., and Brignell, J. E. (1985). *Sensors and Actuators 7* 189–198.

Cornsweet, T. N. and Crane, H. D. (1973). *J. Opt. Soc. Am. 63* 921.

Cornwell, P. J. (1984). *Electron. Prod. Des. 5* 71–73.

Crane, P. M. (1984). *SID International Symposium. Digest of Technical Papers.*

Cumming, G. (1983). *Behav. Res. Methods & Instrum. 15* 72–74.

Curry, David G. (1984). MAGIC 1: A study of manual vs vocal control under heavy task loading, USAFA-TR-84-2.

Curry, David G., Reising, John, and Lizza, Gretchen. (1985). *SID International Symposium. Digest of Technical Papers. 16* 36–39.

deBruyne, P. (1980). *Comput. Graphics SIGGRAPH 1980 Conference Proceedings. Seventh Annual Conference on Computer Graphics and Interactive Techniques. 14* 25–31.

Ebeling, F. A., Goldhon, R. S., and Johnson, R. L. (1972). *SID International Symposium. Digest of Technical Papers. 3* 134–135.

Epps, Brian W., and Snyder, Harry L. (1986). *SID International Symposium. Digest of Technical Papers. 17* 302–305.

Foley, James D., Wallace, Victor L., and Chan, Peggy. (1984). *IEEE CG and A. Nov.* 13–48.

Geffner, S. L. (1970). *Memories, Terminals, and Peripherals, Proceedings of the 1970 IEEE International Computer Group Conference.*

Godman, Stanford. *Information Theory* (Prentice-Hall (Dover, 1968), 1953).

Goldman, O. H., and Wilford, J. E. (1978). *IBM Tech. Disclosure Bull. 21* 1580–1581.

Goodman, D., Dickinson, J., and Francas, M. J. (1985). *Behav. & Inf. Technol. 4* 189–200.

Goodwin, N. C. (1975). *Hum. Factors 17* 289–295.

Grover, F. W. *Inductance Calculation* (Dover, New York, 1962).

Haller, R., Mutschler, H., and Voss, M. (1984). *INTERA '84. First IFIP Conference on Human-Computer Interaction.*

Harris, T. R. (1985). *Proceedings of the Eleventh Annual Northeast Bioengineering Conference.*

Hasegawa, M., Ogasawara, N., Takamatsu, M., Nakatsuji, H., Katoh, T., and Mitsugi, I. (1982) *Natl. Tech. Rep. 28* 920–932.

Heap, P. (1981). *Electron. Today Int. 10* 51.

Hoke, J. (1983). *Syst. Technol.* 18–24.

Ii, L. B., and Malden, A. E. (1982). *IBM Tech. Disclosure Bull. 25* 1568–1569.

Istvan, N. (1980). *Wireless World 86* 84.

Jackson, A. (1982). *International Conference on Man/Machine Systems. Manchester, England.*

Johnson, E. A. (1967). *Ergonomics 10* 271–277.

Jones, B. E. and Zia, K. (1981). *Trans. Inst. M. C. 3* 13–20.

Karat, J., McDonald, J. E., and Anderson, M. (1984). *INTERA '84. First IFIP Conference on 'Human-Computer Interaction'. London, England.*

Kesselman, Murray. (1973). *Proceeding of the SID 14* 52–61.

Kieras, David, and Polson, Peter G. (1985). *Int. J. Man Machine Studies 22* 365–394.

King, Andrew A., and White, Richard M (1985). *Sensors and Actuators 8* 49–63.

Kley, V. (1983). *Comput. Graphics World 6* 69–72.

Knight, A. A., and Dagnall, P. R. (1967). *Ergonomics 10* 321–330.

Komada, S., Mori, M., and Watanabe, T. (1985). *SID International Symposium. Digest of Technical Papers. 16* 28–31.

Leggett, J., and Williams, G. (1984). *Int. J. Man Machine Studies 21* 493–520.

Levine, J. L. (1984). *Comput. Biol. Med. 14* 77–89.

Lian, W. J., and Middlehoek, S. (1986). *Sensors and Actuators 9* 259–268.

Long, John. (1984). *Human Factors 26* 3–17.

Lyon, R. F. (1981). *VLSI Systems and Computations. CMU Conference on VLSI Systems and Computations.*

Martin, James. *Design of Man-Computer Dialogues* (Prentice-Hall, 1973).

Martindale, D. (1984). *Proceedings of Graphics Interface '84.*

Merchant, J. (1975). *IEEE Trans. Biomed. Eng. 21* 390.

Mori, Y., Yamamoto, K., and Imada, H. (1984). *Natl. Tech. Rep. 30* 310–316.

Nagayama, T., Shibuya, J., and Kawakita, T. (1985). *SID International Symposium. Digest of Technical Papers. 16* 32–35.

Ngo, Peter Dinh-Tuan. (1975). *SID International Symposium. Digest of Technical Papers. 6* 110–111.

Nobbe, T. A. (1985). *Mach. Des. 57* 106–110.

Nomura, H., and Saitoh, A. (1984). *IBM Tech. Disclosure Bull. 27* 3423–3424.

Norman, Donald A. (1984). *Int. J. Man Machine Studies 21* 365–375.

Norton, Harry N. *Handbook of Transducers for Electronic Measuring Systems,* (Prentice-Hall, Englewood Cliffs, NJ, 1969).

Parker, R. (1982). *Comput. Des. 21* 157–180.

Perlowin, J. M., and Wattenbarger, H. E. (1985). *IBM Tech. Disclosure Bull. 27* 5453–5455.

Phillips, H. (1979). *Electron. Eng. 51* 19.

Potts, J. (1985). *Gov. Data Syst. 14* 14–16, 28.

Rabin, R. (1985). *Proceedings CADCON West. Digital Design. Circuits Manufacturing.*

Richardson, B. L. (1972). *SID International Symposium. Digest of Technical Papers. 3* 132–133.

Sato, Y., Kishimoto, T., and Akajshi, T. (1982). *Trans. Inst. Electron. & Commun. Eng. Jpn. Sect. E E65* 301.

Sato, Y., and Kishimoto, T. (1983). *Rev. Electr. Commun. Lab. 31* 676–682.

Schlosser, P., and Kable, R. (1985). *1985 SID International Symposium. Digest of Technical Papers.*

Seibel, R. (1972) in: *Human Engineering Guide to Equipment Design*, ed., H. P. VanCott and R. G. Kindade.

Shannon, C. E., and Weaver, W. *A Mathematical Theory of Communication* (Illinois University Press, 1949).

Shannon, T. C. (1985). *DEC Prof. 4* 66–70.

Shaw, S. (1985). *Res. & Dev. 27* 91–92, 97.

Smythe, William R. *Static and Dynamic Electricity,* Third edition, (McGraw-Hill, New York, 1968).

Sokolnikoff, I. S., and Redheffer, R. M. *Mathematics of Physics and Modern Engineering.* (McGraw-Hill, New York, 1966).

Sporton, T. M. (1982). *Trans. Inst. M. C. 4* 150–152.

Stammers, R. B., and Bird, J. M. (1980). *Hum. Factors 22* 581–589.

Sugimura, K., Inokuchi, S., and Sakurai, Y. (1979). *Trans. Inst. Electron. & Commun. Eng. Jpn. Sect. E. E62* 577–578.

Sutton, J. (1984). *Computerworld 18.*

Suzuki, M., Ito, Y., Mochizuki, T., and Hamao, S. (1978). *Trans. Inst. Electron. & Commun. Eng. Jpn. Sect. E. E61* 307.

Tamura, S., Tanaka, K., and Okazaki, K. (1980). *Appl. Opt. 19* 1738–1739.

Tanaka, Toshinori, and Kobayashi, Shunsuke (1986). *SID International Symposium. Digest of Technical Papers. 17* 318–320.

Tanie, K. (1984). *Proc. 4th Int Conf. on Robot Vision and Sensing Controls.* 241–250.

Tassinari, A. F. (1973). *Proceedings of 1973 IEEE Southeast-Conference.*

Teschler, L. (1984). *Mach. Des. 56* 84–91.

The Wedge Operators Manual (Talos Systems Inc., 1980).

Thornburg, D. D. (1983). *Digest of Papers Spring COMPCON 83. Intellectual Leverage for the Information Society. IEEE. San Francisco, CA, USA.*

Thrope, G. B., and Letechipia, J. (1985). *Proceedings of the Eighth Annual Conference on Rehabilitation Technology, Technology — A Bridge to Independence.*

Turner, J. A., and Ritchie, G. J. (1970). *AFIPS Conference Proceedings 1970, Spring Joint Computer Conference.*

Turner, J. A., and Ritchie, G. J. (1973). *SID International Symposium. Digest of Technical Papers. 4*

C. Vees. (1985). *Nachrichtentech. Z. (NTZ) 38* 24–26.

Waaben, S., Federico, J., and Curran, R. K. (1986). *SID International Symposium. Digest of Technical Papers. 17*

Walker, E. L. (1980). *IBM Tech. Disclosure Bull. 23* 278–281.

Whitfield, D., Ball, R. G., and Bird, J. M. (1983). *Ergonomics 26* 1033–1053.

Wilton, J., and McLean, R. S. (1983). *Proceedings of the Fourth Canadian Symposium on Instructional Technology.*

Xing, Y. Z., and Boeder, C. P. W. (1985). *Sensors and Actuators 7* 153–166.

2

Human Factors Considerations in the Design and Selection of Computer Input Devices

LYNN Y. ARNAUT

Hewlett-Packard
Sunnyvale, California

JOEL S. GREENSTEIN

Clemson University
Clemson, South Carolina

2.1 Introduction

A list of the more common computer input devices includes keyboards, touch screen devices, graphic tablets, mice, trackballs, joysticks, and light pens. Additionally, although the ability of computers to recognize speech is limited at this time, speech recognition systems are now being employed effectively in certain applications, particularly those in which it is not possible or desirable to dedicate the hands to computer data entry. This chapter presents recommendations for the design and selection of a number of manual computer input devices. In Section 2.2, the human factors considerations affecting the design of each type of input device are considered in turn. Section 2.3 presents human performance and preference data to aid in the selection of an appropriate device type for a given application. Chapter 7 considers the use of voice as an alternative or additional medium for the input of information to a computer, while Chapter 3 focuses specifically on the keyboard, certainly the most ubiquitous input device in today's computer workstations.

2.2 Design Considerations

2.2.1 Touch Screen Devices

A touch screen device produces an input signal in response to a touch or movement of the finger on the display. Touch screens have traditionally been used with CRTs, but it is also possible to use them with other display technologies. There are two principles of touch screen operation; either an overlay senses pressure or beams projected across the screen are interrupted. The different touch screen technologies will be described briefly so the advantages and disadvantages of each device for different applications can be discussed.

In the first category are conductive, capacitive, and cross-wire devices. The conductive touch screen has two conductive layers, each with an electrode grid in both the X and Y directions. When pressure is applied, the two surfaces touch and a circuit is completed. The voltage levels from the X and Y axes are encoded into X and Y coordinates (Pfauth and Priest, 1981; Schulze and Snyder, 1983).

The capacitive touch screen device operates through the use of a conductive film deposited on the back of a glass overlay. A capacitive touch screen is depicted in Figure 2.1. The body's capacitance causes an electrical signal to be generated when an individual touches the overlay (Ritchie and Turner, 1975).

A less common version of the pressure-sensitive touch screen is the cross-wire device. This device uses both horizontal and vertical wires set in transparent sheets placed on the display (Schulze and Synder, 1983). A current is applied to either the vertical or horizontal wires and a signal is produced when the wires are touched at an intersection. One problem with these screens is that the wires may obscure parts of the display.

Most pressure-sensitive devices sense inputs in only two dimensions. An exception is the touch screen developed by Herot and Weinzapfel (1978). Two strain gauges are mounted on each side of the display, one to measure forces perpendicular to the glass overlay, such as occurs in a pointing motion, and one to measure forces parallel to the glass, as might occur when drawing. Force and torque values for X, Y, and Z axes are generated

Figure 2.1. A capacitive touch screen device. (Courtesy of MicroTouch Systems Inc., Woburn, Massachusetts.)

based on the output from the strain gauges, and these values are used to calculate X and Y coordinates and cursor acceleration (Schulze and Snyder, 1983). Drawing is made easier through the use of the strain gauges, but training may be required to use such a device due to the addition of the force vectors.

The second type of touch screen is activated when the finger interrupts a signal. In an acoustic touch screen, a glass plate is placed over the CRT screen and ultrasonic waves are generated on the glass by transducers placed along the edges (de Bruyne, 1980; Hlady, 1969). When a waveform is interrupted, the horizontal and vertical waves are reflected back and detected by the transducer, and X and Y coordinates are calculated based upon the time between wave transmission and detection. A problem peculiar to the acoustic touch screen is that there is a short period of time after a transducer emits a wave before it can act as a detector. Thus, there is a $1\frac{1}{2}$ to 2 inch strip on the outside of the glass that does not respond to touch input (Pfauth and Priest, 1981).

On an infrared touch screen, light emitting diodes are paired with light detectors and placed along all sides of the display, as shown in Figure 2.2.

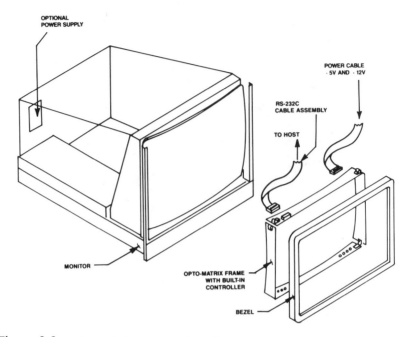

Figure 2.2. Schematic diagram of the infrared touch screen device. (Courtesy of Carroll Touch, Inc., Round Rock, Texas.)

When the operator touches his or her finger to the screen, two light beams are interrupted and the resulting X and Y coordinates for that position are calculated. The characteristics of the different touch screen technologies are summarized in Table 2.1.

Comparison of Touch Screen Devices. When choosing a touch screen, it is important to consider characteristics of the different technologies to provide the best match between the touch screen and its intended application. Logan (1985) has identified eight characteristics important in determining touch screen performance. These characteristics are: resolution, parallax, durability, optical clarity, installation and design, ease of use, environmental considerations, and cost. Several of these factors will be discussed in this section.

Resolution. Conductive screens tend to have the highest resolution; they may have from 1000×1000 to 4000×4000 discrete touch points. Capacitive screens typically have approximately 256×256 resolution. Infrared screens may have as few as 25×40 touch points due to limitations on the number of light beams that can be placed around the screen (Logan,

Table 2.1. Characteristics of Touch Screen
Technologies

	Touch Screens[a]				
	TW	IR	AC	PS	CO
Characteristics					
May obscure display	X				
Unreliable detection	X				
Limited resolution		X			
Parallax		X	X	X	
Sensitive to ambient lighting		X			
Inadvertent activation		X	X		
Does not use whole screen			X		
Awkward drawing device	X	X	X		X
Extra training required				X	
Reduced light from screen					X
Relatively easily damaged					X

SOURCE: Greenstein and Arnaut, 1987. Reproduced by permission of John Wiley & Sons, Inc.

[a] TW: Touch wire
  IR: Infrared
  AC: Acoustic
  PS: Pressure sensitive
  CO: Conductive

1985). Acoustic touch screens may have somewhat higher resolution than
infrared panels, but less than the other technologies.

For applications requiring high resolution, then, infrared and acoustic
devices may be unsuitable. However, even if high resolution is not required, additional touch points allow greater pointing precision because
the software can average all the points that have been touched. Additionally, the greater the number of touch points, the easier it is to map them to
the targets presented on the screen; screen design may thus become less
complicated and more flexible. If a target is not placed directly under a
touch point, errors in selection may occur (see, for example, Beringer and
Peterson, 1985).

Parallax. Parallax occurs when the touch surface or detectors are separated from the targets. For all touch screen technologies, the touch surface
will always be slightly above the target due to the glass surface of the display
between the phosphor and the finger. The addition of an overlay separates
the finger and the target even more. This problem can be alleviated by
requiring the user to be directly in front of the target and to place the finger
perpendicular to the screen. Unfortunately, this requirement offsets the

advantage of the naturalness of the required input, especially for targets at the side of the display.

For infrared touch screens, the parallax problem is increased. Because light beams travel in a straight line, the beams must be above the surface of the curved CRT. When the user touches the screen, the beam may be broken at a point that is not directly above the target (see Figure 2.3). This separation is even greater at the CRT edges. There have been some attempts to alleviate this problem by curving the rows of LEDs; however, Logan (1985) reports that a reduction of only 50 percent of the parallax has been achieved.

Durability. Touch screen durability is primarily a problem in dirty environments and when the touch screen is in continual use; for example, many touch screens are placed in public places such as hotels, banks, and office buildings to provide information to users. In this case, the touch screen must not be damaged easily. The conductive touch screen uses plastic sheets that may be scratched fairly readily. The glass surface on an acoustic touch screen may also be scratched; in addition to possibly obscuring the screen, dirt or scratches may falsely activate the device. The capacitive and infrared screens tend to be the most resistant to damage (Logan, 1985; Pfauth and Priest, 1981).

Optical Clarity. Optical clarity is of primary importance when an individual uses a touch screen for extended periods of time, such as in an office

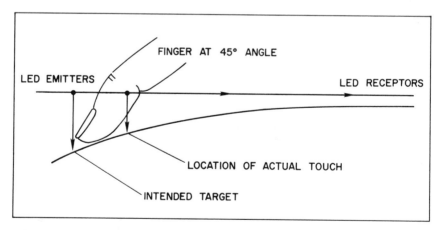

Figure 2.3. Parallax due to the removal of the infrared light beams from the display surface. (From Logan (1985), Copyright 1985, by Hearst Business Communications, Inc., and reproduced by permission.)

environment. A decrease in display quality can lead to strain and fatigue for the operator. Infrared touch screens are the best in preserving optical clarity since there is no overlay to obscure the display (Schulze and Snyder, 1983). Acoustic touch screens have a glass overlay, and thus they may not reduce the display clarity as much as the conductive and capacitive devices. The overlays on the latter devices tend to reduce the amount of light transmitted from the display.

Environmental Limitations.   Dirt and static electricity (which attracts dust) can be problems for touch screens. As previously indicated, the acoustic device may be activated by dirt or scratches on the glass; infrared beams can also be broken by dirt or smoke. An additional problem unique to the infrared device is that ambient lighting may affect the response of the device. However, the illumination in the workplace may be sampled and stored in memory to be used as a correction factor (Schulze and Snyder, 1983).

Although not affected by lighting or inadvertent activation like the acoustic and infrared screens, capacitive and conductive devices may be sensitive to changes in temperature and humidity. Finally, all the devices may be activated with a stylus with the exception of the capacitive touch screen. Since the capacitive screen utilizes the capacitance of the human body, it must be activated by a finger and may therefore be inappropriate in cold environments or those in which the user may wear a glove.

In general, the targets will probably not become obscured with any of the devices through regular use; Logan (1985) states that most touch screens are coated so that grease will not adhere to the surface. Fingerprints may be apparent on the display surface when an infrared device is used, although in general the screen or overlays can be easily cleaned.

Ease of Use.   Perhaps the most important yet least well-defined touch screen characteristic is the ease of learning and operation. Although touch screens require a natural pointing gesture and thus require minimal training in the initial concept, they may respond in unexpected ways and confuse the user. For example, as indicated earlier, the LED beams for an infrared device are above the screen. The user does not need to touch the device to activate the display; however, if the user does not understand this, there may be a problem with inadvertent activation and incorrect target selection due to parallax.

Another factor is the pressure required to activate an overlay. If too much pressure is required, the activation may take longer and lead to user discomfort (Logan, 1985). Finally, touch screens with low resolution may be frustrating for the operator; if the touch points are not centered over the targets, an incorrect response or no response at all may be registered.

Empirical Evidence. Only one study to date has provided any objective performance data to aid in deciding between the various touch screen technologies. Schulze and Snyder (1983) performed a comparison of five touch screens: acoustic, capacitive, conductive film, cross-wires, and infra-red. They found that the infrared device provided the highest display clarity due to the fact that no overlay was placed over the screen. The capacitive device resulted in the least display noise. In a second experiment, subjects performed three tasks: 1) searching for and touching a specified alphanumeric character, 2) assigning seats on an aircraft, and 3) hierarchical menu selection. On the basis of errors and total time to complete these three tasks, the authors reported that the infrared and cross-wire devices provided the best performance. Overall, the cross-wire device received the highest subjective rankings from the participants.

Parameters of Touch Screens.   The characteristics of touch screens discussed in the previous section reflect hardware dimensions that may affect the performance of a touch screen in different applications. Once a touch screen technology is chosen for a given application, it is possible to design the controlling software and the displayed images to improve performance further. In the following section, several potential design parameters will be discussed.

Touch Key Design.   Valk (1985) compared the ten touch screen buttons or keys shown in Figure 2.4 in an attempt to determine guidelines for their design for an industrial process control application. The touch-sensitive section of each key was white and the state of the key (on or off) was highlighted by an orange background for most keys. The keys were presented individually to the participants, who were required to indicate the initial key state and then to change that state.

The dependent measures included the number of incorrect touches, the correctness of the key state identification, the time taken to change the state, and the touch location. Based upon these measure, Valk identified key characteristics that tended to lead to confusion. Keys with adjacent color-coded squares with a label in each square led to more confusion than those with both labels in one square. Keys that indicated motions incompatible with the necessary direct press required (such as the sliding switch in key 5) also led to a decrease in performance. Keys that could be activated in any area rather than a single part tended to decrease confusion, as did the presence of recognizable designs (such as the light switch and

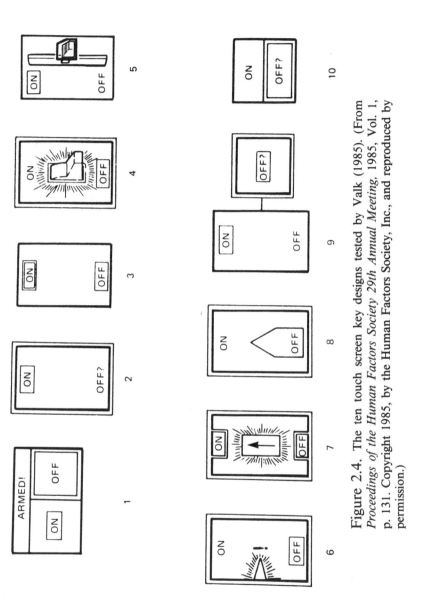

Figure 2.4. The ten touch screen key designs tested by Valk (1985). (From *Proceedings of the Human Factors Society 29th Annual Meeting*, 1985, Vol. 1, p. 131. Copyright 1985, by the Human Factors Society, Inc., and reproduced by permission.)

pointer in keys 4 and 8). Subjects also tended to touch the on and off labels in each key, even if a press was required elsewhere. Overall, key 10 led to the most errors.

Key Size. Two other factors affecting performance with touch screen keys are their size and the separation between them. Beaton and Weiman (1984) performed a study with a conductive touch panel in which they varied the horizontal and vertical size and separation of touch keys. They tested two key heights (5.08 and 10.16 mm), two key widths (10.16 and 20.32 mm), three horizontal separations (from 0.0 to 20.32 mm), and five vertical separations (from 0.0 to 20.32 mm). Subjects were required to press the touch key containing a consonant-vowel-consonant (CVC) trigram that matched a target CVC. Key height significantly affected error rate; the taller key led to fewer errors than the shorter key. The other key dimensions did not significantly affect performance. However, the vertical separation interacted with key height; for the 10.16 mm keys, there was an increase in errors as the vertical separation increased, while the opposite trend occurred for the 5.08 mm keys. Preference data suggested that the largest keys (10.16 mm high by 20.32 mm wide) were preferred, along with a horizontal separation of 10.16 mm and a vertical separation of 5.08 or 10.16 mm.

In a second experiment, Beaton and Weiman investigated the effects of viewing angle on touch key size. The basic effects of key size were replicated. In addition, the authors report that as viewing angle increased, the error rate did not increase as much for the wide key as it did for the narrow key.

Weiman, Beaton, Knox, and Glasser (1985) performed a similar experiment with an infrared touch screen. They used key heights of 6.4 and 12.8 mm and key widths of 9.4 and 18.8 mm, and the same CVC target selection task just described. The results essentially replicate those of Beaton and Weiman (1985); the taller keys led to better performance, and the tall, wide keys were preferred. The separation between keys was not as critical, and when the keys were large enough the separation did not affect performance. The authors suggest that optimal key matrix designs should provide dense vertical arrangements of tall keys and that wide keys are preferred. It should be noted, however, that a limited number of key sizes were included in these experiments. Thus, while providing guidelines for key design, these experiments do not indicate the optimal size of keys. In addition, they do not indicate whether there are expected differences in the speed of performance since error rate was the only dependent measure studied.

Feedback and Acceptance of Input. It is possible to provide users with feedback of both the current cursor location and of the correctness of their actions. It is also possible to modify the software to accept only certain inputs as valid. Both of these techniques may be used to improve performance by making users aware of the results of their actions and by making the effects of spurious inputs or movements negligible.

Weiman et al. (1985) studied the effects of both of these design parameters. They provided users with two types of location feedback: in one condition, a tracking cursor followed the user's finger in the active touch area; in the other, the tracking cursor appeared and, additionally, the key that the cursor was in was highlighted. They also included two types of software algorithms designed to reduce the selection error rate. One algorithm, called "last key," only accepted touches that were contained within a known key site. The other algorithm, called "last touch," accepted as input only the last touch coordinates instead of responding to the first touch.

While the main effect of feedback was not significant when compared with a group receiving no feedback, the combination of feedback and encoding algorithm did improve menu selection accuracy. Any feedback plus the last-touch algorithm improved performance over a baseline group with neither of these modifications, and feedback plus the last-key algorithm improved performance even more.

Beringer and Peterson (1985) performed a study to examine response biases inherent in touch screen performance and the effects of operator training and software compensation on these errors. In their first experiment, a 9 × 6 matrix of circles was presented to the subjects. One of the circles had a break in it, and the task was to identify and touch this target. The screen was tilted away from the subjects at 90, 75, 60, and 45 degrees, respectively. Results indicated that users tended to touch slightly below the target. This effect was more pronounced for targets near the top of the display and for the larger screen angles. The authors state that these errors were probably due to parallax and a need to extend the arm farther for the top targets.

In their second experiment, Beringer and Peterson compared two methods of decreasing this reponse bias: providing training for the operators and incorporating software to compensate for the bias. The task was to touch a square target on a blank field. Operator training was accomplished by providing feedback in the form of a square around the touch point. Also, software models based on the performance of individual subjects were developed to provide the automatic reponse bias compensation. Both methods reduced the response errors. The work of Beringer and Peterson (1985), along with that of Weiman et al. (1985), indicates that feedback and software modifications may increase accuracy and the ease of touch screen use.

Advantages and Disadvantages of Touch Screen Devices. One of the most obvious advantages of touch screen devices is that the input device is also the output device. That is, there is direct eye-hand coordination. Consequently, there is a direct relationship between the user's input and the displayed output. A second advantage is that possible inputs are limited by what is displayed on the screen; thus, no memorization of commands is required, and input errors are minimized. In addition, the possible inputs can change as the display changes so that the operator may be led through an appropriate sequence of inputs.

With the exception of Herot and Weinzapfel's (1978) pressure-sensitive device that can be used for drawing, the only input required by a touch screen device is a natural pointing gesture. Training is thereby minimized for a touch screen device and so is the need for operator selection procedures. Individuals can become quite skilled at fast target selection in a relatively short period of time. Consequently, there may be high user acceptance of such a device.

Touch screens have several disadvantages. Because the output surface is also the input medium, the user must sit within arm's reach of the display. This requirement may constrain both the workplace design and the mobility of the operator. The user must continually lift his or her hand to the display and may thus experience arm fatigue; additionally, the user's finger or arm may block the screen.

Another disadvantage is that regardless of the inherent touch screen resolution, there is limited target resolution possible due to the size of the operator's finger in relation to the screen. The use of a stylus may reduce this problem, but the pointing gesture becomes less natural, and the user must then pick up a device before touching the screen. If a finger is used, touch screen devices are inappropriate for selection of small items.

Since the touch screen must be fitted onto a display, there may be a problem with retrofit if the display has already been purchased; some technologies may not fit some displays, and some displays may not have any screens made to fit them. Finally, for the input of unstructured data, data entry using a touch screen will be slower than it will be with a keyboard. The advantages and disadvantages of touch screen devices are summarized in Table 2.2.

Types of Tasks. Due to the nature of the touch screen device, it is best suited to certain task types. Pfauth and Priest (1981) state that these devices are best used when working with data already displayed on the screen,

Table 2.2. Advantages and Disadvantages of Touch Screen Devices

Advantages	Disadvantages
1. Direct eye-hand coordination	1. Arm fatigue
2. No command memorization needed	2. Limited resolution
3. Operator may be led through correct command sequence	3. User must be close to display
4. Minimal training needed	4. Slow data entry
5. High user acceptance	5. Finger/Arm may obscure screen
	6. Overlays may lead to parallax
	7. Retrofit

SOURCE: Adapted from Greenstein and Arnaut, 1987. Reproduced by permission of John Wiley & Sons, Inc.

while they are inefficient for inputting new graphic information or for freehand drawing. Touch screen devices are quite useful in menu-selection tasks. In addition, it has already been stated that selection or entry of single characters is slow and may be beyond the resolution capabilities of the touch screen device.

Touch screen devices are useful in applications where it is time-consuming or perhaps even dangerous to divert attention from the display. There is evidence, for example, indicating that touch entry devices may work well in air traffic control tasks (Gaertner and Holzhausen, 1980; Stammers and Bird, 1980). Other research indicates that touch screens are useful in tactical display workstations (Davis and Badger, 1982). These devices are also beneficial in reducing workload in situations where the possible types of inputs are limited and well defined. For instance, Beringer (1979) states that touch screen devices may decrease workload if used in plane cockpits for navigation. Similarly, touch screen devices are potentially beneficial in high-stress environments due to the limited number of possible inputs (Pfauth and Priest, 1981). Finally, if many potential users are unfamiliar with the system, touch panels may prove helpful; for example, touch screen devices have been used successfully with information displays in shopping malls, banks, and hotels.

2.2.2 Graphic Tablets

Graphic or data tablets consist of a flat panel that is placed on a table in front of the display. The surface of the tablet represents the display, and movement of a finger or a stylus on the tablet provides information for cursor location. There are two types of graphic tablets. Digitizing tablets or digitizers have a special stylus or puck attached to the tablet by a cable. The stylus produces signals indicating coordinate values for cursor positioning.

The other type of graphic tablet is typically called a touch tablet or a touch-sensitive tablet. Figure 2.5 shows a touch tablet. This device responds to a touch by a finger or pen, and it uses information from the tablet instead of a stylus to calculate cursor position. The majority of human factors evaluations of graphic tablets have used touch tablets rather than digitizers. Thus, unless otherwise indicated, it can be assumed that a touch tablet was used for any research cited.

There are several graphic tablet technologies. Representative technologies will be described briefly so that the characteristics and advantages of each may be discussed. The characteristics of these technologies are briefly summarized in Table 2.3.

Matrix-encoded digitizers work through the use of electrical or magnetic fields. As the special stylus or puck is passed over the tablet surface, it detects signals produced by horizontal and vertical conductors or wires in the tablet, as shown in Figure 2.6. These signals are used to determine X and Y coordinates for the cursor. One advantage of this system is that it allows for high resolution of cursor control. With a voltage-gradient tablet, a conductive sheet forms the surface of the tablet. A potential is applied to the point of the stylus, and a decrease in potential on the plate at the stylus position is measured. Using the distance from the sides of the tablet as a reference, X and Y coordinate values are calculated (Ohlson, 1978; Ritchie and Turner, 1975). For this method to work, the stylus must be in direct

Figure 2.5. A touch tablet. (Courtesy of Elographics, Inc., Oak Ridge, Tennessee.)

Table 2.3. Characteristics of Graphic Tablet Technologies

Characteristics	Graphic Tablet[a]					
	ME	VG	AD	EA	AT	ML
High resolution	X	X				
Three-dimensional capability			X			
Requires stylus	X	X	X	X		
Produces noise			X			
Sensitive to ambient noise			X			
Inadvertent activation					X	X

SOURCE: Greenstein and Arnaut, 1987. Reproduced by permission of John Wiley & Sons, Inc.

[a] ME: matrix-encoded
VG: voltage-gradient
AD: acoustic digitizing
EA: electroacoustic
AT: acoustic touch
ML: multilayer

contact with the tablet surface. Thus, no paper may be placed on the tablet for such operations as tracing or digitizing.

Acoustic digitizing tablets operate through the use of a stylus that generates a spark at its tip (see Figure 2.7). The sound impulses are detected by two strip microphones mounted on adjacent sides of the tablet. By determining the delay between the time the sound originated and its reception,

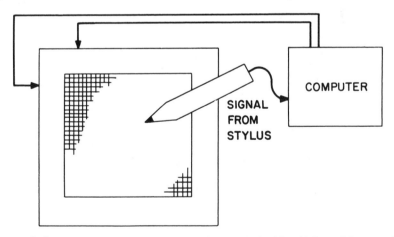

Figure 2.6. Schematic diagram of a matrix encoded tablet. (Adapted, by permission, from Newman and Sproull (1973), *Principles of Interactive Computer Graphics,* Mc-Graw-Hill.)

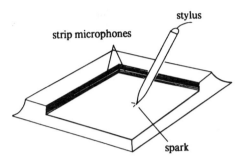

Figure 2.7. An acoustic digitizing tablet. (Reprinted, by permission, from New-man and Sproull (1979), *Principles of Interactive Computer Graphics, McGraw-Hill.*)

X and Y coordinate values may be calculated. Ohlson (1978) states that the acoustic tablet does not provide high resolution.

An alternative acoustic technique, called the electroacoustic method, requires that electric pulses be generated on the tablet. These pulses are detected by the stylus, and the delay between pulse generation and recep-tion is used to calculate the cursor position. Electroacoustic tablets are quieter than acoustic tablets and are less sensitive to noise in the environ-ment (Newman and Sproull, 1979).

The acoustic touch tablet may be used without a special stylus. High-frequency waves are produced on a glass surface. When these waves are interrupted by a finger or pen, they are reflected back to the tablet edge. Acoustic couplers detect the reflection, and as with the acoustic digitizing tablet, the delay between the wave generation and reception is used to calculate X and Y coordinates. One disadvantage of this technique is that if the arm and/or hand touch the tablet surface, inadvertent activation may result.

There are several tablets available that use two or three conducting sheets. When these sheets are pressed together by a passive stylus or finger, an electrical potential is generated and X and Y coordinate values are calculated based upon the origin of the signal (Ritchie and Turner, 1975). As with the acoustic touch tablets, the user's arm may not be in contact with the tablet, else inadvertent operation may result.

There are other types of touch tablets that may be used without concern for inadvertent activation caused by arm pressure. For example, Scott (1982) discusses a touch-sensitive digitizer that responds only to a point of pressure, such as that from a pen. For a more detailed discussion of these and other technologies, see Mims (1984) or Ritchie and Turner (1975).

Parameters of Graphic Tablets. In this section, several ways in which graphic tablets may be modified according to task, user, and environmental demands are discussed. The flexible parameters include the method of cursor control, the control-display relationship, the configuration and sizing of the tablet, confirmation and feedback, stylus versus finger control, and the ability to sense inputs in more than two directions.

Method of Cursor Control. One feature of the tablet subject to modification is the way the cursor responds to a movement or placement on the tablet. For example, when an individual places his or her finger on the tablet, the display cursor may move from its current position and appear at a position that corresponds to the location of the finger on the tablet. Movement of the finger on the tablet will produce cursor movement such that the cursor location is continually referenced to the actual coordinates of the finger on the tablet. This method may be referred to as an *absolute* mode of cursor control.

A second possibility is that when the finger is placed anywhere on the tablet, the display cursor remains in its current position. Movement of the finger in this case leads to a corresponding cursor movement relative to this cursor location; consequently, this method is referred to as a *relative* mode of cursor control. Relative mode may be likened to movement of a cursor by a trackball. The difference between the absolute and relative mode may be described as a difference in the information provided for cursor location; in absolute mode both cursor position and movement information are provided, while only cursor movement information is given in relative mode.

The nature of the task may dictate which method should be used. Arnaut and Greenstein (1986) found that an absolute mode of target acquisition resulted in faster target selection rates than did relative mode, as did Epps, Snyder, and Muto (1986). Similarly, Ellingstad, Parng, Gehlen, Swierenga, and Auflick (1985) reported that there was less RMS-error on a compensatory tracking task when absolute mode was used. However, there may be instances in which the tablet must be small in comparison to the display; for example, a tablet may be inserted in a keyboard. In this case, the display would typically be much larger than the tablet, and absolute mode would require that a high control-to-display gain be used. Relative mode might be preferred since the gain will then not be dictated by the size of the tablet. (See the next section for a discussion of the relationship between gain, tablet size, and method of cursor control).

Control-Display Relationship. The amount of movement of the display cursor in response to a movement on the tablet, or what is referred to as *control-display gain,* may be changed. (See Chapanis and Kinkade (1972) for a general discussion of control-display relationships.) The tablet gain can interact with the method of cursor control in the design of an interface. When a tablet is used in absolute mode, the control-display gain dictates that size of the tablet. For example, a gain of 1.0 means that the tablet is the same size as the display, while a gain of 2.0 means that the tablet is half the size of the display. This is true for absolute mode because the coordinates of the tablet are directly translated into a position on the display. With relative mode, the finger can be anywhere on the tablet since the finger provides movement information only. Thus, the size of the tablet is free to vary with relative mode. However, if the size of a tablet used with relative mode and a given gain is such that a movement across the entire tablet surface does not move the cursor across the entire display, then the user will have to make several sweeping movements with his or her finger to move the cursor across an appreciable part of the display. In this case, the tablet operation approaches that of a trackball. This situation would arise when a small tablet is used with a low gain.

Arnaut and Greenstein (1986) found that for a touch-sensitive tablet with a display size of approximately 31.75 cm (12.5 in), a gain between 0.8 and 1.0 resulted in better performance on a target selection task than did higher or lower gains. This result occurred for both relative and absolute modes. The superiority of this range of gains is probably due to the fact that with higher gains, while gross movements to the vicinity of the target are faster, fine positioning movements into the target are more difficult. With lower gains, any improvements in fine positioning performance are outweighed by the additional time required for gross movement. For a tablet in absolute mode, the size of the tablet would therefore be either the same size or slightly larger than the display when the gain is from 0.8 to 1.0, while a tablet in relative mode could be made any size regardless of the gain.

A touch tablet in relative mode is typically programmed to displace the cursor by an amount proportional to the displacement of the finger across the tablet, independent of the finger velocity during execution of this displacement. It is possible, however, to program such a tablet to include a gain component that depends on finger velocity in addition to the gain component that depends solely on finger displacement. In this case, the displacement of the cursor increases in proportion to the finger's velocity as well as the finger's displacement. A rapid movement of the finger of a given displacement will move the cursor a greater distance than a gradual movement with the same displacement. Because human control inputs tend to be rapid during gross movement and more gradual during fine positioning, the addition of a velocity-gain component offers the possibility of high overall gain during gross movement, diminishing to a lower gain during fine positioning. Using this approach, the overall gain can be adjusted to enhance gross movement speed, as well as fine positioning accuracy.

Becker and Greenstein (1986) compared a pure position-gain system with a position- and velocity-gain touch tablet (referred to as a lead-lag compensation system). The results indicated that while the target selection rate was faster for the lead-lag system, there were more entries into the target prior to confirmation and a slight increase in errors as compared to a pure position-gain system. The authors suggest that the improvement in target selection rate for the lead-lag system more than offsets the slight decrease in accuracy for many applications.

Tablet Configuration. Although the fact that graphic tablets are separate from the display means that there is an indirect relationship between the output and input devices, it also means that they are more flexible than touch screen devices. The size of the tablet may vary from one that can fit on or next to a keyboard to an entire digitizing table. Additionally, the low profile of the tablet in comparison to a joystick or trackball means that inadvertent activation is less likely. Also, the tablet can be made easily transportable.

In addition to allowing flexibility in sizing, the flat surface of the tablet itself may be configured in many ways. For example, for ease and correctness of positioning, a template may be placed over the tablet to correspond with positions on the display in a menu-selection task. This is especially useful for a task in which menu or function positions do not change. Alternatively, for applications other than target or function selection, an overlay may indicate allowable operations that are not directly referenced to the display. For example, one software package designed to teach music basics includes a template imprinted with a keyboard. The keys on the template correspond to notes that can be heard and displayed on the screen, but the keyboard itself is not displayed (Holden, 1984).

Brown, Buxton, and Murtagh (1985) suggest a more sophisticated use of the tablet. They state that the tablet surface may be divided into separate regions analogous to display windows. Each region may then be configured to become a different virtual input device; that is, each area may respond to inputs differently in order to emulate the characteristics of other input devices. For example, one window may have specific areas that can be treated like buttons. Another window may be in relative mode and may be used much like a trackball. This flexibility may be extremely useful in system prototyping; the use of virtual input devices simultaneously may aid in making hardware decisions for later versions of the system. Brown et al. state that such flexibility is possible only with a touch tablet because it is able to provide absolute coordinate locations and because it consists of a plane with fixed coordinate locations. Mice, trackballs, and joysticks do not have these capabilities. In addition, the input device must be separate from the output device for such an application, thus a light pen or a touch screen placed over the displayed output could not be used in such a manner either.

Confirmation and Feedback. Due to the indirect nature of the graphic tablet, Swezey and Davis (1983) suggest that it is important to include a feedback or confirmation mechanism, especially where incorrect entries may be detrimental. An audible click or tone and/or a visual confirmation can be used to signal that an entry has been recognized. Visual and auditory feedback may be especially helpful since no tactile feedback is provided by pressing the tablet. Requiring confirmation and providing feedback have two benefits: first, the operator is aware that an entry has been accepted, and second, inadvertent inputs can be avoided.

One problem related to confirmation that has been identified in several studies of touch tablets is referred to as "fall-out" or "jitter" (Buxton, Hill, and Rowley, 1985; Whitfield, Ball, and Bird, 1983). That is, when the finger is removed from the tablet, the centroid of finger pressure shifts, and the display cursor moves in response. Fall-out may be avoided in several ways. First, a stylus may be used to decrease the area of pressure. Second, the last few data samples may be discarded after lift-off so that the cursor remains in the position it was in just prior to removal of the finger from the tablet. Finally, users could leave their fingers on the tablet and press a separate confirmation button with the other hand.

Ellingstad et al. (1985) studied various methods of confirming an entry. These methods were: 1) lifting the finger off the tablet; 2) lifting the finger off the tablet and pressing a separate area on the tablet; 3) lifting the finger off the tablet and pressing a key located off the tablet; and 4) keeping the finger on the tablet and pressing a separate key off the tablet. Cursor positioning, compensatory tracking, data entry, and a simulated operator's task with function selection and data entry were studied.

The lift-off-only method of confirmation tended to be the fastest, but it led to more errors than the other methods (this is possibly due to fall-out error). Lift-off with a separate enter key consistently produced good performance in terms of errors and reponse time across all tasks. The authors suggest that the latter method is preferred when error correction is not readily available. If error correction procedures are available, or if the targets provided are large enough so that fall-out error is minimal, lift-off only may be a better choice. It should be noted that in the study by

Ellingstad et al., in the condition where subjects were required to lift their finger and press a separate area on the tablet, the same hand was used to press the confirmation area as had been used for positioning. In the other methods in which a key was pressed, the opposite hand was used to confirm. This factor may have caused the lift-off with confirmation on the tablet to take somewhat longer than the other conditions. Thus, in some cases this method may be useful in place of the lift-off with separate enter key it two hands are used.

Stylus versus Finger Control. A touch tablet may typically be used with either a finger or a stylus. The advantage of using a finger is its simplicity; there is no stylus to lose or break. A stylus, however, can provide greater resolution since the area over which it applies pressure is smaller than that of a finger. It also allows an operator to make small movements without requiring the entire hand or arm to move; moving the stylus with the fingers allows fine adjustments to be made. However, certain tablets may be damaged if a stylus is used over extended periods of time; it may be necessary to place a protective layer over the tablet surface. Ellingstad et al. (1985) reported that for cursor positioning, compensatory tracking, data entry, and function-selection tasks, the use of a stylus resulted in faster and more accurate responses than did use of a finger.

Two- versus Three-Dimensional Tablets. Touch tablets can be made to transmit information in more than two dimensions. For example, Buxton et al. (1985) reported that pressure-sensitive tablets have been developed; these tablets can be made to respond differentially to varying amounts of pressure in the same location. Thus, a light touch may be used for drawing, while a heavy touch might indicate function selection. For graphics applications, different degrees of pressure might be used to indicate the widths of lines.

Other types of tablets may also provide three-dimensional information. For example, acoustic digitizing tablets may include a third microphone perpendicular to the tablet in addition to the two microphones along the edges of the tablet. In this way, movements of the stylus in the air above the tablet can be detected and three-dimensional drawings may be created.

Advantages and Disadvantages of Graphic Tablets. Graphic tablets have several advantages. First, the movement required and the control-display relationship are natural to many users. Similarly, Swezey and Davis (1983) suggest that graphic tablets may improve productivity because the user is not required to "translate" a command or movement into a series of key presses. Because the tablet surface is constructed of one piece with no moving parts, tablets are suited for use in "hostile" environments in which input devices may be easily damaged (Buxton et al., 1985). They may also be easily cleaned; thus, they are useful in industrial applications.

For tablets capable of sensing multiple simultaneous inputs, it is possible to use more than one hand and even more than one finger on each hand to input information. A tablet may thus have the capability of simulating a keyboard by assigning locations on the tablet to specific alphanumeric characters. The characters can be displayed on the screen or placed on an overlay. Even tablets that can accept information from only one input location at a time can be used for keyboard data entry, although typing may have to be artificially slowed in this case. It may also be possible to place a modified keyboard with plungers over the tablet. When a key is struck, an entry is registered; the tablet can be programmed to associate that location with a given letter or symbol. In this manner, tactile feedback may be provided, thereby improving the tablet's data entry potential while alleviating the necessity of interfacing a keyboard directly to the system.

In comparison with touch screen devices, in which the user points directly at the screen to input data, Whitfield, Ball, and Bird (1983) suggest that the graphic tablet provides four distinct advantages. First, both the display and the tablet may be positioned separately according to user preference. Second, the user's hand does not cover any parts of the display. Third, there are no problems with parallax due to the viewing angle of the user. Fourth, drift in the display will not affect the input. In addition, the user of a graphic tablet is not likely to experience fatigue associated with continually lifting his or her hand to the screen, as is typical with a light pen or touch screen.

Graphic tablets have several disadvantages. Foley and Wallace (1974) indicate that touch-sensitive tablets may not provide high positioning accuracy, although digitizers can typically provide high resolution. In comparison with a touch screen, graphic tablets do not allow for direct eye-hand coordination, since they are somewhat removed from the display. Large graphic tablets take up space on the work surface, although as depicted in Figure 2.8, small tablets may be inserted in a keyboard for cursor control. For tablets that require a stylus, there may be a problem with loss or breakage of the stylus (Rouse, 1975). Friction may be a problem over extended use periods. It is important to adjust the tablet so that the pressure required does not fatigue the operator. See Table 2.4 for a summary of these advantages and disadvantages.

Types of Tasks. Graphic tablets may be effectively used for several types of tasks. A graphic tablet is virtually the only input device useful for drafting or hard copy data entry (Ohlson, 1978; Rouse, 1975), freehand

Figure 2.8. A touch tablet inserted into a keyboard may be used for cursor control. (Courtesy of Key Tronic Corp., Spokane, Washington.)

sketching (Ellis and Sibley, 1967; Hornbuckle, 1967), or producing a three-dimensional picture (Sutherland, 1974). Parrish, Gates, Munger, Grimma, and Smith (1982), in an attempt to standardize military usage of input devices, recommend that graphic tablets be used for all drawing purposes. Touch tablets are also appropriate when the user must select or point to an item from an array or menu. Because of their inherent graphic nature and the fact that with many tablets all fingers may not be used at one time, alphanumeric data entry with graphic tablets is typically slow.

A digitizer has several advantages over a touch-sensitive tablet (White, 1983). First, it is especially suited for digitizing graphical information such as drawings, maps, and graphs. Thus, it is well suited for many CAD/CAM applications. Digitizers typically have higher resolution than touch-sensi-

Table 2.4. Advantages and Disadvantages of Graphic Tablets

Advantages	Disadvantages
1. Natural control-display relationship	1. May have low positioning accuracy
2. Hand doesn't obscure display	2. Indirect eye-hand coordination
3. No parallax	3. Requires space
4. No arm fatigue	4. May lose or break digitizer stylus
5. Can modify control-display gain	5. Slow character data entry
6. Can use absolute or relative mode	

SOURCE: Greenstein and Arnaut, 1987. Reproduced by permission of John Wiley & Sons, Inc.

tive tablets, in part because of the small tip on the stylus. In addition, digitizers do not respond to pressure from the arm as some touch-sensitive tablets do. On the other hand, a touch-sensitive tablet has the advantage of being operable without a special stylus. Thus, loss of or damage to the stylus is not a problem. Finger-activated tablets also eliminate the extra movement required to pick up the stylus. These tablets are useful for cursor movement applications when digitizing is not required.

2.2.3 Mice

A mouse is a hand-held input device consisting of a small plastic box that can fit under the palm or fingertips, attached to the computer by a wire. Movement of the mouse on a flat surface is used to generate cursor movement. Mice have from one to three buttons that may be pressed to perform such functions as changing menus, drawing lines, or confirming inputs. Movement of the mouse is detected mechanically or optically.

The mechanical technique typically involves mounting a small ball in the bottom of the mouse; essentially this device is then an upside-down trackball. Movement of the ball leads to output from potentiometers or optical encoders that is used to determine orientation information. One problem with mechanical mice is that they may produce noise during movement. Additionally, debris from the table surface may become lodged inside the mouse. However, mechanical mice have the advantage of working on any surface.

Another mouse technology uses optical sensors that emit pulses as the mouse is moved across a special grid. The number of lines in the grid are counted as the mouse crosses the grid, and X and Y coordinates are calculated accordingly. An optical mouse is shown in Figure 2.9. The control-display gain of the mouse may be changed by changing the spacing of the lines on the grid (Somerson, 1983). These mice make no noise and require no moving parts; thus, they will not pick up debris from the surface. However, optical mice require that the special grid be used. Resolution may also be lower than that obtained with mechanical mice (Somerson, 1983).

Parameters of the Mouse. As indicated previously, mice typically have one or more buttons that may be pressed to perform various functions. Price and Cordova (1983) compared two methods of button depression: 1) multiple depressions on one button, and 2) depression of multiple buttons. The authors report that for a task in which one item was repeatedly selected, performance was faster for clicks of single rather than multiple buttons. However, for a task involving several actions (in this case, cursor

Figure 2.9. An optical mouse. (Courtesy of Mouse Systems Corp., Santa Clara, California.)

movement and an indication of the correctness of a mathematical sum), performance using multiple buttons was better than when multiple clicks of the same button were used.

As was the case with the graphic tablet, the gain of the mouse may be changed. Thus, movement of the mouse may result in either more, less, or the same amount of movement of the cursor on the screen. However, unlike the graphic tablet, the mouse will only work in relative mode.

Advantages and Disadvantages of the Mouse. Mice have become popular as computer peripheral devices for several reasons. First, they can work in small spaces because the mouse can be picked up and repositioned. Second, as mentioned earlier, the control-display gain for a mouse can be modified, although this capability is not often made commercially available. A third advantage of mice is that they are inexpensive in comparison to other devices, such as graphic tablets. Fourth, the operator can usually locate and move the mouse while still looking at the screen. For further discussion of these advantages, see Rubinstein and Hersh (1984), Somerson (1983), and Warfield (1983).

There are also disadvantages associated with the mouse (McGeever, 1984; Mims, 1984; Scott, 1982). First, while it is true that the mouse may only require a small surface, it does require some space in addition to that allotted to a keyboard. Thus, it is not compatible with many portable or lap computers. Second, as stated previously, a mouse can only be operated in relative mode, a feature that may limit its usefulness for drawing tasks.

Other limitations of the mouse for graphic applications include an inability to trace a drawing or to handprint characters. Drawing with a mouse is not as natural as drawing with a pen or pencil. Thus, some experience may be necessary to effectively use the mouse for graphic tasks.

In comparison with digitizers, mice typically have lower resolution capabilities. They also do not transmit information as quickly as do most digitizers; the difference may be on the order of a tenfold decrease from digitizer to mouse (McGeever, 1984; Newman and Sproull, 1979). For a brief review of the advantages and disadvantages of the mouse, see Table 2.5.

Types of Tasks. Due to the limitations of the mouse, it is best suited for pointing and selection tasks, while graphic tablets are more suited to drawing and design tasks. In addition, as with the touch screen devices, the mouse is not well suited for single character data entry. Thus, mice are typically used as ancillary devices only and not as the sole input device.

2.2.4 Trackballs

A trackball is composed of a fixed housing holding a ball that can be moved freely in any direction by the fingertips, as shown in Figure 2.10. This input device is similar to the mouse in operation. Two types of trackballs will be discussed: 1) mechanical trackballs that make use of potentiometers, and 2) trackballs using optics. For a more detailed description of these trackballs, see Ritchie and Turner (1975) and Scott (1982).

Movement of a mechanical trackball leads to movement of two shaft encoders. This, in turn, causes output to be generated from internal potentiometers. The output pulses from the potentiometers correspond to changes in the X and Y directions; the display cursor is moved accordingly.

Table 2.5. Advantages and Disadvantages of Mice

Advantages	Disadvantages
1. Work in small spaces	1. Require space beside keyboard
2. Can modify control-display gain	2. May have low resolution and information
3. Inexpensive	transmission rates
4. User can keep eyes on screen	3. Unnatural drawing movements
5. Mechanical mice use any surface	4. Relative mode only
6. Optical mice are noiseless	5. Optical mice require grid
	6. Mechanical mice produce noise and pick up debris

SOURCE: Greenstein and Arnaut, 1987. Reproduced by permission of John Wiley & Sons, Inc.

Figure 2.10. A trackball. (Courtesy of Honeywell, Inc., Disc Instruments Subsidiary, Costa Mesa, California.)

In an optical trackball, optical encoders generate signals or pulses. These pulses are used to determine increments in rotation in each of four directions: up and down on both the X and Y axes.

Parameters of the Trackball. The diameter, mass, and frictional forces of the trackball may all be adjusted. Control-display gain is an additional design parameter that must be specified. Like the mouse, the trackball is solely a relative mode device. In an approach analogous to that discussed for the touch tablet in relative mode, a gain component that depends on trackball velocity can be added to the position gain that depends on trackball displacement. In this case, rapid movements of the ball will result in larger cursor movements per unit of ball rotation than gradual movements. The trackball's gain function may then be adjusted so that both gross movement speed (for which high gain is appropriate) and fine positioning accuracy (which requires lower gain) are possible. Thus, the trackball may be fairly flexible, permitting rapid movements and accurate positioning.

Advantages and Disadvantages of Trackballs. The trackball has several advantages that have contributed to its selection in many military applica-

Table 2.6. Advantages and Disadvantages of the Trackball

Advantages	Disadvantages
1. Direct tactile feedback	1. Not well suited for drawing
2. High resolution	2. No three-dimensional
3. Requires little space	input
4. Allows rapid cursor positioning	
5. Can modify control-display gain	

SOURCE: Adapted from Greenstein and Arnaut, 1987. Reproduced by permission of John Wiley & Sons, Inc.

tions (Ritchie and Turner, 1975; Rubinstein and Hersh, 1984). First, it is comfortable to use for an extended period of time if users can rest their forearm, since they can keep their hand in one place and spin the trackball, stopping it when desired. The trackball also provides direct tactile feedback from the ball's rotation and speed. It provides high resolution of movement. A fourth advantage is that a trackball requires only a small, fixed amount of space, and it can be installed in a keyboard. Finally, due to these advantages and the flexibility of its features described in the previous section, a trackball can achieve rapid cursor movement.

Some disadvantages of the trackball are that it cannot be used for tracing, input of hand-drawn characters, or three-dimensional drawings. The advantages and disadvantages of trackballs are summarized in Table 2.6.

Types of Tasks.   Due to the limitations of the trackball just described, it is best suited for tasks requiring rapid and accurate cursor positioning. While trackballs may be used to draw lines and sketch, Parrish et al. (1982) suggest that they should only be used when requirements for drawing speed and accuracy are not stringent. These authors also suggest that trackballs are excellent for moving and indicating symbols on a display, especially when high speed and accuracy are necessary.

2.2.5 Joysticks

A joystick consists of a lever approximately 2.5 to 10 cm (1 to 4 in.) long, mounted vertically in a fixed base. The joystick operates using one of three basic mechanisms: displacement, force, or digital switches. These technologies will be discussed briefly; Mims (1984), Ohlson (1978), and Scott (1982) provide additional information on these devices.

With a displacement joystick, movements of the lever are detected by

Figure 2.11. A displacement joystick. (Courtesy of Measurement Systems, Inc., Norwalk, Connecticut.)

potentiometers, and there is a continuous relationship between the magnitude of lever displacement and the output signal generated. Both on- and off-axis movements may be made. The lever may be spring-loaded so that it returns to center when released. Figure 2.11 is an example of a displacement joystick.

A force or *isometric* joystick is a rigid lever that does not move noticeably in any direction (see Figure 2.12). Strain gauges measure the force applied to the joystick. The force joystick responds to forces applied in any direction in proportion to the amount of force applied. When the lever is released, the output drops to zero.

Figure 2.12. A force-operated joystick. (Courtesy of Measurement Systems, Inc., Norwalk, Connecticut.)

With a switch-activated or *digital* joystick, movement of the lever generates output by closing one or more of the switches positioned around the base of the lever. Movement in any of eight directions can typically be detected by the switches. The output signal generated by the device is either "on" in one of the eight directions or "off." It is not proportional to the magnitude of the lever displacement. An "on" signal in a given direction results in cursor movement at a constant rate in that direction. When the lever is released, the cursor stops moving and holds its current position. Digital joysticks are limited by the lack of a continuous range of input direction and magnitude. Their design simplicity results in low cost but reduces the flexibility of the device in graphics applications.

Parameters of the Joystick. As with touch tablets, mice, and trackballs, the gain of the joystick may be changed. Jenkins and Karr (1954) conducted a study in which they found that the optimal joystick gain for movement of a pointer was approximately 0.4 (in terms of pointer displacement relative to the linear displacement of the tip of the joystick). The dimensions of the joystick levers and display screens used in graphics applications, however, typically constrain the joystick gain to a range of five to ten in absolute mode, making fine positioning of a cursor difficult. Accordingly, Foley and van Dam (1982) suggest that the joystick is better utilized for graphics tasks as a rate control in which a constant displacement of a displacement joystick (or constant force applied to a force joystick) results in a constant rate of cursor movement rather than a specific cursor displacement. A larger displacement of the displacement joystick (or force applied to the force joystick) results in a higher cursor velocity, while reducing the displacement (or force) to zero halts the movement of the cursor at its current position.

Foley and van Dam note the importance of incorporating a small *dead zone* of zero velocity around the center position of a rate-control joystick so that nulling the joystick input is not difficult. Gain remains an issue in the design of rate-control joysticks. In this case, the gain specifies the cursor speed that results from a unit displacement of the displacement joystick or a unit force applied to the force joystick.

The force-displacement relationship of the displacement joystick is an additional design parameter. The force joystick represents one extreme force-displacement relationship: the displacement of the joystick is negligible regardless of the force applied. At the other extreme, it is possible to design a joystick that offers negligible resistance to displacement. Most displacement joysticks, however, offer at least some resistance to displacement and, in this case, there are two common relationships between the force applied to the joystick and its resulting displacement.

A spring-loaded joystick displays elastic resistance. The application of a constant force to the joystick results in a constant displacement of the joystick. Increasing the force applied to the joystick increases its displacement. This direct relationship between applied force and resulting displacement can be used by the human operator to enhance positioning accuracy. Spring-loading is also beneficial when it is desirable to return the joystick automatically to its center position upon release. Finally, in tracking tasks requiring sudden reversals of cursor movements, spring-loading enhances the operator's ability to execute these reversals.

A joystick may also be designed to offer viscous resistance. In this case, the application of a constant force to the joystick results in a constant rate of joystick movement. Increasing the force applied to the joystick increases the rate of displacement. Viscous damping aids in the execution of smooth control movements and is particularly appropriate if maintaining a constant rate of cursor movement or acquiring a cursor location at a particular time are important aspects of the cursor positioning task.

Finally, it is possible to include a three-dimensional capability on the joystick by allowing the stick to be twisted in a clockwise or counterclockwise direction (Foley and van Dam, 1982). Alternatively, a rotatable knob can be placed on the top of the joystick (Scott, 1982).

Advantages and Disadvantages of the Joystick. The advantages of the joystick include the fact that it requires only a small fixed amount of desk space and can be made small enough to fit into a keyboard. If a palm or hand rest is provided, the joystick may be used for extended periods of time with little fatigue (Ritchie and Turner, 1975). Because the joystick is used in varied applications, military and others, there are many models available. These range from inexpensive, typically switch-activated joysticks to more expensive joysticks that allow the user to modify many of the features discussed earlier.

Disadvantages of the joystick include low accuracy and low resolution (Scott, 1982; Rubinstein and Hersh, 1984). In addition, joysticks cannot be used to trace or digitize drawings, to input hand-drawn characters, or to input single characters. Table 2.7 summarizes the advantages and disadvantages of joysticks.

Types of Tasks. Joysticks tend to be most suited to tracking tasks or to pointing tasks that do not require a great deal of precision (Mims, 1984). Parrish et al. (1982) suggest that a joystick in absolute mode may be used for line drawing if high accuracy and speed are not required. The authors also suggest that joysticks can be useful in placing and moving symbols and in menu selection if rate control is used.

Table 2.7. Advantages and Disadvantages of the Joystick

Advantages	Disadvantages
1. Requires little space	1. Low accuracy
2. Can be used without fatigue	2. Low resolution
3. Many models available	3. Difficult to use for drawing
4. Can modify control-display gain	

SOURCE: Greenstein and Arnaut, 1987. Reproduced by permission of John Wiley & Sons, Inc.

2.2.6 Light Pens

The light pen, depicted in Figure 2.13, is a stylus that generates information when it is pointed at the screen. The light pen contains a light detector or photocell. When the electron beam in a CRT passes over and refreshes the phosphor at the spot where the light pen is pointing, the increase in brightness causes an electrical signal to be sent to the computer. Based on the timing of this signal, the coordinates of the spot on the display are calculated. Light pens have either a shutter or finger-operated mechanical switch that, when pressed, allows light to reach the light detector. In this manner, inadvertent activation is avoided.

Because the light pen is activated by the increase in brightness of the CRT phosphor, it may typically only be used with CRT displays. However, Ritchie and Turner (1975) state that with a complex interface, a storage display or plasma panel may be used. The method of operation also requires that the hardware and software be precise, so that the exact spot on

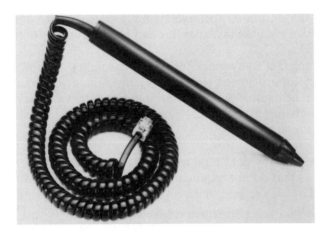

Figure 2.13. A light pen. (Courtesy of FTG Data Systems, Stanton, California.)

the screen may be calculated before the screen is refreshed again. Typically, a refresh interrupt occurs so that the phosphor refresh is halted for a brief, imperceptible period of time during the calculation.

Parameters of the Light Pen. *Modes of Operation.* There are two modes in which the light pen may be used: pick or pointing mode, and tracking mode. In *pointing* mode, a character or figure may be selected by first pointing to a spot on the display and then enabling the light pen. In *tracking* mode, the light pen is used to position a cross-hair or cursor present on the display. The operator aims the light pen at the cross-hair and then moves the pen. As long as the image remains in the light pen's field of view, a line will be traced where the pen is moved. It is necessary to move the light pen at a steady rate or the cross-hair will be lost and tracking will be interrupted.

Field of View and Target Size. The field of view of the light pen can be modified, and the size and spacing of the targets may depend upon the field of view chosen. For instance, a large field of view may make it easier to select a small or dim target, but it also means that the targets must not be close together or an incorrect target may be selected inadvertently.

By increasing the resolution capabilities of the light pen, the target size may not be dictated so much by the field of view and the associated accuracy of the light pen as it is by the operator's capabilities. Hatamian and Brown (1985) state that ±5 pixels in both directions was the lowest resolution accuracy possible until recently. They report on a newly developed light pen accurate to one-quarter of a pixel on a screen with 1000 × 1000 resolution. On a 38 cm screen, this equates to approximately 0.01 cm resolution. This new resolving capability means that the light pen can be used to select very small targets.

However, it is important to realize that while the light pen may be able to select extremely small targets, the human operator may not be capable of such accuracy. For example, Avons, Beveridge, Hickman, and Hitch (1983) studied the use of a light pen by children 4 to 6 years old and 10 to 11 years old for a target-selection task. The diameter of the light pen tip was 10 mm. The mean placement error was 3 mm for the younger children and 1.7 mm for the older children. Based on these results, the authors suggest target sizes of 13 mm and 8 mm for the younger and older children, respectively, to decrease the number of incorrect selections.

The results of Avons et al. indicate that children may not be able to make use of the higher resolution capabilities of the light pen reported by Hatamian and Brown (1985). It is unclear how well adults could use such a device for target-selection tasks. Thus, testing should be performed to determine the appropriate target sizes for adult light pen users. However, the improved resolution capability will still enable the light pen to be more useful in graphics applications.

Advantages and Disadvantages of the Light Pen.   The light pen is the only input device beside the touch screen that uses the output display as the input interface. Since this interface provides a direct relationship between output and input, it therefore allows natural pointing and/or drawing gestures to be used to input data (Mims, 1984; Scott, 1982). The light pen may also be mounted in a device that is worn on the head, providing an input device for handicapped users or for those operators who must use their hands for other tasks, as depicted in Figure 2.14. However, a study by Beringer and Scott (1985) indicates that this may be a fatiguing input method for users. Additional advantages include the availability of inexpensive models and the fact that the light pen does not require extra desk space.

The light pen has several disadvantages (Mims, 1984; Scott, 1982). Because the display is also the surface used to input information, the operator must sit within arm's reach of the display. In addition, holding the light pen to the screen can be fatiguing over long work periods. For example, Avons et al. (1983) report that young children (4 to 6 years old)

Figure 2.14. A light pen may be used as a hands-free input device. (Courtesy of Inkwell Systems, San Diego, California.)

were unable to rest their elbows while using a light pen and, as a result, they encountered more fatigue than did older children (10 to 11 years old). In addition, the light pen and the operator's arm may also obscure parts of the display.

With the exception of the light pen reported on by Hatamian and Brown (1985), the light pen lacks high resolution capabilities. Foley and van Dam (1982) indicate that a light pen can be activated by false targets such as adjacent characters or ambient lighting. Light pens are highly dependent on the accompanying hardware and software, and any problems or inaccuracies in either of these components may lead to inaccuracies in light pen performance. Beaumont (1985) states that there may be perceptible lags in the controlling software.

Parallax may be a problem, especially when pointing to objects at the sides of the display. As with the touch screen, this parallax is a combination of the required near viewing distance due to the fact that the display surface is also the input surface and the separation of the light pen tip and the target due to the screen surface (Avons et al., 1983). Using only the center of the screen to display targets may alleviate this problem; however, this solution limits the usefulness of the device. A more satisfactory solution might be to make the targets large enough at the sides of the screen so that the effects of incorrect placement are minimized; additionally, operator training may prove useful. Finally, the light pen requires the added gesture of picking up and putting down an input device when selection or drawing is required. See Table 2.8 for a summary of the light pen's advantages and disadvantages.

Types of Tasks.   Because use of the light pen involves a natural pointing gesture, this input device is well suited to menu-selection tasks (Rubinstein and Hersh, 1984). While a light pen may be used for drawing, Scott (1982) suggests that it is not accurate for precise sketching needs, especially since a constant rate of movement is necessary in tracking mode. The light pen is not capable of tracing from hard copy since it must be in contact with the screen. Parrish et al. (1982) suggest that light pens are most useful in placing and moving symbols on a display, regardless of required speed.

Table 2.8. Advantages and Disadvantages of Light Pens

Advantages	Disadvantages
1. Direct eye-hand coordination	1. Arm fatigue
2. Inexpensive models available	2. Arm and light pen obscure display
3. No extra space required	3. User must be close to display

SOURCE: Adapted from Greenstein and Arnaut, 1987. Reproduced by permission of John Wiley & Sons, Inc.

2.2.7 Novel Input Techniques

In addition to the input devices already discussed, there are many alternative technologies available. Several of these will be described briefly.

Puck Pointer. In an attempt to combine the features of a mouse and a joystick, the Puck pointer was developed (Barney, 1984). As can be seen in Figure 2.15, this device fits into a space of approximately 25 cm² (4 in²) on a keyboard. Using a light emitting diode, the Puck generates X and Y coordinates through an optical sensor when a small handle placed in the center of the space is moved. The handle is approximately the size of a standard key on a keyboard. The advantages of a Puck pointer are that it is inexpensive and does not require the operator to lift his or her hand off the keyboard. In addition, it may be used for three-dimensional input by pressing the handle down.

Footmouse. The assignment of one component of the input task to a foot-operated control may permit the hands to deal with the remaining aspects of the task more effectively. The Footmouse is a foot-operated cursor control device (Harriman, 1985). It consists of a metal pedal approximately 11.5 cm² (4.5 in²) (see Figure 2.16). Its rubberized surface pivots so that a foot rested on the pedal can depress the pedal at its top, bottom, left, or right edge. Each press moves the display cursor one row or column in the selected direction; continued pressure toward an edge repeats the cursor movement. Because the Footmouse provides only the

Figure 2.15. The Puck Pointer installed in a keyboard. (Courtesy of Lightgate, Oakland, California.)

Figure 2.16. The Footmouse. (Courtesy of Versatron Corp., Healdsburg, California.)

means to move a cursor up, down, right, or left at a constant rate, it is really a foot-operated analog of a cursor-positioning keypad rather than a mouse. This limits the flexibility of the device for graphics applications. A foot-operated control has the additional disadvantage of restricting the posture of the operator, either requiring that one foot be on the control, or, to prevent accidental activation, requiring that both feet be some distance from the control. Still, for tasks in which it is undesirable to assign a hand to cursor positioning tasks, the Footmouse offers a solution.

Eye-controlled Switching. Calhoun, Arbak, and Boff (1984) have begun to investigate the possibility of using eye movement as a method of input to computers in aircraft cockpits. The pilot wears a helmet fitted with an oculometer, which tracks the position of the eyes (see Figure 2.17). Helmet and thus head position are also monitored. Using a cockpit simulator, the authors performed a preliminary investigation of the use of eye control as a method of activating switches. They report that eye-controlled switching appears to be a possible alternative to manual switching, with the total switch operation requiring approximately $1\frac{1}{2}$ seconds for two subjects tested. An alternative eye-control technique requires that the operator wear eyeglasses that track the eye through the use of light emitting diodes. It is also possible to track the eye from a remote point using a television camera. Infrared light shines into the eye, the camera detects the reflection, eye position is calculated, and the display coordinates are determined (Bolt, 1984).

The obvious advantages of this potential input method are speed, accuracy, and the freeing of the hands for other tasks. The disadvantage is that

Figure 2.17. The helmet-mounted oculometer. (From *Proceedings of the Human Factors Society 28th Annual Meeting,* 1984, Vol. 1, p. 259. Copyright 1984, by the Human Factors Society, Inc., and reproduced by permission.)

this method may interfere with visual tracking and surveillance tasks. In addition, the first two technologies require that the operator wear special equipment. Thus, the equipment may be obtrusive.

Gesture-based Input.   Another unique technology utilizes operator gestures as a basis for input. Just as touch screen devices may be used for small screens, a gesture-based system may be used to point with a large screen display. Bolt (1984) describes he development of a technique in which both a small "transmitter" cube and a large "sensor" cube are surrounded by magnetic fields. The sensor is placed several feet away from the transmitter. Movement of the transmitter by the user is sensed by the large cube based upon changes in the magnetic fields. This information is used to calculate X, Y, and Z coordinates. While such a technology is not available for use on a large-scale basis, it illustrates input techniques that may be developed for use in the future.

2.3 Empirical Comparisons

The inherent advantages and disadvantages of each input device can aid in making an initial decision as to which devices are appropriate to a given user population, task, environment, or existing hardware setup. However, often more than one device can satisfy these constraints.

To determine which devices lead to better performance under given conditions, some controlled experiments comparing several input devices have been performed. This section presents these studies. Most research has attempted to determine an optimal device for a given task rather than for a specific set of users. Although not all studies can be easily categorized, four main types of tasks are apparent: target acquisition, menu and text selection, tracking, and text editing and data entry. Research on the use of input devices for graphics applications is lacking.

The research to be presented has several limitations. First, most studies compare a limited number of devices, and the devices used vary across studies. Therefore, it is difficult to compare devices across studies. Second, even if the same device was used in different experiments, researchers may not have optimized the device for their particular interface. This factor may partially account for discrepancies in results for the same input devices used in different experiments. Additionally, differences in tasks and users may also result in performance differences seen with the same device. These factors make it difficult to draw generalizations about the optimum input device for any given task or environment. In spite of these problems, an attempt will be made to draw some conclusions from the studies presented.

2.3.1 Target Acquisition Tasks

The majority of experimental comparisons of input devices have involved what are referred to as target acquisition or menu-selection tasks. That is, a stationary target is displayed and the subject is required to position the display cursor at or inside the target position. In the case of menu selection, the target is one of many potential targets presented on the display at one time; in target acquisition, the designated target is the only one presented. In either case, the subject may or may not be required to confirm the selection by pressing a confirmation key or switch. This section reviews research comparing performance when only one target is presented, and the following section looks at studies in which the user was required to select a target from a menu.

Albert (1982) compared the performance of seven input devices on a target acquisition task. The devices were: touch screen, light pen, graphic tablet with puck, trackball, displacement joystick, force-operated joystick, and keyboard. All input devices used a footswitch to confirm acquisitions; however, the light pen and the touch screen were tested both with and without the footswitch. The task was to position the cursor within a 2.54 cm (1 in.) square target and then confirm that position. The trackball, graphic tablet, and force joystick resulted in the three most accurate performances, while the touch screen and light pen, both without a footswitch, led to the most inaccurate performance. The touch screen and light pen, with or without footswitches, resulted in the fastest positioning speed, while the keyboard and both joysticks were slowest. Albert attributes this second result to the direct eye-hand coordination involved with the touch screen and the light pen. He also suggests that requiring confirmation of input leads to a trade-off; the response becomes more accurate, but takes more time. Preference ratings indicated that subjects preferred the touch screen, light pen, and graphics tablet to the other four devices.

Gomez, Wolfe, Davenport, and Calder (1982) report a comparison of a trackball with a touch-sensitive tablet in absolute mode for a task in which the subjects were required to superimpose a cursor over a target appearing at a pseudorandom location on the screen. A confirmation area was provided on the touch tablet, and a confirmation switch was placed next to the trackball. Half of the subjects had previous experience with a trackball and half did not. Response times across groups were not significantly different for the two devices. However, the trackball resulted in significantly less error than did the touch tablet across groups. The authors attribute this latter result to the higher precision characteristics of the trackball, in particular to the fact that the hand was stabilized with the trackball and not with the touch tablet. The response times for the two devices did not differ as a result of prior subject training. However, both the experienced and the inexperienced subjects had less error when using the trackball than when using the touch tablet. In general, the experienced subjects were more accurate than the inexperienced subjects with each device. A problem with this study is that subjects were allowed to use either a stylus or their finger on the tablet. As indicated earlier, performance with a stylus and a finger may differ and, thus, this factor should be controlled.

Mehr and Mehr (1972) tested the following input devices: 1) a center-return displacement joystick in rate mode; 2) a remain-in-position displacement joystick in absolute mode; 3) a rate-mode thumb-operated isometric joystick mounted in a hand-held grip; 4) a rate-mode finger-operated isometric joystick; and 5) a trackball. Subjects positioned a cursor within a circle presented in the middle of a CRT and then pressed a stop button. The trackball resulted in the shortest positioning times, followed closely by the finger-operated isometric joystick, while the two displacement joysticks resulted in the longest positioning times. The trackball and the isometric finger-operated joystick provided the most accurate performance.

As indicated previously, often cursor devices are not optimized for the particular interface in question before they are tested. In a recent study, Epps, Snyder, and Muto (1986) optimized six input devices on a target acquisition task and then compared their performance. The task included targets that varied in size and distance from the cursor. The devices were: an absolute-mode touch tablet, a relative-mode touch tablet, a trackball, a force joystick, a displacement joystick, and a mouse. All devices required a confirmation action; a separate confirmation key was used for all devices except the mouse, which had its own confirmation button. For the smallest target sizes, the mouse and the trackball led to the best performance in terms of the time to position the cursor in the target. The two joysticks led to the worst performance for small targets. As the target size increased, the differences between the devices were less apparent. Similar results were found with respect to target distance; the mouse and the trackball performed best, especially at small distances, while the two joysticks led to the worst performance.

2.3.2 Menu and Text Selection

In one of the earliest input device comparisons reported, English, Engelbart, and Berman (1967) compared a light pen, a knee control, a Grafacon arm, a joystick in both rate and absolute mode, and a mouse on two menu-selection tasks in which the subject was required to position a cursor at one of several "X"'s on the display. Some method of confirmation (such as pressing a switch or the device handle) was required for all devices. For experienced subjects, the mouse resulted in the shortest selection times, while the longest times occurred with the use of the absolute joystick. Inexperienced subjects performed best in terms of selection time with the knee control and the light pen, and worst with the two joysticks. All subjects made the fewest errors in target selection with the mouse. The light pen and the absolute joystick resulted in the highest error rates for experienced subjects, and the light pen and rate joystick resulted in the highest error rates for the inexperienced subjects.

Card, English, and Burr (1978) compared four input devices on a text selection task. The input devices were: a mouse, an isometric joystick, step keys (that is, keys that move the cursor either up/down or right/left), and text keys (function keys that position the cursor at the previous or next character, word, line, or paragraph). The subjects were required to position the cursor at a target in text displayed on a CRT. The subjects then pressed a button to confirm the selection; for all input devices except the mouse, the button was separate from the device. Total response time was divided into homing time (time in seconds from subject's initiation of the new task to cursor movement) and positioning time (time in seconds from initial cursor movement to selection).

The results were similar to those reported by English et al. (1967) and Epps et al. (1986); the mouse was superior to the other devices in terms of total response time, positioning time, and target selection error rate. This result occurred regardless of either the distance of the target from the current cursor position or the target size. The authors attribute the superiority of the mouse to the continuous nature of the movement allowed by the mouse, and they suggest that less "cognitive load" is needed to translate desired into actual cursor movement.

Karat, McDonald, and Anderson (1984) compared a touch screen, a mouse, and a keyboard for target selection, menu selection, and selection with typing tasks. The menu tasks simulated a computerized appointment calendar and telephone aid. Contrary to Card et al.'s results, these authors found that the touch screen was superior in terms of selection rate and task completion time across all task types; the keyboard was second, and the mouse was the worst in terms of selection rate and task completion times. In addition, subjects preferred the keyboard or touch screen to the mouse for all tasks. One reason for these different results may be that the mouse was the only device that required a confirmation action. As indicated previously, while confirmation may aid in improving response accuracy, it can lead to longer response times.

Whitfield, Ball, and Bird (1983) compared touch screens and touch-sensitive tablets in three experiments. The first experimental task involved selection of a highlighted item from a 4 × 3 matrix of "99"'s. The second task required subjects to select a highlighted item in a 16 × 16 array of three-digit numbers. The third task involved the selection of a triangular target. Several levels of target size were included by surrounding the target with six other markers at varying distances from the center marker. The touch screen did not require a confirmation action. The touch tablet required that the user either press a confirmation key or remove their finger from the tablet to confirm an entry.

Total response times were a combination of both target selection and confirmation time. Across all three tasks, the touch tablet without the confirmation key resulted in the longest response times, while the touch screen led to the shortest times. This result was attributed to the longer confirmation time required by the touch tablet due to a need to reverse finger pressure to confirm an entry. The touch tablet was especially slow with small targets. The authors attribute this result to the direct eye-hand coordination present with the touch screen and absent with the touch tablet. With respect to errors, the two input devices were comparable. An additional comparison with a trackball was made in the third study. The trackball resulted in somewhat slower response times than either the touch screen or the touch tablet. However, the trackball resulted in a lower error rate than the two touch input devices at all levels of resolution. The authors suggest that touch input devices in general should not be used with high resolution targets or when the task is paced. However, they feel that the touch screen and the touch tablet provide comparable performance levels.

Hottman (1981) compared an eight-position isotonic joystick, a 3 × 3 matrix keyboard, and a 2 × 4 matrix keyboard for aircraft applications using a menu-selection task. No confirmation action was required for any device. This task was carried out at the same time as a compensatory tracking task was performed using a two-axis isotonic joystick. The purpose of performing two tasks was to simulate the workload conditions a pilot might experience. No instructions were given regarding the importance of either task. For the menu-selection task, there were no differences in response times across the three input devices. However, the joystick resulted in significantly more positioning errors than either of the keyboards. The author suggests that the superiority of the keyboards was due to the additional tactile feedback they provided.

2.3.3 Tracking Tasks

Two studies have compared input devices for a task in which subjects had to track a moving target, keeping the distance between the cursor and the target at a minimum. In a comparison of a trackball, displacement joystick, and mouse, Swierenga and Struckman-Johnson (1984) had subjects perform a compensatory tracking task (that is, one in which only the direction and distance of the error between the target and the tracking cursor is displayed). They found that tracking error was lower for the trackball and joystick than for the mouse. The trackball and joystick did not differ significantly. Subjective responses indicated that the subjects preferred the joystick to either the trackball or the mouse for this task.

Reinhart and Marken (1985) compared a mouse and an isometric joystick on a pursuit tracking task. Subjects were required to keep a cursor near a target on the display. The target was moved in two dimensions by filtered random noise. Three frequencies of filters were tested: 0.03 Hz,

0.06 Hz, and 0.09 Hz. In terms of RMS error and stability, the mouse led to better performance than the joystick. (Stability was essentially a measure of the expected variance between cursor and target position relative to the observed variance.) Also, as would be expected, performance tended to degrade as the frequency of the noise increased.

2.3.4 Text Entering and Editing Tasks

In an attempt to study more realistic tasks, several researchers have required subjects to enter data or make changes in text on a display. In an early look at text entry, Earl and Goff (1965) found that a point-in data entry method similar to a light pen was superior with respect to input time and errors to a type-in method (a typewriter) in entering alphabetic material. This surprising result is probably due to the nature of the task. The subjects did not use the point-in method to enter one character at a time, but rather to mark or point to three words. In the type-in task, subjects were required to type three words. These results may support the use of menu selection for some data entry tasks but not the use of a point-in method to input individual letters.

Goodwin (1975) compared a keyboard, a light pen, and a light gun (a light pen in a pistol grip with a trigger for a switch) on three tasks. For a sequential cursor positioning task, the subjects had to replace each of the numbers 0 through 9 with an "X". The numbers were in random positions on the display, and they had to be replaced in numerical order. An arbitrary cursor positioning task required the subjects to replace ten randomly positioned "M"'s with an "X", in any order. The third task, check-reading, was to read a passage and indicate the position of ten randomly generated incorrect letters by replacing them with an "X". Goodwin reported that for cursor positioning, both a light pen and a light gun were faster than a keyboard for all three tasks. Errors were not considered.

Haller, Mutschler, and Voss (1984) compared a light pen, digitizing tablet, mouse, trackball, cursor keys, and voice recognizer for a text correction task. This task required the location of eighteen erroneous characters in a page of text and replacement of each with the correct character. Location was performed using one of the six input devices, and correction was performed through the use of either keyboard or voice. The positioning time for the task, excluding correction, was lowest for the light pen and longest for voice input. The average times for the graphic tablet, mouse, trackball, and cursor keys fell between the light pen and voice input, and they did not differ significantly from each other. The average positioning errors were: light pen and cursor keys, 0 percent; voice input, 0.9 percent;

graphic tablet, 1.4 percent; mouse, 4.2 percent, and trackball, 5.6 percent. Both of the correction methods, the keyboard and the voice input, resulted in equivalent performance. The authors suggest that the light pen is well suited for cursor positioning, as are the mouse and trackball, if their gain is sufficiently low.

In another study, Struckman-Johnson, Swierenga, and Shieh (1984) compared a keyboard, a displacement joystick, a trackball, and a light pen for a text-editing task. Fifty words were displayed on the screen, ten of which contained an extra highlighted letter. Using the required input device, the subjects positioned the cursor at the extra letter and pressed the enter key, thereby deleting the letter. In terms of time to complete the task, significant differences were found between all devices. The light pen was the fastest, followed by the trackball, joystick, and keyboard, respectively. With respect to errors, the keyboard and the trackball resulted in the best performance, with the joystick resulting in the worst performance (a measure of errors could not be obtained for the light pen). The trackball was the most preferred device, followed by the light pen, keyboard, and joystick, respectively.

A comparison of a QWERTY keyboard, a numeric keypad, a light pen, and a touch screen was carried out by Beaumont (1985). For all four input devices, one of four possible stimuli appeared on the screen. For the keyboard, the stimuli were "0", "-", ".", and "SPACE". The "SPACE" was replaced by "ENTER" for the keypad, and by "E" for the light pen and touch screen. The subject was required to type the corresponding key for the keyboard and keypad conditions, and to touch one of four boxes on the screen displaying the four stimuli for the light pen and touch screen conditions. The results indicated that all the input devices differed significantly in terms of response speed. The touch screen resulted in the fastest performance, followed by the keypad, the keyboard, and the light pen. Beaumont suggests that the poor performance of the light pen was due to lags in the hardware and the necessity for subjects to press a capacitance switch. The light pen was the only input device requiring the confirmation action of pressing a switch. He also suggests that the keypad and the keyboard had distractors due to the keys surrounding the four that were used, and this factor may have led to the degradation of performance with these devices.

Beringer (1979) reported that the use of a touch screen on a map display led to better performance on a plotting task in terms of errors and time to task completion than did keyboard-based systems. On other tasks, including continuous flight control and navigation information updating, the touch- and keyboard-based systems achieved similar levels of performance.

2.4 Conclusion

Table 2.9 summarizes the results of the comparative studies just discussed. In general, trackballs tend to result in high accuracy for cursor positioning tasks. Touch screens and light pens lead to fast cursor positioning and selection.

Several devices have shown conflicting results in different studies. For example, Epps et al. (1986) found that the mouse was the best device for a target acquisition task, as did English et al. (1967) and Card et al. (1978) for menu and text selection tasks. On the other hand, Swierenga and Struckman-Johnson (1984) reported that the mouse was the worst device for a tracking task, and Karat et al. (1984) reported the same results for both target- and menu-selection tasks. Dissimilar results have also been found for the light pen and the joystick. In addition, not only have there been conflicting results across studies, there have also been conflicts within studies; thus, for instance, Albert (1982) found that the touch screen without a footswitch was the fastest target selection device, yet it also resulted in the most errors. As Albert indicated, confirmation can increase response accuracy, but it also tends to increase response time.

These conflicting results illustrate what Gruenefelder and Whitten (1984) have discussed as one problem with generic human factors research, or research aimed at discovering general human factors design principles. That is, the results of these studies may not apply to different settings and uses of the design. Thus, while a particular mouse may provide faster and more accurate positioning for one task, that mouse may work poorly given another task and another user population. Conversely, two different mice may achieve entirely different levels of performance on the same task with the same users. Future comparisons should be performed with devices that have first been optimized for the task and users at hand. In addition, Gruenenfelder and Whitten suggest that the limitations of a study's results should be investigated so that the generalizability of results may be determined.

In summary, the choice of an input device should involve the following considerations (see Table 2.10). First, the characteristics of the task, users, working environment, and existing hardware should be determined. Not only present, but foreseeable future demands should be considered. Next, the characteristics of the potential input devices should be compared with the requirements of the working environment to narrow down the possible choices. Previous research concerning the input devices under consideration should be reviewed at this point. It is also important to consider user preferences in making the selection. As has been shown, subjective preferences do not always correspond to the device that will provide the best

Table 2.9. Summary of Experimental Comparisons of Input Devices

Study	Task	Most accurate	Shortest positioning	Most preferred
Albert (1982)	Target acquisition	Trackball/Graphic tablet	Touch screen/Light pen	Touch screen/Light pen
Beaumont (1985)	Response selection	—	Touch screen	—
Beringer (1979)	Plotting	Touch screen	Touch screen	—
	Flight control	Touch screen/Keyboard	Touch screen/Keyboard	—
Card et al. (1978)	Text selection	Mouse	Mouse	—
Earl and Goff (1965)	Data entry	Light pen	Light pen	—
English et al. (1967)	Target selection	Mouse	Mouse	—
Epps et al. (1986)	Target acquisition	—	Mouse/Trackball	—
Gomez et al. (1982)	Target acquisition	Trackball	Trackball/Graphic tablet	—
Goodwin (1975)	Cursor positioning	—	Light pen	—
Haller et al. (1984)	Text correction	Light pen/Cursor keys	Light pen	Light pen
Hottman (1981)	Menu selection	Keyboards	Joystick/Keyboards	—
Karat et al. (1984)	Target/Menu selection	Touch screen	Trackball	Keyboard/Touch screen
Mehr and Mehr (1972)	Target acquisition	Trackball/isometric fingertip joystick		—
Reinhart and Marken (1985)	Pursuit tracking	Mouse	—	—
Struckman-Johnson et al. (1984)	Text editing	Keyboard/Trackball	Light pen	Trackball
Swierenga et al. (1984)	Compensatory tracking	Trackball/Joystick	—	Joystick
Whitfield et al. (1983)	Target selection	Trackball	Touch screen	Touch screen

Table 2.10. Guidelines for Selection of Input Devices

---

1. Consider present and future characteristics of users, tasks, working environments.
2. Match input device characteristics to demand requirements.
3. Consider previous research and user preference.
4. Test input device in working environment.
5. Optimize modifiable device characteristics.

SOURCE: Greenstein and Arnaut, (1987). Reproduced by permission of John Wiley & Sons, Inc.

performance. Yet it is important to provide the operators with a tool that will be used.

Once a choice has been made (or, preferably, before the choice has been made), the input device should be tested in the working environment with the user population. Within these constraints, the device should be optimized if such optimization is possible given the features of the input device. In this manner, the device chosen may be matched to the use environment. Given a systematic approach to the selection of an input device, it is possible to provide a tool that will be accepted by the users and that will be matched to the tasks and environment.

References

Albert, A. E. (1982). The effect of graphic input devices on performance in a cursor positioning task. In *Proceedings of the Human Factors Society 26th Annual Meeting* (pp. 54–58). Santa Monica, CA: Human Factors Society.

Arnaut, L. Y., and Greenstein, J. S. (1986). Optimizing the touch tablet: The effect of control-display gain and method of cursor control. *Human Factors, 28*(6), 717–726.

Avons, S. E., Beveridge, M. C., Hickman, A. T., and Hitch, G. J. (1983). Considerations on using a lightpen-interactive system with young children. *Behavior Research Methods & Instrumentation, 15*(1), 75–78.

Barney, C. (1984). 'Puck pointer' combines functions of mouse and joystick in number-pad-sized package. *Electronics Week,* July 23, 26.

Beaton, R. J., and Weiman, N. (1984). *Effects of touch key size and separation on menu-selection accuracy.* (Tech. Report No. TR 500-01). Beaverton, OR: Tektronix, Human Factors Research Laboratory.

Beaumont, J. G. (1985). Speed of response using keyboard and screen-based microcomputer response media. *International Journal of Man-Machine Studies, 23,* 61–70.

Becker, J. A., and Greenstein, J. S. (1986). A lead-lag compensation approach to display/control gain for touch tablets. In *Proceedings of the Human Factors Society 30th Annual Meeting.* (pp. 332–336). Santa Monica, CA: Human Factors Society.

Beringer, D. B. (1979). The design and evaluation of complex systems: Application to a man-machine interface for aerial navigation. In *Proceedings of the Human Factors Society 23rd Annual Meeting* (pp. 75–79). Santa Monica, CA: Human Factors Society.

Beringer, D. B., and Peterson, J. G. (1985). Underlying behavioral parameters of the operation of touch-input devices: biases, models and feedback. *Human Factors, 27*(4), 445–458.

Beringer, D. B., and Scott, J. (1985). The long-range light pen as a head-based user-computer interface: Head-mounted "sights" versus head positioning for computer access by the disabled. In *Proceedings of the Human Factors Society 29th Annual Meeting* (pp. 114–118). Santa Monica, CA: Human Factors Society.

Bolt, R. A. (1984). *The human interface: Where people and computers meet.* Belmont, CA: Lifetime Learning Publications.

Brown, E., Buxton, W., and Murtagh, K. (1985). Windows on tablets as a means of achieving virtual input devices. In *Computer Graphics, Proceedings of SIGGRAPH '85, 19*(3) (pp. 225–230).

Buxton, W., Hill, R., and Rowley, P. (1985). Issues and techniques in touch-sensitive tablet input. In *Computer Graphics, Proceedings of SIGGRAPH '85, 19*(3) (pp. 69–85).

Calhoun, G. L., Arbak, C. J., and Boff, K. R. (1984). Eye-controlled switching for crew station design. In *Proceedings of the Human Factors Society 28th Annual Meeting* (pp. 258–262). Santa Monica, CA: Human Factors Society.

Card, S. K., English, W. K., and Burr, B. J. (1978). Evaluation of mouse, rate-controlled isometric joystick, step keys, and text keys for text selection on a CRT. *Ergonomics, 21,* 601–613.

Chapanis, A., and Kinkade, R. G. (1972). Design of controls. In H. P. Van Cott and R. G. Kinkade (Eds.), *Human engineering guide to equipment design* (rev. ed., pp. 345–379). Washington DC: U.S. Government Printing Office.

Davis, G. I., and Badger, S. (1982). User-computer interface design of a complex tactical display terminal. In *Proceedings of the Human Factors Society 26th Annual Meeting* (pp. 768–771). Santa Monica, CA: Human Factors Society.

de Bruyne, P. (1980). Acoustic radar graphic input device. *Computer Graphics, 14*(3), 25–31.

Earl, W. K., and Goff, J. D. (1975). Comparison of two data entry methods. *Perceptual and Motor Skills, 20,* 369–384.

Ellingstad, V. S., Parng, A., Gehlen, G. R., Swierenga, S. J., and Auflick, J. (1985, March). *An evaluation of the touch tablet as a command and control input device* (Tech. Report). Vermillion, SD: University of South Dakota, Dept. of Psychology.

Ellis, T. O., and Sibley, W. L. (1967). On the development of equitable graphic I/O. *IEEE Transactions on Human Factors in Electronics, 8,* 15–17.

English, W. K., Engelbart, D. C., and Berman, M. L. (1967). Display-selection techniques for text manipulation. *IEEE Transactions on Human Factors in Electronics, HFE-8,* 5–15.

Epps, B. W., Snyder, H. L., and Muto, W. H. (1986). Comparison of six cursor devices on a target acquisition task. In *1986 SID Digest of Technical Papers* (pp. 302–305). Los Angeles, CA: Society for Information Display.

Foley, J. D., and van Dam, A. (1982). *Fundamentals of interactive computer graphics.* Reading, MA: Addison-Wesley Publishing Co.

Foley, J. D., and Wallace, V. L. (1974). The art of natural graphic man-machine conversation. *Proceedings of the IEEE, 62,* 462–471.

Gaertner, K. P., and Holzhausen, K. P. (1980). Controlling air traffic with a touch sensitive screen. *Applied Ergonomics, 11,* 17–22.

Gomez, A. D., Wolfe, S. W., Davenport, E. W., and Calder, B. D. (1982, February). *LMDS: Lightweight modular display system* (NOSC Tech. Report 767). San Diego, CA: Naval Ocean Systems Center.

Goodwin, N. C. (1975). Cursor positioning on an electronic display using lightpen, lightgun, or keyboard for three basic tasks. *Human Factors, 17,* 289–295.

Greenstein, J. S., and Arnaut, L. Y. (1987). Human factors aspects of manual computer input devices. In G. Salvendy (Ed.), *Handbook of Human Factors* (Chapter 11.4, pp. 1450–1489). New York: Wiley.

Gruenenfelder, T. M., and Whitten, W. B. (1984). Augmenting generic research with proto-type evaluation experience in applying generic research to specific products. In *Proceedings of the Interact '84 Conference, First IFIP Conference on 'Human-Computer Interaction'* (Vol. 2, pp. 315-319).

Haller, R., Mutschler, H., and Voss, M. (1974). Comparison of input devices for correction of typing errors in office systems. In *Proceedings of the Interact '84 Conference, First IFIP Conference on 'Human-Computer Interaction'* (Vol. 2, pp. 218-223).

Harriman, C. W. (1985). Alternatives for cursor control: Footmouse, pad, or view system. *InfoWorld, 7*(38), 48-50.

Hatamian, M., and Brown, E. F. (1985). A new light pen with subpixel accuracy. *AT&T Technical Journal, 64*(5), 1065-1075.

Herot, C., and Weinzapfel, G. (1978). One-point touch input of vector information for computer displays. *Computer Graphics, 12*(3), 210-216.

Hlady, A. M. (1969). A touch sensitive X-Y position encoder for computer input. *AFIPS Conference Proceedings, 35*, 545-551.

Holden, E. (1984). Chalk Board's Powerpad and Leonardo's Library. *Byte, 9*(3), 268-272.

Hornbuckle, G. D. (1967). The computer graphics user/machine interface. *IEEE Transactions on Human Factors in Electronics, HFE-8*, 17-20.

Hottman, S. B. (1981). Selection of remotely labeled switch functions during dual task performance. In *Proceedings of the Human Factors Society 25th Annual Meeting* (pp. 240-242). Santa Monica, CA: Human Factors Society.

Jenkins, W. L., and Karr, A. C. (1954). The use of a joystick in making settings on a simulated scope face. *Journal of Applied Psychology, 38*, 457-461.

Karat, J., McDonald, J. E., and Anderson, M. (1984). A comparison of selection techniques: Touch panel, mouse, and keyboard. In *Proceedings of the Interact '84 Conference, First IFIP Conference on 'Human-Computer Interaction'* (Vol. 2, pp. 149-153).

Logan, J. D. (1985). Touch screens diversify. *Electronic Products*, Nov. 1, 61-67.

McGeever, C. (1984). Graphics and digitizers. *InfoWorld, 6*(36), 46-48.

Mehr, M. H., and Mehr, E. (1972). Manual digital positioning in 2 axes: A comparison of joystick and trackball controls. In *Proceedings of the Human Factors Society 16th Annual Meeting* (pp. 110-116). Santa Monica. CA: Human Factors Society.

Mims, F. M., III. (1984). A few quick pointers. *Computers and Electronics*, May, 64-117.

Newman, W. M., and Sproull, R. F. (1979). *Principles of interactive computer graphics*, New York: McGraw-Hill.

Ohlson, M. (1978). System design considerations for graphics input devices. *Computer, 11*, 9-18.

Parrish, R. N., Gates, J. L., Munger, S. J., Grimma, P. R., and Smith, L. T. (1982, February). *Development of design guidelines and criteria for user/operator transactions with battlefield automated systems. Phase II Final Report: Volume II. Prototype handbook for combat and materiel developers* (Tech. Report). Synectics Corp., U.S. Army Research Institute for the Behavioral and Social Sciences.

Pfauth, M., and Priest, J. (1981). Person-computer interface using touch screen devices. In *Proceedings of the Human Factors Society 25th Annual Meeting* (pp. 500-504). Santa Monica, CA: Human Factors Society.

Price, L. A., and Cordova, C. A. (1983). Use of mouse buttons. In *Proceedings of the CHI '83 Conference on Human Factors in Computing Systems* (pp. 262-266). New York: ACM.

Reinhart, W., and Marken, R. (1985). Control systems analysis of computer pointing devices. In *Proceedings of the Human Factors Society 29th Annual Meeting* (pp. 119-121). Santa Monica, CA: Human Factors Society.

Ritchie, G. J., and Turner, J. A. (1975). Input devices for interactive graphics. *International Journal of Man-Machine Studies, 7*, 639–660.

Rouse, W. B. (1975). Design of man-computer interfaces for on-line interactive systems. *Proceedings of the IEEE, 63*, 847–857.

Rubinstein, R., and Hersh, H. M. (1984). *The human factor: Designing computer systems for people.* Burlington, MA: Digital Press.

Schulze, L. J. H., and Snyder, H. L. (1983, October). *A comparative evaluation of five touch entry devices* (Tech. Report No. HFL-83-6). Blacksburg, VA: Virginia Polytechnic Institute and State University, Department of Industrial Engineering and Operations Research.

Scott, J. E. (1982). *Introduction to interactive computer graphics.* New York: Wiley.

Somerson, P. (1983). The tale of the mouse. *PC Magazine, 1*(10), 66–71.

Stammers, R. C., and Bird, J. M. (1980). Controller evaluation of a touch input air traffic data system: An "indelicate" experiment. *Human Factors, 22*, 581–589.

Struckman-Johnson, D. L., Swierenga, S. J., and Shieh, K. (1984, January). *Alternative cursor control devices: An empirical comparison using a text editing task* (Final Report: Task II.2). Vermillion, SD: University of South Dakota, Human Factors Laboratory.

Sutherland, I. E. (1974). Three-dimensional data input by tablet. *Proceedings of the IEEE, 62*, 453–461.

Swezey, R. W., and Davis, E. G. (1983). A case study of human factors guidelines in computer graphics. *IEEE Computer Graphics and Applications, 3*(8), 21–30.

Swierenga, S. J., and Struckman-Johnson, D. L. (1984, January). *Alternative cursor control devices: An empirical comparison using a tracking task* (Final Report: Task II.3). Vermillion, SD: University of South Dakota, Human Factors Laboratory.

Valk, M. A. (1985). An experiment to study touchscreen "button" design. In *Proceedings of the Human Factors Society 29th Annual Meeting* (pp. 127–131). Santa Monica, CA: Human Factors Society.

Warfield, R. W. (1983). The new interface technology: An introduction to windows and mice. *Byte, 8*(12), 218–230.

Weiman, N., Beaton, R. J., Knox, S. T., and Glasser, P. C. (1985, September). *Effects of key layout, visual feedback, and encoding algorithm on menu selection with LED-based touch panels* (Tech, Report No. HFL-604-02). Beaverton, OR: Tektronix, Human Factors Research Laboratory.

White, G. M. (1983). Video pointing devices: Enter the touch tablet. *Byte, 8*(12), 218–219.

Whitfield, D., Ball, R. G., and Bird, J. M. (1983). Some comparisons of on-display and off-display touch input devices for interaction with computer generated displays. *Ergonomics, 26*, 1033–1053.

3 Keyboards

JOEL S. GREENSTEIN

Clemson University
Clemson, South Carolina

WILLIAM H. MUTO

Texas Instruments, Inc.
Dallas, Texas

3.1 Introduction

Of the various devices available for transmitting information from the human to the computer, the keyboard is certainly the most generally applied. It is clearly the device of choice for applications involving significant amounts of textual input. It is also the computer input technology most affected by historical precedent. The data entry keyboard achieved some degree of design standardization long before its linkage to the computer. While this linkage has had a substantial effect on the design of current keyboards, the functionality, layout, mechanics, and dimensions of these devices are still in many ways a reflection of nineteenth-century technology.

3.2 Fixed-Function and Variable-Function Keyboards

In many applications, an initial consideration in the selection of a keyboard concerns whether each key shall be dedicated to a single function. Basic hand-held calculators and touch telephones employ fixed-function

123

keyboards (See Figure 3.1). Fixed-function keyboards have several advantages relative to variable-function keyboards:

- Simplicity of operation—typically only one key is pressed at a time and the same function is always performed by the same key.
- All available functions can be determined by scanning the keys.
- Relatively little software support is necessary.
- Keys can be arranged in logical groups.

Disadvantages of fixed-function keyboards include:

- A large number of required functions requires a large number of keys.
- Frequent visual search and arm and hand movement may be required over a large area.
- Changes require hardware modification.
- It may be difficult to group keys logically for all operating procedures.

The selection of a fixed-function keyboard is appropriate when one set of functions is frequently employed, when functions must be executed quickly, and when correct initial selection of functions is critical to satisfactory operation of the system.

The functions of variable-function keys are generally varied in one of two ways: mode change keys may be used, permitting the user to vary a

Figure 3.1. A fixed-function keyboard. (Courtesy of Casio, Inc.)

key's function among a small number of alternatives, or the functions of the keys may be placed under software control with the user informed of the key-function relationships via a labeled keyboard overlay or an associated video display unit. Applications representative of the use of variable-function keyboards include uppercase/lowercase typewriters and advanced hand-held calculators (mode change keys), keyboard overlays associated with software packages (different overlays for different packages), and menu items offered on a video display associating a specific key press with each menu item (Figures 3.2, 3.3, and 3.4). General advantages of variable-function keyboards include:

- Fewer keys are needed relative to a fixed-function keyboard of equivalent power.
- Less visual search and arm and hand movement are required.

Software controlled key-function relationships have several additional advantages:

- The operating procedure and sequence can be guided by programmed instructions displayed on the associated video display.

Figure 3.2. A keyboard that uses two mode change keys to change the functions associated with the remaining keys. The primary function of each key is indicated on the face of the key. The alternate functions are indicated by the gold label printed above the key (activated by pressing the like-colored "F" key followed by the function key) and the blue label printed on the lower face of the key (activated by pressing the like-colored "G" key followed by the function key). (Photograph courtesy of Hewlett-Packard Company.)

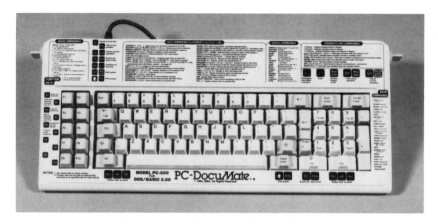

Figure 3.3. A keyboard for which the current functions of the keys are indicated on a labeled overlay. (Photograph courtesy of Systems Management Associates, Inc., Raleigh, North Carolina.)

Figure 3.4. A keyboard for which the current functions of the top row of eight keys are depicted at the bottom of the associated video display. (Photograph courtesy of Hewlett-Packard Company.)

- Changes require software rather than hardware modification.
- Labels can be logically grouped for each operating procedure.
- Keys for functions inappropriate to the current situation may be made inactive.

There are also certain disadvantages associated with variable-function keyboards:

- With mode change keys, the user must press more than one key to execute some of the functions. This additional complexity increases entry time and number of errors. It also becomes difficult to label the keys clearly with their multiple functions and to group labels logically for all procedures.
- With software controlled function assignment, the user must select the currently appropriate function-to-key assignment. It is, therefore, likely that he or she will require more training than would the user of a fixed-function keyboard. The training problem is complicated further when the user employs a variety of software packages. There can easily be a lack of equivalence in function-to-name and function-to-key assignments among the different software packages. Thus, a given function may go by different names, a given name may represent different functions, and a given function may be associated with different keys across the software packages.

The selection of variable-function keyboards appears to be appropriate when there are frequently used subsets of functions, when the pacing of

Table 3.1. Advantages and Disadvantages of Fixed- and Variable-Function Keyboards

Fixed-Function Keyboards	Variable-Function Keyboards
Advantages	
1. Simplicity of operation	1. Fewer keys
2. Function is evident from key	2. Less visual search
3. Minimal software support	3. Less arm and hand movement
4. Logical key grouping	4. Can be modified by software changes
Disadvantages	
1. Numerous functions require numerous keys	1. Increased function selection time
2. Frequent visual search	2. Decreased clarity of key labeling
3. Frequent arm and hand movement	3. Increased prompting and feedback requirements
4. Changes require hardware modification	4. Increased training requirements

SOURCE: Greenstein and Arnaut, 1987. Reproduced by permission of John Wiley & Sons, Inc.

Table 3.2. When to Use Fixed- and Variable-Function Keyboards

Use fixed-function keyboards when:	Use variable-function keyboards when:
1. One set of functions is frequently employed	1. Several subsets of functions are frequently used
2. Functions must be executed quickly	2. Pacing of entries is not forced
3. Correct function selection is critical	3. Sophisticated prompting and feedback are available

SOURCE: Greenstein and Arnaut, 1987. Reproduced by permission of John Wiley & Sons, Inc.

entries is controlled by the user, rather than forced by the system, and when relatively sophisticated prompting and feedback are available. Additionally, software controlled function assignment seems particularly appropriate to applications that experience continual modification.

The relative advantages and disadvantages of fixed- and variable-function keyboards are summarized in Table 3.1. The circumstances in which each of these types of keyboards tends to be more useful are indicated in Table 3.2.

3.3 Keyboard Layout

The arrangement of components within a workspace is guided by the importance, frequency-of-use, function, and sequence-of-use of the individual components. These general considerations apply to the layout of keys on a keyboard as well. Hanes (1975) elaborates upon these fundamental notions to provide a more detailed set of guidelines for keyboard layout:

1. Determine the characters and numbers of keys required.
2. Arrange the keys according to their frequency of use and user characteristics. The most frequently used keys should be assigned to the stronger fingers. To enhance keying speed, the keys should also be arranged to maximize alternation of key presses between hands.
3. Follow historical precedent.
4. Follow established standards.
5. Group frequently used keys under the resting position of the hand where the user can determine their locations by touch.
6. Group related functions together.
7. Group logically and according to sequence of use.
8. Locate according to importance.
9. Code the keys so that the user can easily locate important or frequently used keys and key groups. In addition to key labels, keys can be coded by variations of shape, color, surface texture, and spacing.

10. Consider all factors, including the intended applications, costs, and manufacturing requirements.

These rules can conflict. Users experienced with one layout may be very reluctant to accept a new layout if a substantial amount of retraining will be necessary to improve their proficiency. Thus, the importance of guideline 3 may complicate the application of guideline 2.

Keyboards for computer input typically include alphanumeric, function, auxiliary numeric, and cursor control key groups (see Figure 3.5). Most of the attention to date has focused on the layout of the alphanumeric group, composed of the uppercase and lowercase alphanumeric characters, ten numerals, punctuation marks, and special symbols such as the ampersand and asterisk.

The QWERTY layout (named after the leftmost six keys in its top row of letters) is generally used in English–speaking countries and specifies the location of the alphabetic characters, as well as most of the numerals and symbols. Minor variations from this layout have been adopted elsewhere,

Figure 3.5. A general-purpose alphanumeric keyboard for computer input. Separate alphanumeric, editing, cursor control, and auxiliary numeric key groups are positioned from left to right. Above the alphanumeric keyset, a row of 12 programmable function keys is arranged in three groups of four keys each. Three screen control keys are located above the editing key group, and three lights indicating the keyboard's operational status are above the auxiliary numeric keypad. (Courtesy of International Business Machines Corporation.)

the AZERTY layout being used in France and the QWERTZ layout in German – speaking countries.

The function keys provide such rudimentary functions as mode changes ("SHIFT" key) and communication ("ENTER" key). Such frequently used functions are typically included within the periphery of the alphanumeric keyset. Other specialized functions, such as for text editing (insert, delete), may be offered by additional function keysets on the keyboard. These keysets may also be programmable, enabling their functions to vary with the application in which the keyboard is employed.

An auxiliary numeric keypad provides an efficient adjunct to the alphanumeric keyset in applications requiring numeric data entry. A cursor-control keyset provides a key-oriented means to control current position on an associated video display.

3.3.1 The QWERTY Layout

The QWERTY keyboard layout has been adopted as the basis for a standard alphanumeric keyboard arrangement (American National Standards Institute, 1982). Considerations that led to the adoption of this arrangement included the many QWERTY keyboards in use, as well as the time and money already invested in the training and texts for this arrangement (Lohse, 1968; Ancona, Garland, and Tropsa, 1971). The standard describes the arrangement of 44 basic printing keys on the keyboard, two shift keys, and the space bar, as well as the characters that appear on the printing keys for the unshifted and shifted modes. It provides for a maximum of four additional keys and recommends character assignments for these keys. Finally, it allows for certain character substitutions on some of the keys to provide character sets appropriate to specific applications, such as word processing and information interchange. Figure 3.6 illustrates a keyboard with alphanumeric keys arranged in the QWERTY layout.

The widespread acceptance of the QWERTY keyboard is reason enough to caution against deviation from this layout. Although the considerations which led to the creation of this layout are unclear (Noyes, 1983b), recent data on the typing of English text indicate that the QWERTY arrangement offers other advantages as well. Kinkead (1975) timed and analyzed 115,000 keystrokes from 22 touch typists to determine the differences in keying time between hands, rows, columns, and individual keys. Alternate-hand keying was found to be 24% faster than same-hand keying. Keystrokes to the bottom row were slower than those to the top and middle rows. Keying by the index and middle fingers was more rapid than keying by the ring and little fingers. Successive keystrokes by the same finger resulted in the slowest keystrokes. These data suggest, then, that an effi-

Figure 3.6. The QWERTY keyboard layout. (Courtesy of Key Tronic Corp., Spokane, Washington.)

cient keyboard would use the frequency of character digrams (sequences of two letters) to ensure that most keystrokes alternate from hand to hand; would assign the least frequent letters to the bottom row, and to the ring and little fingers; and would minimize successive keystrokes by the same finger. Kinkead's analyses indicate that the QWERTY layout conforms to these constraints remarkably well.

The QWERTY layout is not without its disadvantages, however, and these disadvantages have motivated the development of many alternative arrangements. Noyes (1983b) provides a historical review of the origins of the QWERTY keyboard and other keyboard layouts put forth since to improve upon it. Some of the criticisms directed at the QWERTY layout over the past 50 years include (Noyes, 1983b):

- It overloads the left hand — 57% of typing is carried out by the nonpreferred hand for the majority of the population.
- It overloads certain fingers. (The differential strength of fingers, however, is perhaps less an issue with today's electronic keyboards than it was with earlier manual typewriters.)
- Too little typing is carried out on the home row of keys (32%). Too much typing (52%) is carried out on the top row. (Most critics of the QWERTY layout have assumed that home-row keying is the fastest. Kinkead (1975) noted, however, that while this may have been so on manual typewriters, top-row keying appears to be fastest for skilled typists on electric typewriters.)

- Excessive row hopping is required in frequently used sequences, often from the bottom row to the top row and down to the bottom again.
- Many common words are typed by the left hand alone.
- Forty-eight percent of all motions to reposition the fingers laterally between consecutive strokes are one-handed rather than easier two-handed motions.

3.3.2 The Dvorak Layout

Of the many efforts to improve upon the QWERTY layout, the Dvorak layout has proven the most enduring. A variant of this layout has, in fact, been accepted by the American National Standards Institute as an alternative standard (American National Standards Institute, 1983). Figure 3.7 illustrates a keyboard utilizing the Dvorak layout.

The Dvorak Simplified Keyboard was arranged on the basis of the frequencies with which letters and letter sequences occur in English text. It was designed to the following criteria (Noyes, 1983b):

- The right hand was given more work (56%) than the left hand (44%).
- The amount of typing assigned to different fingers was proportional to their skill and strength.
- Seventy percent of typing was carried out on the home row—the most frequently used letters were arranged on this row. Only 22% and 8% of typing was carried out on the top and bottom rows, respectively.

Figure 3.7. The Dvorak keyboard layout. (Courtesy of Key Tronic Corp., Spokane, Washington.)

- Letters often occurring together were assigned positions so that alternate hands could strike them.
- Finger motions from row to row and difficult, awkward reaches from the home row were minimized.
- Thirty-five percent of the words typically used were typed exclusively on the home row.

Seibel (1972) notes that a typist's stage of learning on a data entry device has a large effect on performance. In the study of data entry performance, effective elimination of stage-of-learning as a confounding variable requires extended periods of practice. (Seibel suggests at least six months and often a year or more.) As a result, the conduct of a valid experimental comparison of skilled typing with the QWERTY and Dvorak layouts is an extremely difficult and expensive proposition. And, in fact, no studies reported in the literature have been accepted generally as valid.

Yamada (1980) reviews the development and testing of the Dvorak Simplified Keyboard and provides an extensive set of references. While the testing of the Dvorak layout has generally been criticized for lack of careful experimental control, it is worthwhile to note some of the claims that have been made on the basis of these tests. Succinctly, it has been claimed that, relative to the QWERTY layout, the Dvorak layout is easier to learn, is less fatiguing to use, and permits faster data entry with fewer errors (Yamada, 1980).

Kinkead (1975) used keying time data collected from skilled typing on a QWERTY keyboard to predict the speed increase possible with a Dvorak layout. He predicted a keying speed advantage of only 2.3% for the Dvorak layout, this advantage largely the result of the larger proportion of alternate-hand keying possible with the Dvorak layout. Kinkead's assumption that key-to-key time data from QWERTY keying are also valid for Dvorak keying is suspect, however. Seibel (1972) notes that average times for low motor difficulty entries tend to be faster in isolation than when mixed with higher motor difficulty entries. Because the Dvorak layout was designed to minimize the awkward finger movements that commonly occur in QWERTY typing, it is quite possible that it would achieve reduced key-to-key times relative to those achieved with the QWERTY layout.

Thus, Kinkead's prediction of a 2.3% speed advantage for the Dvorak layout is probably pessimistic. Seibel (1972) offers a guess that the upper limit of the daily production advantage for such an arrangement would be about 10%.

The advantages of the QWERTY and Dvorak keyboard layouts are summarized in Table 3.3.

Table 3.3. Advantages of QWERTY and Dvorak Keyboard Layouts

Advantages of the QWERTY Layout	Advantages of the Dvorak Layout
1. Widespread acceptance and use	1. Increased efficiency
2. Accepted as an American National Standard	2. Accepted as an American National Standard
3. Most keystrokes alternate between hands	3. Increased use of alternate-hand keying
4. Bottom row contains least frequent letters	4. Increased use of home row
5. Ring and little fingers key least frequent letters	5. Amount of keying assigned to fingers is proportional to finger strength and skill
6. Relatively few successive keystrokes by same finger	6. Minimal awkward finger movement
	7. Increased use of right hand

SOURCE: Greenstein and Arnaut, 1987. Reproduced by permission of John Wiley & Sons, Inc.

3.3.3 The Alphabetical Layout

It seems reasonable to assume that the familiar order of an alphabetically arranged keyboard would enhance both the speed and accuracy of occasional users employing a hunt-and-peck approach to data entry. In contrast to the arbitrary appearing structure that the QWERTY and Dvorak layouts present to the inexperienced user, an alphabetical layout should provide an easily understood structure that aids in the search for desired keys. Several studies of alphabetical layouts have been reported in the literature, and their results are consistent. The alphabetical layout does not appear to offer any practical performance advantages relative to the QWERTY layout.

Hirsch (1970) reported the results of a study that sought to determine whether the performance of unskilled typists might be improved through use of an alphabetically ordered keyboard. After seven hours of practice, subjects using the alphabetical keyboard were still unable to type more quickly with this layout than they had typed in the pretest, without practice, on the QWERTY layout. A second group of subjects, after seven hours of practice on the QWERTY layout, showed a significant improvement in typing rate over their QWERTY pretest scores. Hirsch concluded that the alphabetical layout is certainly not better than, and perhaps not as good as, the QWERTY layout for relatively low-skilled typists. He offered two explanations for the superiority of the QWERTY layout. First, many of the most frequently used letters happen to be clustered in the center of the QWERTY layout, permitting the hunt for a letter to focus upon a small visual area. Second, while hunt-and-peck use of the QWERTY layout involves a purely visual search that can often be focused upon a small area, use of the alphabetical layout may first involve a memory search to locate the letter's position in the alphabet, followed by a visual search for the key on the board. The focused visual search with the QWERTY layout may be more efficient than the combination of memory and visual search required with the alphabetical layout.

Michaels (1971) conducted a second experiment comparing performance on the QWERTY and alphabetical keyboard layouts. Subjects ranging in typing skill from almost none to secretarial level operated the keyboards for ten half-hour sessions. Half of the subjects started on the alphabetical layout and half on the QWERTY layout, with the two groups switching keyboards after five sessions. There were no significant differences in the performance of low-skill subjects across the two keyboard arrangements. For the medium- and high-skill subjects, keying speed and overall work output were significantly greater on the QWERTY keyboard. This last result is to be expected given the prior experience these subjects had with the QWERTY layout.

Norman and Fisher (1982) tested two alphabetically arranged keyboards and a randomly structured keyboard with subjects who classified themselves as nontypists. Potential subjects were first given a ten-minute pretest on the QWERTY keyboard. Those who typed less than 25 words per minute were then tested for ten minutes on each of the other three keyboards. The results revealed a small (10%) increment in typing speed for the two alphabetical keyboards over the random layout but no difference between the alphabetical keyboards. The speed achieved on the QWERTY keyboard pretest was 66% greater than that later reached with the alphabetical keyboard and 82% greater than that reached with the random keyboard. Norman and Fisher concluded that the potential assistance an

Table 3.4. The Performance of Unskilled Typists Using the QWERTY and Alphabetical Layouts

Practice Time	Hirsch (1970) 7 Hours	Michaels (1971) 2.5 Hours	Norman and Fisher (1982) 10 Minutes
QWERTY	Significant increase in typing rate over the QWERTY pretest rate	No significant difference between the two layouts	QWERTY pretest rate 66% higher than rates attained on two alphabetical layouts
Alphabetical	No significant increase in typing rate over the QWERTY pretest rate		Rates 10% higher than rate attained on randomly arranged keyboard

SOURCE: Greenstein and Arnaut, 1987. Reproduced by permission of John Wiley & Sons, Inc.

alphabetical structure might provide the user in keying is negated by the mental computation required to make use of the structure.

Thus, an alphabetically ordered key layout does enhance the performance of unskilled users relative to a randomly structured layout. But the increment in performance is modest. When the basis of comparison is the QWERTY layout, performance with the alphabetical arrangement is at best no better, and may not be as good. Finally, users who have already developed some degree of skill with the QWERTY layout perform significantly better with the QWERTY layout than with the alphabetical layout. Table 3.4 summarizes the results of the three studies cited for the performance of unskilled typists.

3.3.4 QWERTY Versus Alternative Alphanumeric Layouts

The QWERTY layout is the standard arrangement for alphanumeric data entry. Whatever its origins, it is a reasonably efficient layout as well. More efficient arrangements have been derived, and the Dvorak layout has been accepted as an alternative standard. But the increases in productivity achieved with the improved keyboard arrangements have apparently not been sufficient to overcome the cost of their adoption.

The cost of adopting an alternative layout today, however, is lower than ever before. New keyboard technologies have substantially lowered manufacturing costs. Reconfigurable keyboards and programmable machine logic permit easy switching of key arrangements within the constraints of the traditional four-row layout (see Figure 3.8). The capability to produce a low-cost switchable keyboard for both the QWERTY and alternative arrangements removes two barriers to the adoption of alternative layouts. Those already skilled in the use of the QWERTY layout are assured its continued availability, and those considering the investment of time and effort to acquire skill on a more efficient layout can be assured of the alternative layout's general availability.

Of the alternative layouts that have been proposed, the Dvorak layout has the advantage of an enduring following as well as an accepted standard legitimizing its use. The Dvorak layout represents a more efficient arrangement than the QWERTY standard, although the increment in efficiency to be expected is still unclear. It may have ease-of-learning and ease-of-use advantages as well. Designed in the 1930s for use with mechanical typewriters and English text entry, the Dvorak layout is probably not the optimal arrangement for today's input technologies and tasks. One might wish for a more modern alternative layout based on analysis of current usage and validated through controlled testing. But history has shown that

(a)

(b)

Figure 3.8. A reconfigurable keyboard: (a) the keyboard, (b) rearranging the keys. (Courtesy of Texas Instruments, Inc.)

those willing to invest great effort into keyboard redesign are likely to find their efforts ignored.

Kinkead (1975) argues that reassignment of keys within the conventional layout will achieve only small improvements in raw typing speed. If new arrangements are to represent real improvements, then they must demonstrate advantages in other areas as well, such as training time, error rates, and fatigue. Kinkead notes, however, that opportunities for increasing speed of data entry remain. He reports speed improvements of 7 to 8% using automatic carriage returns, for example.

Rather than invest great effort in keyboard rearrangement, emphasis might be placed on the availability of features that permit rapid and easy error correction. The DWIM ("Do what I mean") error correction facility within the INTERLISP programming environment provides an example of such an approach. This facility corrects various classes of input errors, in some cases automatically without interruption of the user's input process.

3.3.5 Numeric Keypad Layout

The generally accepted keypad for numeric data entry consists of ten keys, one for each of the ten digits, arranged in a three-by-three matrix, with the zero key below the matrix. Two key arrangements are commonly encountered on the three-by-three matrix. The first, found on hand calculators, assigns the digits 1, 2, 3 from left-to-right on the bottom row, with the digits 7, 8, 9 from left-to-right on the top row. The second, used on touch telephones, assigns the digits 1, 2, 3 from left-to-right on the top row, while the digits 7, 8, 9 are assigned from left-to-right on the bottom row. These layouts are illustrated in Figure 3.9.

The highly practiced user can perform about equally well with either the calculator or the telephone arrangement (Seibel, 1972). The selection of a particular arrangement becomes an issue in situations where less dedicated use is made of the keypad or when the user must alternate between the two arrangements. Lutz and Chapanis (1955) sought to determine whether a population stereotype existed for the arrangement of digits on each of six

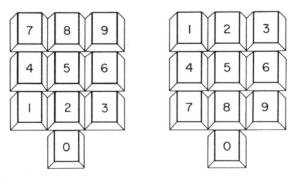

Figure 3.9. Numeric keypad layouts: (a) calculator layout, (b) telephone layout. (Greenstein and Arnaut, 1987. Copyright 1987, John Wiley & Sons, Inc., and reproduced by permission.)

different ten-key keyset configurations. They found that subjects generally expected to find numbers arranged in left-to-right order in horizontal rows starting with the top row. For the three-by-three plus one-key-below arrangement, the telephone layout was expected by 55 of the 100 subjects. The calculator layout was a distant second choice, selected by 8 of 100 subjects.

Conrad and Hull (1968) conducted an experiment to compare speed and accuracy of data entry with the calculator and telephone layouts. One group of subjects entered eight-digit codes exclusively with the calculator layout, a second group with the telephone layout, and a third group alternated frequently between the two layouts. Subjects claimed no previous experience with either of the layouts. There was no significant difference in speed of entry between the calculator and telephone conditions. The telephone layout did, however, achieve somewhat greater accuracy than the calculator layout (6.43% of the codes were entered incorrectly with the telephone layout, 8.16% with the calculator layout). Subjects working exclusively with the telephone layout were also faster and more accurate than subjects alternating between the telephone and calculator layouts.

For the occasional user, then, the telephone layout offers both conceptual compatibility and performance advantages over the calculator layout. It is also undesirable, given the results of the Conrad and Hull study, to require users to alternate between the two arrangements. Unfortunately, while the telephone layout is accepted internationally as the standard for pushbutton telephones, the calculator layout is the established standard for adding and calculating machines (American National Standards Institute, 1979). With computers now providing telecommunicating as well as calculating functions, the results of the experiments cited above favor selection of the telephone layout for an auxiliary numeric keypad. Current practice, however, indicates that the calculator layout is the de facto standard arrangement on computer keyboards. The considerations guiding the selection of a numeric keypad layout are summarized in Table 3.5.

Table 3.5. Numeric Keypad Layout Considerations

1. The telephone layout is consistent with many new users' expectations.
2. Occasional users achieve increased accuracy with the telephone layout.
3. Highly practiced users perform well with either the telephone or the calculator layout.
4. Alternation between layouts degrades performance.
5. The calculator layout is the de facto standard on computer keyboards.

SOURCE: Adapted from Greenstein and Arnaut, 1987. Reproduced by permission of John Wiley & Sons, Inc.

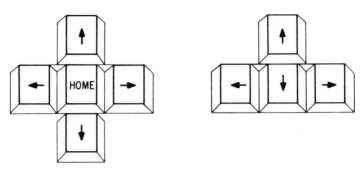

Figure 3.10. Cursor-control key layouts. (Greenstein and Arnaut, 1987. Copyright 1987, John Wiley & Sons, Inc., and reproduced by permission.)

3.3.6 Cursor-Control Key Layout

Cursor-control keys provide a key-oriented means to control current position on an associated visual display. Typically, cursor-control keysets direct the cursor to the left, right, up, down, and, perhaps, to a "home" position on the display screen. The human factors literature provides little specific guidance regarding layout of cursor-control keys.

Figure 3.10 illustrates two reasonable cursor-control key configurations. Both offer a clear relationship between key location and key function. The inverted "T" layout might be particularly appropriate for applications in which the user tends to move downward through displayed data. In such a situation, this layout positions the three most frequently used keys on one compact and easily touch-operated home row.

3.3.7 Function Key Layout

The location of function keys on a keyboard is guided by the general considerations of importance, frequency-of-use, function, and sequence-of-use. Beyond these general considerations, guidelines for function key layout tend to be highly application-specific. A study reported by Hollingsworth and Dray (1981) does, however, indicate a means for limiting the complexity of selecting the appropriate key from among many on a function keyboard. This study investigated the effect of backlighting those keys corresponding to permissible response options at different stages in the use of a function keyboard. The keyboard consisted of two horizontal rows of eight keys. All 16 keys were uniformly backlit until a stimulus was presented. Upon stimulus presentation (a function key label presented on a video display), the backlighting of 4, 8, or all 16 of the keys switched to a

Table 3.6. Function Key Layout Considerations

1. Locate according to importance, frequency-of-use, function, and sequence-of-use.
2. Indicate the current subset of appropriate function keys.
3. Guard against inadvertent activation of critical functions by remote key location, large activation force, or simultaneous key depression.

SOURCE: Greenstein and Arnaut, 1987. Reproduced by permission of John Wiley & Sons, Inc.

discriminably higher intensity level. The key corresponding to the label on the display was always one of the high intensity keys. The subject's task was to press the key indicated on the video display. Reaction time was substantially shorter when the target key was one of only four high intensity keys than when the lighting pattern carried no information (all 16 keys at high intensity). Hollingsworth and Dray suggest that even greater reductions in response time might be achieved if the lighting pattern could be made available before stimulus presentation. Their work indicates that complex function keyboards should be designed to provide response cueing.

An additional consideration in the design and placement of some function keys may be the effect of inadvertent operation. Unfortunately, measures taken to prevent inadvertent entries invariably slow intentional entries as well. However, where accidental invocation of a particular function is highly undesirable, the following approaches can be taken:

- The key corresponding to the function may be located so that inadvertent operation is unlikely.
- The key corresponding to the function may be designed to require a larger activation force than other keys.
- Invocation of the function may require the simultaneous activation of two or more nonadjacent keys.

General considerations guiding the layout of function keys are summarized in Table 3.6.

3.4 One-Handed Alphanumeric Keyboards

Van der Heiden and Grandjean (1984) observed designers using a computer-aided design workstation to perform three types of design tasks. The workstation included an alphanumeric keyboard and a graphic tablet for inputting commands and data. The three tasks observed were mechanical design, printed circuit board design, and electrical schematic design. The authors found that 14 to 24% of the actual work time at the workstation involved use of the keyboard. Frequently used command strings were integrated into a graphic tablet menu and could be activated more efficiently with the tablet than the keyboard. For the mechanical design and printed circuit board design tasks, the tablet was involved in approximately 45% of the work. This usage dropped to 26% of the work time for the electrical schematic design task, where the keyboard was used to insert large amounts of nonstandardized alphanumeric data on the schematics. Operators typically positioned the tablet directly in front of them, in line with their video display unit. The keyboard was usually placed to the side of the tablet.

That the keyboard is a secondary input device for many applications introduces at least two operational difficulties. First, conventional alphanumeric keyboards are designed for two-handed operation. Thus, operation of this secondary input device leaves no hand available to operate the primary input device (which generally *can* be operated with one hand). Second, conventional alphanumeric keyboards take up a substantial amount of space in the workstation. If a two-handed keyboard is to be operated efficiently and comfortably, this space should be directly in front of the operator, in line with his or her displays. This space may be allocated to a graphic tablet, however, if *it* is the primary input device. The keyboard is then placed to the side of the tablet, requiring the operator to twist away from the displays or to reposition the keyboard in line with the displays when keying is necessary. The first approach is uncomfortable. The second approach is time-consuming and inconvenient, particularly if the task requires coordinated inputs from the tablet and the keyboard.

The problems encountered when an alphanumeric keyboard is a secondary input device might be mitigated by employing a keyboard designed for one-handed operation. Such a keyboard would free one hand to operate the primary input device. Because the keyboard need only be accessible by one hand, it can be operated effectively when positioned off to the side of the primary work area. One-handed keyboard designs can achieve space efficiency as well. Thus, the space requirements of a secondary alphanumeric input device can be reduced, providing additional room for other input devices and working documents. This section reviews several design approaches for one-handed alphanumeric keyboards. Few of these approaches have seen successful application in commercial products, and there is little data available to indicate their suitability for general use. They do, however, warrant further study as secondary input devices for certain computer workstation applications.

3.4.1 Sequential Keyboards

Sequential keyboards are operated one key at a time. Conventional two-handed alphanumeric keyboards are primarily sequential in operation.

They deviate from a purely sequential mode when they require the simultaneous depression of two or more keys to generate, for example, an uppercase letter or a special function. The use of purely sequential keyboards has been studied for data entry in aircraft cockpits. This application does not typically require both uppercase and lowercase character sets or a wide variety of special characters. It does, however, place severe size constraints on the keyboard, and it requires that the keyboard be operable by one hand. These constraints effectively rule out the use of a conventional two-handed alphanumeric keyboard. Figure 3.11 illustrates two sequential alphanumeric keyboard designs for use in aircraft cockpits.

Hornsby (1981) compared data entry performance using two alphanumeric keyboards designed for use in aircraft cockpits. The *full alphanumeric keyboard* had a separate key for each letter of the alphabet and for each of the ten digits. The letter keys were arranged in one seven-by-four matrix and the number keys in another four-by-three matrix. Any letter or digit could be entered with one keystroke using this keyboard. The *reduced alphanumeric keyboard* arranged the letters and digits within a three-by-four matrix with three letters and one number to a key. While entry of a

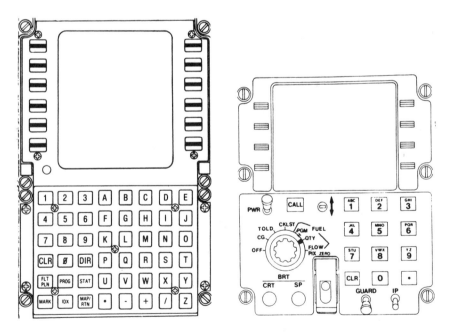

Figure 3.11. Two sequential alphanumeric keyboard designs. (From Butterbaugh and Rockwell 1982. Copyright 1982, by the Human Factors Society, Inc., and reproduced by permission.)

digit required one keystroke using this keyboard, entry of a letter required two. The first stroke designated one of the 12 keys in the matrix. The second, entered on a separate row of three unlabeled keys, specified the letter desired on the just-designated key. Subjects used the keyboards to enter flight initialization information, flight plans, and flight plan modifications. Error rates were low with either of the keyboard designs. With the reduced alphanumeric keyboard requiring two keystrokes for each letter entry, however, entry rates were substantially slower with it (approximately 70% slower for letter entries) than with the full alphanumeric keyboard.

Butterbaugh and Rockwell (1982) also studied the entry of flight plan information using keyboards intended for aircraft cockpit applications. A keying logic that allocated an individual key to each letter of the alphabet and to each digit was compared with three other keying logics that arranged the letters and digits within a four row by three column touch telephone style key matrix. All of the keying logics generated the digits with a single key press. The first logic generated letters with a single key press as well, while the latter three logics required two or three keystrokes to generate each letter. Again, not surprisingly, the keying logic which required only one key press per letter achieved the highest data entry rate by a substantial margin.

It is clear that one-handed keying logics that generate each character with a single key press achieve much higher data entry rates than logics that require a sequence of key presses to produce a single character. Even the *single* key press keyboards reviewed in this section were designed for hunt-and-peck rather than touch operation. Thus, high data entry rates should not be required or expected with these keyboards. In applications involving frequent use by trained operators, data entry rates could be enhanced by a touch-operable design. The primary advantage of the multiple key press per character keysets is their small size. The use of such keysets seems justified only when space constraints are severe and data entry requirements are minimal.

One-handed sequential keyboards are most appropriate for applications involving only a modest amount of alphanumeric data entry. The operation of such keyboards is easily learned. Thus, they impose minimal training requirements on the operator, and they can be operated easily by occasional users.

3.4.2 Chord Keyboards

Chord keyboards require simultaneous presses of two or more keys to generate many of their characters. This enables a small number of keys to generate a relatively large set of characters. Figure 3.12 depicts a basic

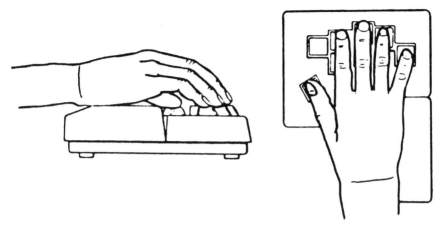

Figure 3.12. A chord keyboard. (From Kirschenbaum, Friedman, and Melnik (1986). Copyright 1986, by the Human Factors Society, Inc., and reproduced by permission.)

one-handed chord keyboard. Thirty-one ($2^5 - 1$) different combinations of key presses can be generated with five keys on such a keyboard. If a second thumb key is added, and the thumb is used to press at most one or the other of the thumb keys, an additional 16 (2^4) key press combinations can be generated. Alternatively, if a shift key is added to permit the five keys to operate in either of two modes, another 31 characters can be added to the original character set. With any of these designs, each of the four fingers may remain on its own home key, permitting straightforward and rapid touch operation of the keyboard.

While the chord keyboard enables one-handed touch typing of a large character set, there are disadvantages associated with this design approach. It is difficult to label the keys clearly because each key is associated with more than one character and many characters involve more than one key. To use the keyboard effectively, the operator must learn the set of relationships between characters and chords. Certain of these chords may not only be difficult to learn, they may also be difficult for the fingers to execute.

Ratz and Ritchie (1961) and Seibel (1962) measured the times required to execute the 31 chords possible with a five-key chord keyboard. The two studies determined very similar rank orderings for the production times of these chords. The five single-key responses were executed most quickly. Chords produced by a consecutive group of fingers tended to be of intermediate difficulty. The most difficult chords tended to require one or two fingers to be held up while their neighbors on each side depressed keys

(Ratz and Ritchie, 1961). The chords with the longest execution times tended to have the highest error rates as well (Seibel, 1962).

Most of the research and development of chord keyboards has focused on highly specific applications, most notably mail sorting. Noyes (1983a) provides a historical review of the development of chord keyboards beginning in the 1940s with particular attention to the mail sorting application. Some recent work with chord keyboards has focused on their use for general alphanumeric data input. This work suggests that chord keyboards hold a good deal of promise for frequent users requiring a one-handed data input device.

Gopher, Hilsernath, and Raij (1985) reported some results of their ongoing work with one- and two-handed chord keyboards for alphanumeric data entry. Their one-handed keyboard includes five conventional typing keys positioned to conform to the fingertips and two shift keys, each of which can provide an additional mode for the five typing keys. The 31 chord combinations of the unshifted mode are sufficient to produce the alphabet. Additional characters and editing functions can be provided by the shifted modes. The more frequently used letters are associated with the easier chord combinations. Using a chart of the letter-chord relationships, subjects typing Hebrew text were able to memorize the complete set of letter chords in less than an hour. By the end of the first hour of typing, they were operating the keyboard by touch without reference to the chart. After 20 hours of practice, subjects were typing 30 to 35 words per minute with error rates of one to two percent. Students learning to use a conventional QWERTY keyboard typically require much more practice to attain this level of typing proficiency.

Rochester, Bequaert, and Sharp (1978) developed a one-handed chord keyboard with a number of interesting features. Figure 3.13 illustrates the layout of the keyboard. The two row by five column array of square keys is operated by the index, middle, and ring fingers. The row of four rectangular keys is operated by the thumb and can be repositioned to the right side of the keyboard for left-handed operation. Rounded depressions, or dimples, are placed on the finger keys so that when a finger presses a dimple, one, two, or four keys are depressed. The 27 dimples on the keyboard are labeled to permit hunt-and-peck typing. Using the dimples, the entire alphabet can be typed with chords generated by single finger presses. Two or three fingers can also be used simultaneously to produce strings of letters, such as "the" and "fro." In fact, the letters have been assigned to the dimples to maximize the average number of characters of English text that can be produced per chord. The thumb keys are spaced to permit the thumb to depress two adjacent thumb keys as part of a chord. As a result, there are eight different thumb actions that can be combined with the

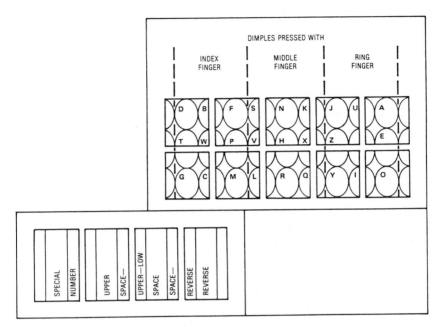

Figure 3.13. The Rochester, Bequaert, and Sharp chord keyboard. (From Rochester, Bequaert, and Sharp (1978). Copyright 1978, by the Institute of Electrical and Electronics Engineers, Inc., and reproduced by permission.)

chords formed by the fingers. Together, the provision for multiple key presses using a single finger and using more than one finger allow three fingers and the thumb of one hand to generate 4407 unique key combinations on this 14-key keyboard.

According to the developers of this keyboard, users require about an hour of training to make use of the keyboard's capabilities in a hunt-and-peck mode. Three of four subjects with 150 to 200 hours of training on the keyboard attained touch typing speeds of more than 40 words per minute; the fourth reached a speed of approximately 25 words per minute. The developers conclude that learning times on the keyboard are similar to those with a conventional QWERTY keyboard for typing speeds up to 40 words per minute.

The small amount of data available suggest that it is significantly more difficult to acquire typing proficiency with this keyboard design than with the more basic chord keyboard developed by Gopher and his colleagues. The design is certainly notable, however, for enabling one finger to depress several keys simultaneously. This feature, coupled with appropriate keyboard labeling, enables both hunt-and-peck and touch operators to generate the entire alphabet with single-finger key presses and one hand. The Rochester, Bequaert, and Sharp keyboard is not the only design that displays these features; Noyes (1983a) describes a 12-key chord keyboard patented by Stewart (1973) that also incorporates these features. No information on the performance attainable with that keyboard appears to be available in the open literature.

Not a great deal of work has yet been devoted to optimizing the chord keyboard for alphanumeric data entry. In the absence of any standards based on previous experience, future implementations must address a number of design issues. Appropriate numbers of keys and key locations must be determined and the relationships between characters and chords must take into account the learning, retention, and execution capabilities of the user. Paradoxically, these issues are especially complex in designs intended for one-handed operation. Depending on the application and the user, a one-handed keyboard may be used by the right hand, the left hand, or, at different times, by either hand. An effective design should enable the user to transfer his or her keying skill from hand to hand.

Chord keyboards offer the potential of reasonably high data entry rates with one-handed operation. They impose a different set of training requirements on their users than sequentially operated keyboards, however. While a sequentially operated keyboard requires touch-operable design and training for *efficient* operation, chord keyboards require design for hunt-and-peck operation or training if operation is to be possible at all. Still, the work reported by Gopher, Hilsernath, and Raij (1985) suggests that with some training and practice, chord keyboard users can achieve impressive data entry rates.

Because chord keyboards require learning and retention of the relationship between characters and chords, they are not appropriate for occasional use. In fact, if a chord keyboard is the only input device provided for alphanumeric input, the occasional user may be denied access to the system. Chord keyboards offer particular promise for the frequent user. If this user is already using one hand to perform another task, they are uniquely capable of providing the means for rapid input of nonstandardized data.

3.5 Keyboard Mechanics, Feedback, and Dimensions

Alden, Daniels, and Kanarick (1972) conducted an extensive review of the literature on keyboard design and operation. They conclude that a good deal of research has been conducted, but there are few definitive findings on which to base design standards. The sponsorship and motivation of much of this keyboard research has resulted in work primarily concerned with the evaluation of specific products. While the work may determine one keyboard design to be superior to another, it often does not isolate the effects of individual keyboard parameters on user performance. Keyboard design research is also frequently proprietary and thus is not published in the open literature.

3.5.1 Keyswitch Mechanisms and Timing Characteristics

Keyswitch Mechanisms.   Although simple in concept, a keyboard design that provides the optimal combination of high reliability, high user acceptance, and low cost has been an elusive target. In an effort to satisfy design requirements, manufacturers have developed a number of switch technologies. The following briefly describes some of the major technologies and considers their advantages and disadvantages.

Mechanical Contact.   The simplest switch mechanism employs mechanical contacts that are brought together as the key plunger is depressed (Figure 3.14). Although low in cost, one problem with mechanical contacts is that they suffer from contact bounce, which can generate false signals. This problem usually necessitates the use of appropriate debounce circuitry. Another disadvantage of mechanical contact switches is that con-

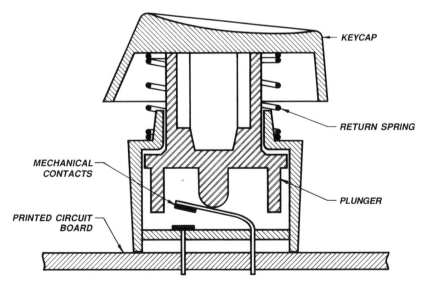

Figure 3.14. An example of a mechanical contact keyswitch.

tacts can be contaminated by particulates or oxidation. Such contamination results in increased contact resistance, causing unreliable operation or even total switch failure. Methods used to combat contamination include gold plating of contacts or contact designs with wiping actions that are self-cleaning. Such approaches, however, tend to increase cost or reduce key switch longevity. Key life is in the range of 5 to 10 million actuations, but survival rate often drops rapidly above 5 million operations.

Reed. Although reed switches employ what are essentially mechanical contacts, problems caused by contamination are eliminated by enclosing the switch contacts in a sealed capsule, which is usually made of glass. Depression of a key moves a magnet close to the encapsulated reeds on which the switch contacts are mounted. The attraction of the magnet on the reeds causes them to be brought together until the contacts touch. Because the sealed capsule prevents contamination of the switch contacts, the long-term reliability (after passing through the "infant mortality" portion of the life cycle) is generally good. Key life of 50 million operations is possible. The biggest disadvantage of reed switches is their high cost relative to other technologies. As a result, reed switches have declined in popularity for the past several years.

Capacitance. One of the most popular keyboard technologies uses capacitance changes to signal key activation. In its most common form, the capacitance switching mechanism (shown in Figure 3.15) employs a foam pad that is bonded to the bottom of the key plunger. A sheet of conductive foil is attached to the bottom of the foam pad. As a key is pressed, the foil, which acts as a capacitive plate, is brought into contact with a printed circuit board mounted under the array of key plungers. The change in capacitance as the foil contacts the circuit board passes a low-level signal onto detector circuits, which signals key activation. Because capacitance switching does not depend on the closing of a circuit through low resistance contacts, some contamination of surfaces is tolerable before keyboard operation is affected. As a result, capacitance keyboards exhibit high reliability. Typical key life characteristics range from 10 to 50 million keystrokes. Because of its relatively low cost and high reliability, capacitance switching has become the dominant "full travel" technology.

Hall Effect. In Hall effect keyboards, a magnetic transducer (typically an integrated circuit) is mounted near a magnet, which is affixed to the key plunger. Depression of a key moves the magnet closer to the magnetic transducer, causing the transducer to output a voltage change signaling key activation. Because the switching mechanism employs solid state elec-

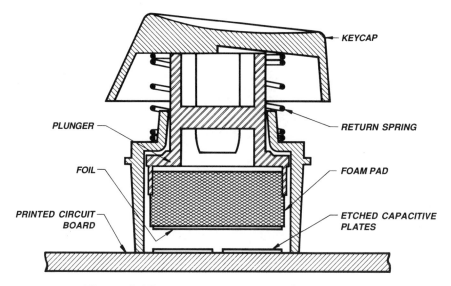

Figure 3.15. An example of a capacitance keyswitch.

tronics, Hall effect keyboards exhibit extremely high reliability. Key life of more than 100 million actuations per key is typical. In addition, because individual keyswitches can be sealed, Hall effect keyboards are often used in military, marine, industrial, and aerospace applications where reliability is a critical factor. The disadvantages of Hall effect switches are relatively high cost and large size of individual keyswitch modules. The latter rules them out for low profile (30 mm) configurations.

Full Travel Membrane. Although essentially a contact switch technology, full travel membrane keyboards present a low cost, reliable keyboard alternative. A matrix of full travel (approximately 4 mm) key button assemblies is mounted above a three-layer sandwich of circuit materials that comprise the switching mechanisms for all keys on the keyboard (Figure 3.16). The top and bottom layers of the sandwich are thin sheets of flexible film (typically, clear polymer) with a conductive silver composition deposited onto facing sides of the flexible film. The silver composition is "printed" in a pattern that forms the electrical contacts for each key station and all electrical interconnections. Between the conductive layers is a third layer that provides a gap between contacts through holes in the layer. The entire three-layer switch assembly is bonded to a sheet metal base plate. When a key is pressed, a switch closure is accomplished by deflecting the top film layer through the hole in the separation layer so that the conduc-

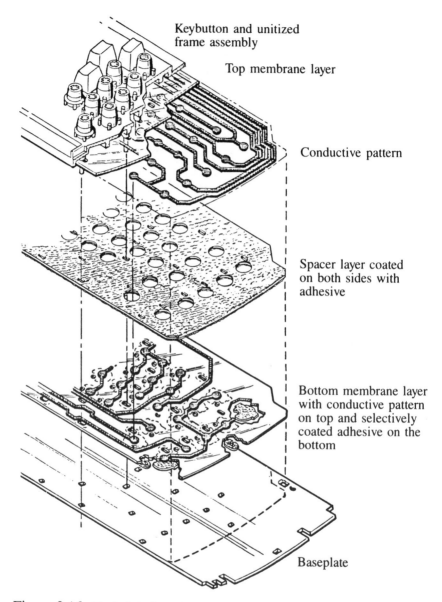

Keybutton and unitized
frame assembly

Top membrane layer

Conductive pattern

Spacer layer coated
on both sides with
adhesive

Bottom membrane layer
with conductive pattern
on top and selectively
coated adhesive on the
bottom

Baseplate

Figure 3.16. Exploded view of a full travel membrane keyboard showing unitized frame, space layer, adhesive layers, and base plate. (Copyright 1985, by International Business Machines Corporation; reprinted with permission.)

tive material on the top film layer comes in contact with the conductive material on the bottom layer. Although early membrane keyboards had a reputation for poor reliability, recent advances in materials and manufacturing techniques have greatly improved their performance and reliability. Typical key life characteristics for full travel membrane keyboards now exceed 10 million keystrokes (Defosse, Williams, Gostomski, and Cobb, 1985). A major contributor to the low cost of full travel membranes is the use of the switching sandwich, which contains all the switches for the keyboard. This arrangement is significantly less expensive than keyboards that employ individual switching modules and somewhat less expensive than units that employ printed circuit boards (typically used in capacitance keyboards). Unfortunately, the technology requires specialized tooling and stringent manufacturing (clean room) environments. Consequently, full travel membrane technology is less suitable for custom or low-volume keyboard applications.

Keyboard Life Requirements. An important specification required in selecting or developing a keyboard is keyboard life, usually specified as the number of key actuations made on each key without failure. This specification is important because if it is set too low, the keyboard is likely to fail prematurely in the working environment. If set too high, keyboards may be unnecessarily costly when certain components are designed to accommodate the extended life requirement. An important objective, then, is to match the keyboard life requirement to the needs of the application in question.

Keyboard life requirements for keyboard-intensive applications such as word processing and electronic typewriters are typically in the range of 20 million actuations per key. "Worst case" estimates for design life are based on assumptions. For example, estimated keyboard usage is approximately 120 hours per month at an input rate of 12,000 keystrokes per hour (approximately equivalent to 40 words per minute). Assuming that the "E" key (the most frequent letter in English text, which constitutes about 13.8% of all typed characters) will be the limiting factor at 20 million keystrokes, it is estimated that the alphabetic keyboard array will receive approximately 145 million keystrokes. At the assumed usage rate of 12,000 characters per hour for 120 hours per month, the calculated keyboard life would be approximately 8.4 years.

Assuming that most graphic workstation users will seldom maintain equivalent rates for sustained periods, it is likely that more modest keyboard life requirements will be acceptable. Keyboards on most popular personal/professional microcomputers, for example, have life cycle requirements of 10 million cycles per key (Defosse et al., 1985).

Keyboard Timing and Rollover Characteristics. One of the problems in the design of early electric typewriters was the jamming of the print mechanism when two or more keys were pressed simultaneously. To combat this problem, manufacturers designed interlocks that would mechanically prohibit the depression of a second key as long as the first key remained depressed.

Not being hampered by relatively slow electromechanical mechanisms, it would seem that electronic keyboards with even modest specifications would be able to accept inputs at the limits of human capabilities. How valid is this assumption? Much to the dismay of keyboard designers, typists have often shown an ability to exceed a given keyboard's response capabilities. How does this happen? One common mistake is to base design parameters on gross average typing speeds (commonly, in words per minute). For example, let it be assumed that the fastest typist a given system is likely to encounter types at 125 words per minute. Assuming an average of five keystrokes per word, this would be equivalent to about 625 keystrokes per minute or approximately 10.4 keystrokes per second. Based on these calculations, the average time between keystrokes would be approximately 96 ms. A look at a distribution of interkeystroke interval times for a typical typist (Figure 3.17) indicates that a substantial proportion of keystrokes have a duration of less than 96 ms. A keyboard designed to scan keys of the keyboard matrix at that threshold would lose any keystrokes that follow shorter interkeystroke intervals.

The main source of the problem, of course, is that keystroke times are more variable than can be predicted by average typing speed or average time between characters. As shown in Figure 3.17, although the average interkeystroke interval is approximately 125 ms, a substantial number of keystroke intervals are either shorter or longer than the average. The shortest intervals, in fact, are remarkably quick. For example, it is common for typists of even average skill to type short bursts of two to three character sequences with interkeystroke intervals in the range of 20 to 30 ms. Furthermore, certain keystroke combinations such as "he" in "the" have been observed with intervals as short as 4 ms (Daniels and Graf, 1970).

How is it possible that humans can perform with such rapidity? Several mechanisms have been suggested for the rapidity of a typist's keystrokes. August Dvorak, in 1936, suggested that operator's keystrokes tend to overlap. In a two-letter sequence, for example, the second finger begins to make its keystroke before the first has been completed (Salthouse, 1984). Dvorak's hypothesis was verified about four decades later when Gentner, Grudin, and Conway (1980) used high-speed motion pictures (taken at 100 frames per second) to study finger movements of transcription typists.

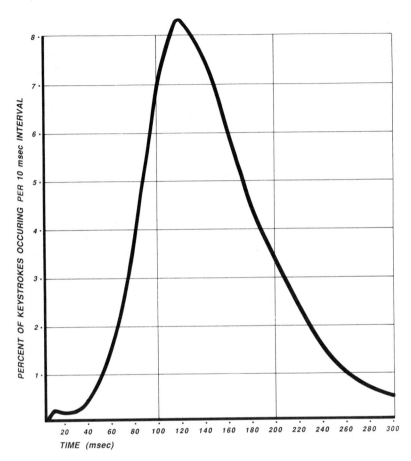

Figure 3.17. Distribution of interkeystroke intervals for a group of typists. (Based on a study reported in Kinkead (1975).)

Detailed analysis of the films indicated that finger movements are highly overlapping, with 96% of the finger movements being initiated *before* the previous key is completely depressed. Analysis of finger movement times indicated that the average time for complete finger movement (261 ms) was much longer than interkeystroke times (124 ms), indicating that two or three fingers are often in motion simultaneously.

What implications do these observations have for the design of keyboards?

1. Interkeystroke interval data of skilled typists indicate that a significant proportion of keystrokes occur very quickly—around 20 to 30 ms. If

the minimum acceptance time of the keyboard is made significantly longer, the number of errors due to character omissions will increase.

2. In applications where rapid keyboard entry is likely, the overlap of finger motions means that more than one key will be depressed at any given time. A keyboard feature that allows a keystroke to be accepted while another key or keys (depending on the specific design) is depressed is known as rollover. A keyboard with no rollover disallows other keystrokes as long as one key is depressed. Several versions of rollover exist. Figure 3.18 shows the timing characteristics of several rollover schemes.

- Two-key rollover (also known as shadow rollover) allows a second key to be depressed when one key is already down. The second key, however, will output a signal only as the first key is released. If the second key is released before the first key, the second keystroke will be ignored. If two keys are pressed simultaneously, all output is blocked.

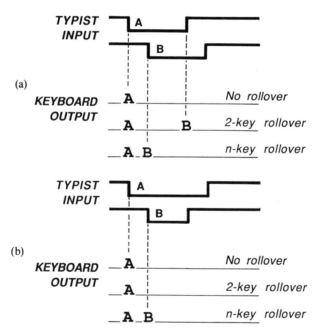

Figure 3.18. Action of keyboards with no rollover, two-key rollover, and *n*-key rollover: (a) the effect on keyboard output when two keys are pressed simultaneously and the first key is released before the second, (b) when two keys are pressed simultaneously and the second key is released before the first.

- Three-key rollover provides valid data for two sequentially depressed keys. Depression of a third key does not produce a character output until one of the first two keys is released.
- n-key rollover allows a keyboard to accept all keystrokes and generate all valid characters regardless of the number of keys that are depressed at the same time. Electronic memory is used to keep the signals in stroked sequence.

Daniels and Graf (1970) conducted a study comparing keyboards with n-key rollover and two-key rollover to a keyboard with no rollover. Although no differences were found in typing speed among the three configurations, subjects were found to make approximately 30 percent fewer errors with n-key rollover than with two-key rollover. The error rate for the no rollover keyboard (10.2 errors/minute) was more than nine times that of the n-key rollover keyboard.

Although n-key rollover reduces errors by allowing unlimited overlap of key depressions, it is unlikely that typists will depress more than three or four keys at once. Therefore, the capability to accept an unlimited number of overlapping keystrokes may be unnecessary. In fact, according to DeFosse, et al. (1985), human factors data have shown that the number of errors caused by simultaneous depression of three or more keys is insignificant (0.009%). These findings have led DeFosse et al. to include three-key rollover in the design of keyboards for a popular line of electronic typewriters.

3.5.2 Tactile Feedback

The return mechanism of a keyswitch is responsible both for restoring the key upon release to its uppermost position and for providing resistance to the downward motion of the key as it is being pressed. This resistance varies as a function of key displacement and is a major determinant of the tactile feel of the keyboard. Key activation forces from 0.9 to 5.3 ozf (0.25 to 1.47 N) and total key displacements between 0.05 and 0.25 inches (1 to 6 mm) appear to be preferred by operators, although, within limits, force and displacement appear to have little effect on the keying performance of experienced users (Alden et al., 1972). Typical production keyboards for computer input have key activation forces ranging from 0.4 to 1.2 N with key displacements between 3 and 5 mm.

There are few studies in the open literature dealing with the relationship between keying force and resulting key displacement. Most keyboards exhibit a buildup of force as the key is depressed; a number of keyboards exhibit a reduction of the required force in the region of activation, followed by a second increase in force thereafter. Brunner, Marken, and Briggs (1984) conducted a study involving three keyboards with different force-displacement relationships. The first keyboard used a snap-spring that buckles at a specific point in the downward travel of the key (see Figure 3.19). This couples a pivot plate to a capacitance plate mounted on the substrate directly beneath. The snap-spring mechanism produces a buildup of resistance on the downstroke with a sharp drop-off at the point of activation (Figure 3.20). This keyboard exhibited the longest key travel, the heaviest key activation resistance, and the most pronounced hysteresis (the tendency of a keyswitch to remain closed even after partial reduction of applied force; hysteresis is used to reduce the possibility of inadvertent multiple entries).

The second keyboard had an elastomer keyswitch consisting of two collapsible domes—a small dome mounted on top of a larger primary dome (Figure 3.21). This produced a double-peaked force-displacement curve (Figure 3.22). The first peak gives way as the primary dome collapses and the capacitive membrane switch is contacted. The second peak follows switch closure, giving way as the smaller, secondary dome collapses. This keyboard, which operates without hysteresis, uses an electronic polling mechanism to control for unintended switch contacts. A key press signal is issued only if switch closure is detected on at least two successive polls.

The third keyboard used a linear spring mechanism with a capacitive foam pad (Figure 3.23). The spring exhibited light, linearly increasing resistance to switch closure, rapid doubling of resistance at switch closure due to compression of the foam-backed mylar contact pad, and very little hysteresis (Figure 3.24).

Preference and performance data were obtained for both occasional and

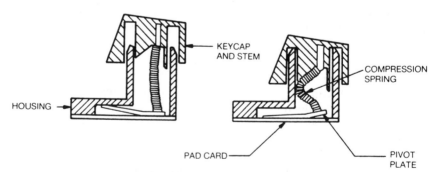

Figure 3.19. Cross-sectional view of a snap-spring keyswitch. (From Brunner, Marken, and Briggs (1984). Reprinted with permission of MICRO SWITCH, a division of Honeywell, Inc.)

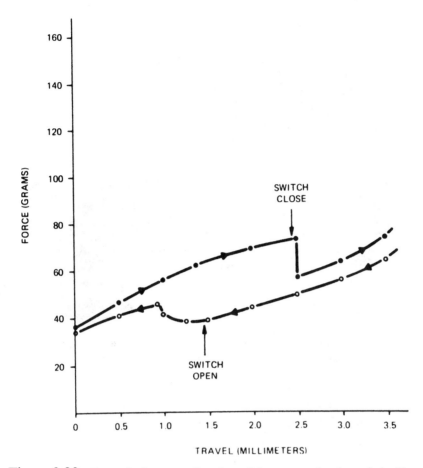

Figure 3.20. Force-displacement function of the snap-spring keyswitch. (From Brunner, Marken, and Briggs (1984). Reprinted with permission of MICRO SWITCH, a division of Honeywell, Inc.)

expert typists. After one hour of use, the general preference scores for the snap-spring and elastomer keyboards (which included measures to control inadvertent multiple entries and provided force feedback at or prior to switch closure) were approximately equal and significantly higher than those for the linear spring/foam pad keyboard (which exhibited very little hysteresis and little force feedback at or prior to switch closure). The error-adjusted throughput rate achieved with the elastomer keyboard (which used electronic polling to control inadvertent multiple entries and exhibited a reduction in resistance prior to switch closure) was approximately 10 percent greater than the rates for the snap-spring and linear

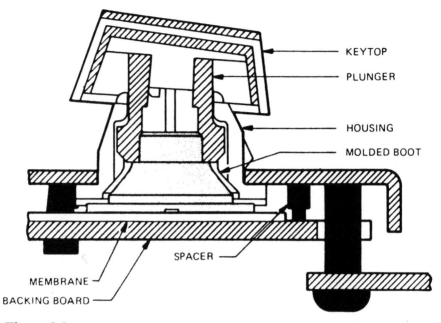

Figure 3.21. Cross-sectional view of an elastomer keyswitch. (From Brunner, Marken, and Briggs (1984). Reprinted with permission of MICRO SWITCH, a division of Honeywell, Inc.)

spring/foam pad keyboards. Finally, occasional typists using the linear spring/foam pad keyboard committed a disproportionately large number of inadvertent entries, inserting extra characters into otherwise correctly typed words.

The paucity of data available in the open literature makes the specification of an appropriate keyswitch return mechanism difficult. In general, operators appear to favor keyboards that provide a gradual buildup in force followed by an abrupt decrease in force at or near the switch actuation point. The addition of a second peak later in the force-displacement curve appears to enhance operator preference further. Nonetheless, springs (or other mechanisms) that provide linear force-displacement characteristics are widely accepted by keyboard operators.

Several manufacturers have attempted to enhance the tactile feedback provided by simple linear spring mechanisms through the incorporation of additional springs or foam pads. These additions are used to produce a progressive (and often abrupt) increase in force toward the bottom of the key's travel. Such mechanisms are often judged by operators to be "fatigu-

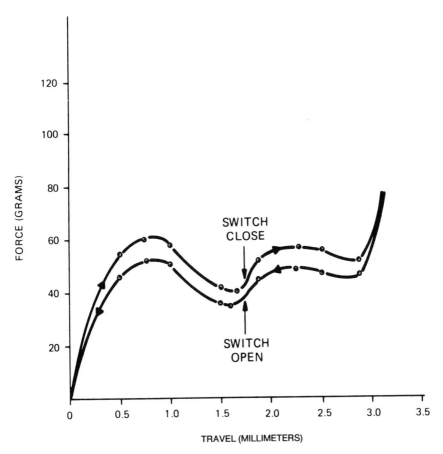

Figure 3.22. Force-displacement function of the elastomer keyswitch. (From Brunner, Marken, and Briggs (1984). Reprinted with permission of MICRO SWITCH, a division of Honeywell, Inc.)

ing" and "hard to push," and are often among the least favored in keyboard tests assessing operator preference. Other characteristics that operators find undesirable include key wobble (side-to-side movement), key binding (a sharp increase in resistance when the key is pressed off-center), and excessive noise associated with key actuation. Because of the many variations possible in the specification of key switch actuation and return mechanisms and because the associated variables may interact, it is important to validate new keyboard designs and selections through operator testing.

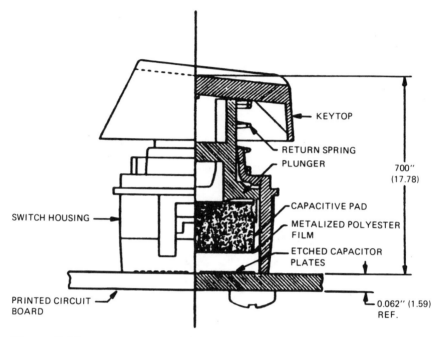

Figure 3.23. Cross-sectional view of a linear spring/foam pad keyswitch. (From Brunner, Marken, and Briggs (1984). Reprinted with permission of MICRO SWITCH, a division of Honeywell, Inc.)

3.5.3 Visual and Auditory Feedback

The major source of feedback for the highly skilled user of a full travel keyboard appears to be the kinesthetic-proprioceptive-tactual feedback that the user receives by actually making the movement and striking the key (Seibel, 1972). Visual feedback does appear to be important during training and for the correction of errors, however (Alden et al., 1972; Klemmer, 1971). Rosinski, Chiesi, and Debons (1980) investigated the effect of displaying typed input on the input performance of novice, semi-skilled, and professional typists. They found that, regardless of skill level, the presence or absence of visual feedback did not affect input speed or number of input errors. There was, however, a significant effect of visual feedback on error correction. Greater amounts of visual feedback permitted the subjects to review their performance and correct their errors. The authors conclude that there is no advantage gained by providing visual feedback if the main interest is in the initial speed and accuracy of input. But where errors must be monitored and corrected, or when editing is necessary, visual feedback is advantageous.

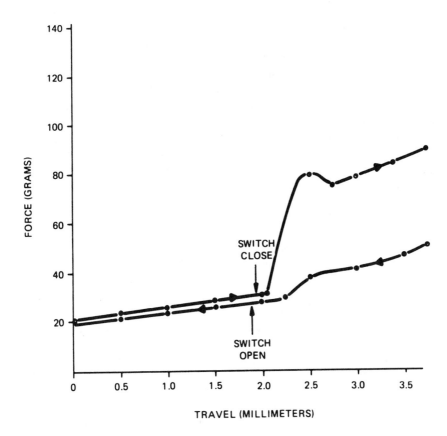

Figure 3.24. Force-displacement function of the linear spring/foam pad key-switch. (From Brunner, Marken, and Briggs (1984). Reprinted with permission of MICRO SWITCH, a division of Honeywell, Inc.)

The effect of supplemental auditory feedback upon keying performance with a full travel keyboard is less clear. Pollard and Cooper (1979) investigated the effect of auditory feedback on numeric data entry performance with a touch telephone keypad. The four feedback conditions included multifrequency tones, single tone, click on depression and release, and a baseline condition in which no supplemental feedback was provided. The authors found no significant differences in keying speed, error rate, or user preference across the four conditions. They conclude that the naturally occurring sounds of operation, as well as the tactual and kinesthetic sensations experienced during keying, provide adequate feedback and eliminate the need for additional, electronically generated feedback.

Monty, Snyder, and Birdwell (1983) investigated the effect of auditory feedback upon text entry performance with several alphanumeric keyboards. They reported a small (2%) but significant improvement in text entry time when electronically generated click options were employed. Subjects also indicated a substantial preference for the supplemental auditory feedback. Brunner et al. (1984) also studied the effect of auditory feedback on text entry performance with an alphanumeric keyboard. They utilized an elastomer key action keyboard that was noiseless in operation. The keyboard provided for auditory feedback with an option for electronic click at the instant of switch closure. The addition of auditory feedback appeared to result in slightly higher throughput and, upon initial exposure, subjects indicated a preference for the keyboard with auditory feedback. After an hour of use, however, preference differences were not significant.

The effects of the different forms of feedback possible with full travel keyboards are summarized in Table 3.7.

While the effect of supplemental feedback (whether kinesthetic, visual, or auditory) on input performance with full travel keyboards appears to be small, there are keyboard technologies for which supplemental feedback may achieve more substantial results. The flat panel membrane keypad, consisting of mechanical contacts on two layers of material separated by a spacer layer less than 1 mm thick, is one such technology (see Figure 3.25). Switch activation occurs when the user depresses the flexible upper layer through holes in the spacer layer. When pressure is removed from the membrane, it breaks contact with the shorting pad and returns to its original position.

Flat panel membrane keypads offer several engineering advantages. They are inexpensive to produce, their thin profile offers considerable design flexibility, they are easy to label and relabel, and their switches can be protected from hostile environments, dust, and spills. Their design lacks much of the feedback inherent in full travel keyboards, however. Key travel is negligible (0.15 to 0.20 mm), the keys are noiseless in operation, and while key locations are depicted graphically on the membrane, the smooth surface offers no tactual cues for key location. Pollard and Cooper

Table 3.7. Sources of Feedback with Full Travel Keyboards

1. Kinesthetic-proprioceptive-tactual: major source of feedback, especially for skilled users
2. Visual: important during training and for error correction and editing tasks; does not affect input accuracy and speed
3. Supplemental auditory: may provide modest enhancement, but inherent feedback is typically sufficient

SOURCE: Greenstein and Arnaut, 1987. Reproduced by permission of John Wiley & Sons, Inc.

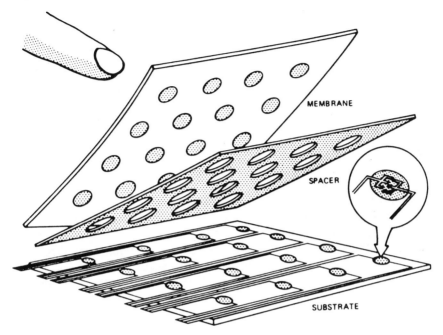

Figure 3.25. Membrane switch technology. (From Cohen Loeb (1983). Reprinted with permission from the *AT&T Technical Journal.* Copyright 1983, AT&T.)

(1979) compared keying performance with full travel and flat panel membrane telephone keysets. Subjects entered ten-digit sequences on each keyset. An auditory tone as well as visual feedback were provided upon digit entry with the membrane keyset. While 3.17% of the sequences entered on the full travel keypad contained errors, there were errors in 11.55% of the sequences entered with the membrane keypad. The authors note, however, that preliminary work with the membrane keypad without provision of any supplemental feedback resulted in error rates as high as 20%. Thus, supplemental feedback appears to enhance performance with flat panel membrane keypads.

This conclusion is reinforced by research reported by Roe, Muto, and Blake (1984). Their work addressed the additional key discriminability provided by embossed key edges as well as the supplemental feedback provided by metal domes and auditory tones on flat panel membrane keypads. The metallic domes increased key travel (from 0.25 mm without domes to 0.41 mm with domes) and provided some snap-action and auditory feedback. The study focused on applications where only occasional entries are made. The results of this study indicated that the pairing of auditory tones with embossed key edges and/or metal domes best enhanced performance and preference scores with flat panel membrane keys.

Flat panel membrane keypads are typically used in applications involving only occasional data entry. Cohen Loeb (1983) suggests that with extended practice and additional design optimization, these keyboards may prove effective in more intensive data entry applications as well. She compared data entry performance using a flat panel membrane keyboard with that using a full travel keyboard for subjects with different levels of typing skill. Auditory feedback was provided with both keyboards. Touch typists performed considerably better on the full travel keyboard than on the membrane keyboard (the excellent touch typists, for example, typed 26% fewer words per minute with the membrane keyboard). The advantage of the full travel keyboard was considerably smaller for nontouch typists, who typed 6.5% fewer words per minute with the membrane keyboard. Although subjects were provided only three hours of exposure to the membrane keyboard, rapid learning effects were apparent. Cohen Loeb concludes that the cost advantages and design flexibility offered by flat panel membrane keyboards warrant additional research and development.

The advantages and disadvantages of flat panel membrane keypads are summarized in Table 3.8.

3.5.4 Keyboard Dimensions

Keys. The size and spacing of keys on general purpose alphanumeric keyboards are largely based on design conventions rather than on empirical data. Key dimensions of 0.5 inches (13 mm) with center-to-center spacings of 0.75 inches (19 mm) are typical (Alden et al., 1972). Key tops are typically rectangular or square with slightly concave surfaces to assist proper finger placement.

Table 3.8. Advantages and Disadvantages of Flat Panel Membrane Keypads

Advantages	Disadvantages
1. Inexpensive	1. Negligible inherent feedback
2. Thin profile	2. Supplemental kinesthetic-tactual feedback necessary
3. Protective switch enclosure	3. Supplemental auditory feedback necessary
4. Ease of labeling	4. Input rates equivalent to full travel keypads not yet demonstrated
5. Ease of cleaning	

SOURCE: Adapted from Greenstein and Arnaut, 1987. Reproduced by permission of John Wiley & Sons, Inc.

Keyboard Height and Slope. In 1979, West Germany's Deutsche Institut fur Normung (DIN) established standards (66-234) for office computer workstations that included specifications for keyboards. The DIN specifications were adopted by the German Trade Cooperatives Association (TCA) to form standard ZH1/618, which became part of Germany's equipment and safety laws in 1982 (with deadline for full compliance by January 1, 1985). The specifications require that the height of the "home row" cannot exceed 30 mm from the table top with inclination as low as possible (preferably less than 15 degrees from the horizontal). Keyboards with home row heights greater than 30 mm must be equipped with palm rests. Manufacturers (including those in the United States) were soon marketing low-profile, "ergonomic" keyboards.

Despite widespread adoption, the exact justification for the 30 mm height requirement is unclear. Cakir, Hart, and Stewart (1980) pose the following argument:

. . . every millimeter that can be spared in keeping the thickness of the keyboard to a minimum helps to reduce the postural loading on the user by ensuring the correct working level.

. . . it is desirable that the thickness of the keyboard, i.e., the distance from the base of the keyboard to the home row of keys, should not exceed about 30 mm (Cakir et al., 1980, p. 126).

These recommendations are based on the following assertions. First, in order to minimize postural loading and resultant fatigue, the operator's working level (distance between the underside of the thighs and the palms of the hand) should be set so that the individual is sitting in a nearly upright position with hands and forearms horizontal. Second, of the elements that occupy the working level (operator's thigh thickness, tabletop and support thickness, minimum knee clearance, and keyboard thickness), the keyboard thickness appears to be the only feasible candidate for modification so that the working level envelope is not exceeded.

Although intuitively appealing, there appears to be little experimental evidence supporting the prescription that an operator's hands and forearms should be horizontal, nor are there data indicating the extent to which deviations from the horizontal affect typing performance, operator preference, or the frequency of related pathology in typists. Because of these uncertainties, several investigators have questioned the validity of the current keyboard recommendations.

Miller and Suther (1981) conducted a study in which 37 typists representing 5th, 50th, and 95th percentiles were asked to select preferred settings for various adjustments of a visual display terminal workstation. Adjustments were made for seat height, keyboard support height, keyboard slope angle, display height, and display angle. After all adjustments were set, subjects were asked to type a page of text and were encouraged to make workstation adjustments if necessary. Keyboard support surface heights ranged from 560 mm (22.0 inches) to 725 mm (28.5 inches) with a mean of 630 mm (24.8 inches). Since the keyboard home row height (from the keyboard support) was 77 mm (3.0 inches), the total home row height from the floor ranged from 637 mm (25.1 inches) to 802 mm (31.6 inches), with a mean of 707 mm (27.8 inches).

Emmons and Hirsh (1982) conducted a study comparing keyboards with home row heights of 30, 38, and 45 mm (1.2, 1.5, and 1.8 inches, respectively). Measures of keystroke rates and errors indicated that keyboard heights of 38 and 45 mm were significantly superior in performance to the 30 mm height. Questionnaire data indicated that the 45 mm keyboard was most preferred and the 30 mm keyboard least preferred. One problem with the Emmons and Hirsh data is that keyboard height was adjusted by varying the keyboard tilt (5, 12, and 18 degrees). This "confound" makes the source of performance and preference differences ambiguous (Burke, Muto, and Gutmann, 1984).

In a similar study, Burke et al. (1984) investigated the effects of keyboard height on user performance and preference. Forty-eight skilled typists were asked to type on keyboards with home row heights of 35 mm, 64 mm, 84 mm, and 104 mm (1.4, 2.5, 3.3, and 4.1 inches, respectively). All keyboards were placed on a 26 inch (660 mm) high typing table at a fixed angle of 11 degrees. Although there were no differences in typing speed or errors, questionnaire data showed statistically significant preference for 64 mm and 84 mm keyboard heights over both high (104 mm) and low (35 mm) extremes. Burke et al. conclude that there is a range of acceptability for keyboard height (although the exact parameters and tolerances are unclear) that is believed to include heights ranging from approximately 64 mm to 84 mm and excludes heights of 35 mm and 104 mm.

Abernethy (1984) has observed that the 30 mm home row height causes a curling of the hands, which could be a contributing factor in early fatigue. To address this concern, a study was conducted in which 20 typists were asked to type on an adjustable workstation that allowed adjustment of the keyboard angle from 8 degrees to greater than 30 degrees. Participants were asked to adjust the keyboard to the angle they would find comfortable enough to work with all day. Results indicated that at a typing stand height of 673 mm (26.5 inches), the average selected angle was 14.4 degrees (standard deviation, 1.7 degrees). At the typical U.S. desk top height of 750 mm (29.5 inches), the average angle was 16.1 degrees (standard deviation, 2.3 degrees).

Despite the lack of conclusive data, the 30 mm home row height is becoming the de facto worldwide keyboard height standard. Most low-profile keyboards that satisfy the 30 mm home row specification, however, do so only when placed at an angle of about 5 degrees. At this angle, many operators will complain that the keyboard is "too flat" or "too low." Consequently, it is advised that low-profile keyboards be provided with adjustments that allow the operator to set the keyboard tilt angle in the range of 5 to 15 degrees.

3.6 Keyboard Testing: Assessing Operator Performance and Preference

Most important keyboard characteristics can be quantified in terms of physical measurements such as peak force, force versus displacement, keyswitch bounce duration, and auditory noise. Even with apparently good specifications, however, the "goodness" of a keyboard cannot be assured unless keyboard designs (or selections) are validated with hands-on tests involving representative operators of the workstation in question. Operator tests can supply answers to questions such as: a) Can operators perform effectively on the keyboard? b) If not, what are the keyboard's design characteristics that hinder performance? c) Do operators like the test keyboard? d) What are the features that are not liked? e) Is the test keyboard liked as well as (better or worse than) keyboards of competitive systems (or other benchmarks)? Despite the fact that such testing can yield answers critical to the success of the keyboard (and in some cases to the success of the entire workstation), it is unfortunate that operator tests, when done at all, are often conducted in a manner that yields results of questionable validity. This section focuses on some of the major issues in operator/keyboard testing including measurement techniques and means to avoid common testing pitfalls. The reader is urged to consult sources in experimental design, experimental psychology, and statistical analysis techniques for more information. Two excellent examples are by Meister (1985) and Chapanis (1959).

The first issue in operator testing is to select the measures to be used. Essentially, operator testing provides quantifiable measures for two classes of keyboard assessment criteria: *user input performance* and *user preference*.

3.6.1 Performance Measures

The predominant performance measures in keyboard testing are used to quantify *typing speed* and *error rates*. Statistically significant differences in typing speed among keyboards can be useful not only in selecting keyboards that enable high throughput rates but also to provide a means for detecting keyboard design deficiencies that hinder input rates (such as poor key layout, poor tactile feel, improper keyboard timing, and poorly designed keycaps). In a similar manner, error rates are often useful in discovering keyboard deficiencies that contribute to the occurrence of apparent keying errors. Examples of such deficiencies include keyswitch bounce, inadequate key rollover, and keystation " cross talk."

Standardized Typing Tests. The simplest and most common tool for measuring typing performance is the standardized typing test. These tests typically require the operator to type a calibrated text passage during a timed interval of one to five minutes. After the typing period, the number of words typed are tallied, then divided by the duration of the test to determine typing rate in words per minute. One of the first considerations before running the test is selection of the test length. Results of short duration tests tend to be more variable than those of tests of longer duration and, consequently, tend to be less representative of true typing performance. During short duration tests, relatively small fluctuations in speed may be amplified simply because they constitute a larger portion of the total test data, whereas the same fluctuations in longer tests will have a lesser effect on the outcome. Long duration tests on the other hand, present another potential problem — typing fatigue. This can be especially important when testing several keyboards in a series, where fatigue could cause biases in both performance and preference against keyboards positioned later in the test series. Fatigue effects can be minimized in several ways. First, limit the duration of typing tests to approximately two to five minutes. Second, provide rest breaks between typing sessions. Breaks should be about equal in duration to the typing tests. Third, counterbalance or randomize the order in which keyboards are presented to operators.

Typing errors in standardized typing tests are usually counted and subtracted from the gross typing speed to compute "net words per minute." For keyboard assessment, it is recommended that typing errors and gross typing speed be collected and maintained as separate measurements (dependent variables).

An important factor in performance measurement is the nature of instructions given to operators. Although there is some evidence to the contrary, it appears that, under some circumstances, operators make a speed-versus-accuracy trade-off (Alden et al., 1972). When instructions stress speed, operators tend to type faster but with decreased accuracy. Likewise, when instructions stress accuracy, operators tend to type more accurately but at a slower rate. In general, instructions should advise operators to type "normally" — typing as fast *and* as error-free as possible.

Interkeystroke Intervals. Among the most useful measures of typing speed is the interkeystroke interval, the measurement of the time interval between individual keyboard signals (downstrokes). Interkeystroke interval measures have several advantages over words-per-minute typing test measures. First, interkeystroke interval data tend to have more precision than conventional typing speed measures. Typical interkeystroke interval data resolve keystroke events to one millisecond, while words-per-minute measurements are rounded to the nearest word (usually assumed to average about five or six characters per word). Second, interkeystroke interval data tend to be less affected by errors in testing. For example, if a typist stops typing for several seconds during a typing test (for example, when losing his or her place in the text), words-per-minute measures are likely to be affected more than interkeystroke interval measures. The reason is that the break in typing may have been a significant portion of the total typing test duration. But in the interkeystroke interval statistics, it constitutes a single event (which can be detected and eliminated as an "outlying" data point). Another advantage of interkeystroke interval data is that they can be used to uncover problems not easily discovered by other means. For example, a sequence containing repetitions of the same character with an interkeystroke interval of less than 10 ms is almost certainly attributable to keyboard error (e.g., switch bounce) rather than to operator error. This supposition is based on the fact that typical "one finger digrams" range from about 100 ms to 200 ms (Gentner, 1983).

The typical apparatus used for measuring interkeystroke timing intervals employs a mini- or microcomputer, which monitors keyboard output in parallel with the keyboard's normal output. As keyboard signals are outputted, the monitoring computer records the keystroke identifier code (in some cases, key upstrokes as well as downstrokes) and a time stamp (generated by the computer's real time clock). Interkeystroke intervals, error detection (e.g., deviation from standard text, specific keystroke error combinations), and subsequent statistical computations are usually calculated in postexperiment processing rather than in real time. Postprocessing minimizes the possibility of lost data and allows for more flexibility in the analysis. Some of the useful performance measures include mean interkeystroke intervals, intervals between (specified) letter pairs (digrams) or three-letter combinations (trigrams), interkeystroke interval by frequency, and frequency of specified keystroke combinations.

3.6.2 Preference Measures

One of the most important objectives of operator testing is to determine the operators' order of preference among several keyboards—for the keyboard as a unit or in terms of specific keyboard attributes such as tactile feel, keycap shape, keyboard layout, and casework color.

Keyboard Ranking. In the simplest form of evaluation, the user types on each of the test keyboards and indicates his or her order of preference for each of the keyboards. This procedure is adequate in dealing with a small number of keyboards (three or fewer); however, in dealing with a larger number of keyboards, the task of ordering preferences can become exceedingly difficult, especially when differences are subtle. The source of the problem is that, as the number of test keyboards increases, the ability of the operator to form a mental impression of each keyboard and retain that impression until all comparisons are made becomes less reliable.

One of the simplest and most reliable alternatives to simultaneous overall rankings is the use of *pair-wise comparisons*. The operator is asked to evaluate only two keyboards at a time and to indicate which keyboard of the two is preferred. The operator is asked to indicate choices until all possible pair-wise comparisons are made. Subsequent scoring is accomplished by counting the number of "preferred" votes for each keyboard and then ranking the keyboards based on the frequency of "preferred" choices for each subject. The statistical significance of keyboard rank sums can be determined with, for example, the Friedman Rank Sum Statistic (Hollander and Wolfe, 1973).

Questionnaires. Questionnaires are the most familiar means of obtaining operators' opinions, attitudes, and judgments of keyboard units or of specific keyboard design characteristics. When properly designed and administered, questionnaires are able to capture the direction (e.g., positive, negative, favorable, unfavorable) of the user's judgment, as well as how strongly the user feels about that particular dimension. Among the most useful questionnaire items are bipolar or semantic differential rating scales. Each scale contains five or seven segments and uses labels at either end of the scale to represent opposite extremes of a selected dimension. Respondents are asked to indicate their ratings by marking the segment that best describes their leanings toward one of the bipolar descriptors. The rating scales contain an odd number of segments to allow a neutral rating. Investigators typically recommend the use of five or seven segments. The use of more than seven segments has been found to reduce the reliability of the measure and does not contribute to measurement precision. A few examples of keyboard rating dimensions are shown in Table 3.9.

Also useful in questionnaires are open-ended questions. Open-ended questions allow the respondent to answer a question in narrative form. They can be useful in gathering information on problems not otherwise

Table 3.9. Examples of Keyboard Rating Dimensions

Like								Dislike

Easy to push keys	/	Hard to push keys
Fast	/	Slow
Comfortable	/	Uncomfortable
Expensive	/	Cheap
Feels good	/	Feels bad
Restful	/	Tiring
Keys too small	/	Keys too large
Like	/	Dislike
Responsive	/	Sluggish
Simple	/	Confusing
Quiet	/	Noisy
No key wobble	/	Much key wobble
Easy to get used to	/	Difficult to get used to
Touch too light	/	Touch too heavy
Key travel too shallow	/	Key travel too deep
Acceptable	/	Unacceptable

anticipated by the questionnaire. They can also be useful in collecting operator comments that are often the most poignant descriptors of the sentiment (good or bad) toward keyboard attributes. In general, directed questions such as What are the things you like best about the keyboard? and What are the things you like least about the keyboard? are preferable to response areas designed for "comments."

3.6.3 Major Pitfalls in Operator Testing

The following section briefly discusses some of the major issues in operator testing and ways to avoid the major problems associated with them.

Carefully Consider Subject Selection and Sample Size. The main objective of user testing is to predict performance and preference of the intended operator population from a sample of subjects. It is essential, therefore, that individuals be selected on the basis of how well they represent the characteristics of intended operators in terms of such factors as gender, skill levels, experience, and familiarity with particular equipment. Special care should be taken to exclude subjects who might exhibit biases that could affect the experimental outcome. Chapanis (1959) suggests

never use subjects who have designed the equipment or have any stake in its potential usefulness. Such subjects, which include design engineering, office personnel, supervisors . . . are usually not typical . . . of those who will operate the equipment in actual use. Even if they were typical, they must be disqualified because of their "ego involvement" in the outcome of the tests. (pp. 245–246)

It often makes sense to partition subject selection based on proportions of operator characteristics in the overall population. If, for example, your intended operator population contains a certain proportion of females, your subject selection should contain an equal proportion of females. When it is not possible or practical to use proportional stratified sampling, random selection from a representative population is an acceptable alternative.

When using formal statistical methods, the number of subjects needed for a test ultimately depends on the sampling error that the researcher is willing to accept. Twenty-five or thirty subjects are typically sufficient to detect performance and preference differences among keyboards.

Elimination or Control of Extraneous Variables.   One problem in operator testing is that subjects' responses can be affected by factors not directly related to the variable or variables of interest. It is important, therefore, to eliminate or minimize differences between keyboards that are not related to the variable being tested. For example, the main objective of a test evaluating operators' perceived typing comfort on two keyboards with differing spring mechanisms would be to provide operators' ratings of factors inherent in the keyboard mechanisms such as key force, key travel, and force-displacement profile. Other factors that have been shown to affect typing comfort judgments such as keyboard height, keyboard slope, and operator seating height should be eliminated as possible contaminating factors by making sure that these factors are identical for both keyboards. A test that does not control for such extraneous variables has questionable validity.

As with the keyboard itself, it is also important to minimize possible extraneous variables introduced by the test environment and procedures. Therefore, test procedures, instructions, and the test environment should be made equivalent across individual keyboard test conditions. When it is not possible to eliminate extraneous variables, instructions should be used to explain the differences and to request that operators exclude those differences from their judgments. Biases can be introduced by instructions given to subjects before and during testing. It is prudent, therefore, to employ standardized written or oral materials to instruct subjects on the details of the procedures. Preliminary tests should be conducted to ensure that instructions convey the desired meaning to subjects.

Keyboard Presentation Sequence. In a keyboard test requiring each subject to operate and evaluate several keyboards (an example of a *repeated measures* test paradigm), it is possible that the use of one keyboard will affect the subject's responses to subsequent keyboards. A test that presents the keyboards to every subject in the same order could introduce biases in the test that would otherwise not exist. One method for mitigating this potential bias is *counterbalancing*, where all possible keyboard presentation sequences are administered to an equal number of subjects. When counterbalancing is not possible, another alternative is randomization, where the presentation order is selected at random for each subject. Some behavioral scientists argue that neither randomization nor counterbalancing can completely negate the possible biases introduced by repeated measures tests. The alternative is to use a test paradigm that requires each subject to operate and evaluate one keyboard only. Although this eliminates the potential bias, the increase in variability introduced by the variability between individuals greatly increases the number of subjects required to achieve statistically valid results. As a result, the use of such randomized block designs is not always practical. Carefully considered repeated measures tests using either counterbalancing or randomization techniques can yield reliable and valid results.

Statistical Methods. After data are collected, it is very tempting to form conclusions based on graphical representations of the raw data or summary statistics (such as mean or median scores). One of the main problems with this approach is that numeric differences existing between keyboards may be spurious; that is, the outcome could be the result of chance. Thus, in repeated runs of the keyboard test, the same (apparent) difference would be expected during a proportion of the experimental runs even though no actual effect exists. If the probability of such a difference due to chance is too high (a typical criterion is 5%), the difference is said to be statistically nonsignificant; the conclusion is that no differences exist between the test keyboards. The choice of proper statistical analyses depends on the design of the experiment and the nature of the data. For example, to test the difference between two keyboards, the most common parametric test is the Student's t-test. For tests involving multiple keyboards or when keyboards are combined with other factors, analysis of variance (ANOVA) is among the most often used analysis techniques. It is beyond the scope of this chapter to discuss the various types of statistical techniques available. The reader is urged to consult textbooks in these areas.

3.7 Conclusion

Although there are now a number of new input technologies available that offer efficiency and ease-of-use advantages relative to the keyboard for specific applications, the keyboard remains an integral part of today's computer workstation. It is particularly appropriate for use in applications where the input of nonstandardized textual data is a significant component of the user's task.

The design of today's keyboards is heavily influenced by historical precedent. While technology improvements have gradually worked their way into today's keyboard products, the layout and operating principles of current general purpose alphanumeric keyboards are remarkably similar to those of keyboards marketed a century ago. The costs associated with the adoption of radically different keyboard designs, coupled with human resistance to change, have blocked widespread acceptance of many keyboard innovations.

As the keyboard becomes one of several input devices incorporated into multipurpose computer workstations, its lower costs, increased reconfigurability, and more specialized uses may finally permit introduction of significant design innovations. Because there are few definitive results of keyboard research currently available in the open literature, it is imperative that designers attempting to introduce these innovations conduct tests of their designs with potential users. This testing will help to assure that the new keyboard is compatible with both the capabilities and the preferences of its intended user.

References

Abernethy, C. N. (1984). Behavioural data in the design of ergonomic computer terminals and workstations—a case study. *Behaviour and Information Technology, 3*(4), 399-403.

Alden, D. G., Daniels, R. W., and Kanarick, A. F. (1972). Keyboard design and operation: A review of the major issues. *Human Factors, 14,* 275-293.

American National Standards Institute. (1979). *American national standard for 10-key keyboard for adding and calculating machines. ANSI X4.6-1979.* New York.

American National Standards Institute. (1982). *American national standard for office machines and supplies—alphanumeric machines—keyboard arrangement. ANSI X4.23-1982.* New York.

American National Standards Institute. (1983). *American national standard for office machines and supplies—alphanumeric machines—alternative keyboard arrangement. ANSI X4.22-1983.* New York.

Ancona, J. P., Garland, S. M., and Tropsa, J. J. (1971). At last: Standards for keyboards. *Datamation, 17*(5), 32-36.

Brunner, H., Marken, R., and Briggs, A. (1984). *Effects of key action design on keyboard preference and throughput performance.* Roseville, MN: Honeywell Technology Strategy Center. (Available from MICRO SWITCH, Freeport, IL 61032.)

Burke, T. M., Muto, W. H., and Gutmann, J. C. (1984). Effects of keyboard height on typist performance and preference. In *Proceedings of the Human Factors Society 28th Annual Meeting* (pp. 272–276). Santa Monica, CA: Human Factors Society.

Butterbaugh, L. C., and Rockwell, T. H. (1982). Evaluation of alternative alphanumeric keying logics. *Human Factors, 24*(5), 521–533.

Cakir, A., Hart, D. J., and Stewart, T. F. M. (1980). *Visual display terminals.* Chichester, England: Wiley.

Chapanis, A. (1959). *Research techniques in human engineering.* Baltimore: Johns Hopkins University Press.

Cohen Loeb, K. M. (1983). Membrane keyboards and human performance. *Bell System Technical Journal, 62,* 1733–1749.

Conrad, R., and Hull, A. J. (1968). The preferred layout for numeral data-entry keysets. *Ergonomics, 11,* 165–173.

Daniels, R. W., and Graf, C. P. (1970). *The influence of keyset interlocks on operator performance.* Honeywell Systems and Research Division.

DeFosse, S. F., Williams, G. T., Gostomski, D. A., Jr., and Cobb, R. H. (1985). Development of a membrane switch-type full-travel tactile keyboard. *IBM Journal of Research and Development, 29*(3), 478–487.

Emmons, W. H., and Hirsch, R. S. (1982). Thirty millimeter keyboards: How good are they? In *Proceedings of the Human Factors Society 26th Annual Meeting* (pp. 425–429). Santa Monica, CA: Human Factors Society.

Gentner, D. R. (1983). Keystroke timing in transcription typing. In W. E. Cooper (Ed.), *Cognitive aspects of skilled typewriting* (pp. 95–120). New York: Springer-Verlag.

Gentner, D. R., Grudin, J., and Conway, E. (1980, May). *Finger movements in transcription typing* (Tech. Report 8108). LaJolla, CA: University of California at San Diego, Center for Human Information Processing.

Gopher, D., Hilsernath, H., and Raij, D. (1985). Steps in the development of a new data entry device based upon two hand chord keyboard. In *Proceedings of the Human Factors Society 29th Annual Meeting* (pp. 132–136). Santa Monica, CA: Human Factors Society.

Greenstein, J. S., and Arnaut, L. Y. (1987). Human factors aspects of manual computer input devices. In G. Salvendy (Ed.), *Handbook of Human Factors* (Chapter 11.4, pp. 1450–1489). New York: Wiley.

Hanes, L. F. (1975). Human factors in international keyboard arrangement. In A. Chapanis (Ed.), *Ethnic variables in human factors engineering* (pp. 189–206). Baltimore: Johns Hopkins University Press.

Hirsch, R. S. (1970). Effects of standard versus alphabetical keyboard formats on typing performance. *Journal of Applied Psychology, 54,* 484–490.

Hollander, M., and Wolfe, D. A. (1973). *Nonparametric statistical methods*: New York: Wiley.

Hollingsworth, S. R., and Dray, S. M. (1981). Implications of post-stimulus cueing of response options for the design of function keyboards. In *Proceedings of the Human Factors Society 25th Annual Meeting* (pp 263–265). Santa Monica, CA: Human Factors Society.

Hornsby, M. E. (1981). A comparison of full- and reduced-alpha keyboards for aircraft data entry. In *Proceedings of the Human Factors Society 25th Annual Meeting* (p. 257). Santa Monica, CA: Human Factors Society.

Kinkead, R. (1975). Typing speed, keying rates, and optimal keyboard layouts. In *Proceedings of the Human Factors Society 19th Annual Meeting* (pp. 159–161). Santa Monica, CA: Human Factors Society.

Kirschenbaum, A., Friedman, Z., and Melnik, A. (1986). Performance of disabled persons on a chordic keyboard. *Human Factors, 28*(2), 187–194.

Klemmer, E. T. (1971). Keyboard entry. *Applied Ergonomics, 2,* 2–6.

Lohse, E. (Ed.) (1968). Proposed USA standard—General purpose alphanumeric keyboard arrangement for information interchange. *Communications of the ACM, 11,* 126–129.

Lutz, M. C., and Chapanis, A. (1955). Expected locations of digits and letters on ten-button keysets. *Journal of Applied Psychology, 39,* 314–317.

Meister, D. (1985). *Behavioral analysis and measurement methods.* New York: Wiley.

Michaels, S. E. (1971). QWERTY versus alphabetic keyboards as a function of typing skill. *Human Factors, 13,* 419–426.

Miller, I., and Suther, T. W., III. (1981). Preferred height and angle settings of CRT and keyboard for a display station input task. In *Proceedings of the Human Factors Society 25th Annual Meeting* (pp. 492–496). Santa Monica, CA: Human Factors Society.

Monty, R. W., Snyder, H. L., and Birdwell, G. G. (1983). Keyboard design: An investigation of user preference and performance. In *Proceedings of the Human Factors Society 27th Annual Meeting* (pp. 201–205). Santa Monica, CA: Human Factors Society.

Norman, D. A., and Fisher, D. (1982). Why alphabetic keyboards are not easy to use: Keyboard layout doesn't much matter. *Human Factors, 24,* 509–519.

Noyes, J. (1983a). Chord keyboards. *Applied Ergonomics, 14*(1), 55–59.

Noyes, J. (1983b). The QWERTY keyboard: A review. *International Journal of Man-Machine Studies, 18,* 265–281.

Pollard, D., and Cooper, M. B. (1979). The effects of feedback on keying performance. *Applied Ergonomics, 10,* 194–200.

Ratz, H. C., and Ritchie, D. K. (1961). Operator performance on a chord keyboard. *Journal of Applied Psychology, 45*(5), 303–308.

Rochester, N., Bequaert, F. C., and Sharp, E. M. (1978). The chord keyboard. *Computer, 11*(12), 57–63.

Roe, C. J., Muto, W. H., and Blake, T. (1984). Feedback and key discrimination on membrane keypads. In *Proceedings of the Human Factors Society 28th Annual Meeting* (pp. 277–281). Santa Monica, CA: Human Factors Society.

Rosinski, R. R., Chiesi, H., and Debons, A. (1980). Effects of amount of visual feedback on typing performance. In *Proceedings of the Human Factors Society 24th Annual Meeting* (pp. 195–199). Santa Monica, CA: Human Factors Society.

Salthouse, T. A. (1984). The skill of typing. *Scientific American, 250*(2), 128–135.

Seibel, R. (1962). Performance on a five-finger chord keyboard. *Journal of Applied Psychology, 46*(3), 165–169.

Seibel, R. (1972). Data entry devices and procedures. In H. P. Van Cott and R. G. Kinkade (Eds.), *Human engineering guide to equipment design* (rev. ed., pp. 311–344). Washington, DC: U.S. Government Printing Office.

Stewart, T. F. M. (1973). Improvements in or relating to keyboards: Concerned with marking and use of chord keyboards. British Patent No. 1,492,538.

van der Heiden, G. H., and Grandjean, E. (1984). Ergonomic studies in computer-aided design. *Behaviour and Information Technology, 3*(4), 341–346.

Yamada, H. (1980). A historical study of typewriters and typing methods: From the position of planning Japanese parallels. *Journal of Information Processing, 2,* 175–202.

4 Digitizers and Input Tablets

THOMAS E. DAVIES,

H. GERARD MATTHEWS,

and

PAUL D. SMITH

Summagraphics Corporation
Fairfield, Connecticut

4.1 Introduction

Graphics tablets and digitizers have been used to enter graphical information into computers for several years. In fact, some users, thinking of the
large expensive tablets of the late 1970s, treat graphics tablets as "last
generation's" technology. These old tablets needed regular service with
large disk-corrupting magnets and were unsupported by all but the most
expensive software. Still another group of computer users have never heard
of graphics tablets, or if they have, they think of inexpensive, low-perform-
ance touch tablets, toys suitable only for playing games on home computers.

But today's graphics tablets are sophisticated, powerful tools that are
easy to use, stylish, and inexpensive. The typical system, complete with
interface cables, power supply, and multibutton cursor, is available for
about $500. Typically, these systems have 1000 lines per inch resolution,
on-board diagnostics, are capable of better than 100 reports per second,
can be programmed for a wide range of operating characteristics, and

Input Devices

179

require no maintenance. What's more, these new tablets are supported by hundreds of software packages ranging from simple paintbrush routines to high powered Computer-Aided Engineering (CAE) and Computer-Aided Design (CAD) programs.

Graphics tablets have been standard equipment on workstation products for several years, but recently tablets are being offered as options with several powerful personal computer based software products. This competitive market has fostered research into many ways to make tablets even more powerful while reducing their price.

Development efforts concentrate on improving present technologies with refinements like VLSI and more powerful on-board microprocessors, and are exploring new approaches in both hardware and software.

In this chapter, we discuss tablet technology and applications, and compare graphics tablets with several of the popular input devices such as computer mice, light pens, and trackballs. We introduce the reader to graphics tablets with special emphasis on where tablets might be used and how tablets can improve productivity.

Section 4.2 is entitled Tablet Technology and is a detailed guide to the terminology and technology of graphics tablets. Section 4.3 is entitled Tablet Classes and explains the variety of digitizing equipment related to performance and size. Section 4.4 is entitled Tablet Applications and deals with the general issue of what logical functions input devices must perform, details how tablets compare with other input devices, and explains how graphics tablets are used in a broad range of applications.

4.2 Tablet Technology

4.2.1 Definitions

Currently, there is no recognized industry or market set of standards relating to digitizer tablet characteristics (Ward & Phillips, 1987). As foundation for a description of tablet technology, we will use the terms that follow:

Accuracy: The maximum error in $\pm X$ and $\pm Y$ units between any two points over the tablet's specified area. An example would be a specification of plus or minus 0.010 inch (plus or minus 0.254 mm) accuracy up to one inch from the edge of the active area. This specification indicates that the operator should be able to measure the position of a point with a relative uncertainty of plus or minus 0.020 inch as long as the measurement is taken at least an inch inside the edge of the active area. This could lead to a maximum error of 0.020 inch on the measurement of the distance between any two points.

Specified Area: The area within the tablet's active area that meets the specified accuracy. Specified area may be the same as the active area.

Active Area: The area on the tablet's surface over which X, Y coordinates may be digitized and reported.

Proximity: The distance above the tablet's active area surface where X, Y coordinates may be digitized and reported.

Resolution: Generally, the resolution is held equal along both the X and Y axes, and is specified in lines per inch (lpi) or lines per milimeter (lpmm). Some tablets can be set either way (i.e., 1000 lpi or 40 lpmm). Typical tablet resolutions range from 100 lpi for menu selection applications to 1000 lpi for CAD, mapping, and other precision applications.

Report Rate: The number of X, Y coordinate points per second reported by the digitizer.

Jitter: The magnitude of short-term changes in X, Y coordinate reports for a stationary cursor or stylus.

Stability: The magnitude of long-term changes in X, Y coordinate reports for a stationary cursor or stylus.

Transducer: The hand-held pointing device, either stylus or cursor, moved over the active area to designate the point(s) to be digitized.

Stylus: A penlike pointing device, usually constructed with a tip switch to provide on/off indication at designated point(s). The stylus is primarily used for nonprecision applications such as cursor steering or graphics creation.

Tilt Error: The maximum deviation in $\pm X$, $\pm Y$ units reported by a digitizer tablet due to tilting a stylus ± 30 degrees around a given coordinate position.

Edge Effects: The degradation in digitizer performance (accuracy, resolution) aproaching the edges of the active area.

4.2.2 State of the Art

Digitizer tablets have been developed using a broad spectrum of technologies: optics, acoustics, magnetostriction, electromagnetics, resistance, capacitance. Currently, tablets employing electromagnetic principles dominate the market. They are characterized by stability, high accuracy and resolution, insensitivity to noise, and convenient implementation. However, recent growth in graphics applications and personal computer systems has prompted renewed investigations into all approaches in an effort to match tablet characteristics more closely to the applications. The following is intended to give the reader a basic understanding of prevalent digitizer tablet technologies.

Magnetostrictive. Although one could debate whether magnetostrictive-based digitizer tablets can be considered current, the technology is significant nonetheless. The name Bit Pad®, which has almost become synonymous with digitizer tablets, was used first in 1975 on a series of tablets that used magnetostrictive technology manufactured by Summagraphics Corporation.

Wires or ribbons of materials that exhibit magnetostriction are sometimes referred to as delay lines. These lines will propagate a strain wave down their length at the speed of sound (approximately 500 meters/second). A strain wave may be induced in a delay line by the magnetic "jolt" created by current pulsed through a "send" wire placed perpendicular to the delay line. Conversely, a current pulse will be induced in a receive wire placed perpendicular to the delay line by the magnetic pulse created as the strain wave propagates past the receive wire's position. The distance between the send and receive conductors is readily determined by timing the delay between the send and receive pulses. A magnetostrictive digitizer uses this time-distance relationship.

Imbedded in the tablet's surface are two orthogonal sets of equispaced delay lines; one set runs parallel to the X axis, and the other set runs parallel to the Y axis. An X send wire crosses all the X axis delay lines at one end. When pulsed, a planar strain wave propagates across the tablet surface in the X direction. A hand-held cursor coil acts as the receive conductor. When the passing strain wave induces a current pulse in the coil, the time delay gives the X position of the coil. A second Y send wire is used with the Y delay lines to determine the Y coordinate.

With a strain wave propagation velocity of 500 meters/second, to resolve 0.1 mm (0.004 inch or 250 lines per inch) requires timing resolution of 20 nanoseconds using a 50 MHz clock.

The need to employ such high frequency circuitry makes magnetostrictive-based digitizer tablets one of the more costly approaches.

Electromagnetic. The technology most often chosen to implement high performance digitizer tablets is based on electromagnetic induction — the basic principle of the transformer. A conductor, carrying an alternating current, creates a magnetic field that will induce a current in a second conductor. For digitizer applications, the amplitude and direction or phase of the induced current is significant. Two factors that affect amplitude are the distance between conductors (amplitude increases as distance decreases) and the orientation of one conductor to the other (maximum amplitude when conductors are parallel, decreasing to zero when at right angles). If one conductor is reversed with respect to the other, the direction of the induced current will likewise be reversed. As used in digitizer tablet applications, one conductor, in the form of a circular coil, is movable, such as a cursor over the tablet surface. The second conductor is one selected from many, imbedded in an *X-Y* pattern or grid, beneath the tablet surface. The circular conductor, placed anywhere on the *X-Y* grid of conductors, becomes parallel and thereby favors electromagnetic induction with those *X, Y* grid lines lying closest to its circumference. The *X* lines adjacent to and directly under the circumference of the circular coils would be so favored on each side of the coil. The same is true for the two *Y* lines. However, for those lines that lie on opposite sides of the circular coil, the direction relationship or phase of induced current between the favored *X* lines (or *Y* lines) is reversed. Furthermore, no current is induced with a grid line that bisects the circular coil. This is illustrated by Figure 4.1.

The position of the cursor coil on the tablet surface is determined by reading the phase and relative amplitude of induced current when individ-

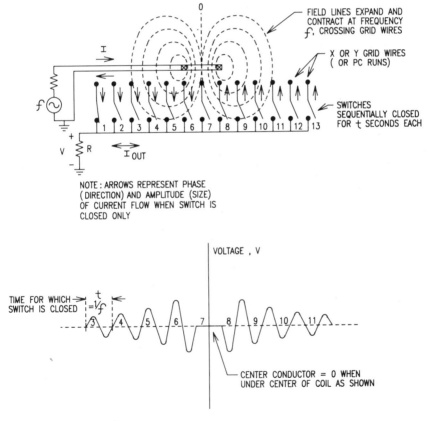

Figure 4.1. Electromagnetic technology.

ual grid lines are selected. The exact position of the cursor coil's center must be interpolated between grid lines from the phase–amplitude readings correlated with the X-Y grid lines in the vicinity of the cursor coil. This may be accomplished in one of two ways: 1) through the use of digitizer circuitry that sweeps grid lines sequentially while demodulating and filtering the induced signal to detect the exact point of phase reversal, or 2) by calculating the point from digitized amplitude–phase data read into microprocessor memory. Either technique will resolve X-Y coordinates to 0.025 mm (0.001 inch or 1000 lines per inch).

Since the X-Y grid lines are merely accurately spaced conductors, they are conveniently and economically implemented using a double-sided printed circuit board that also facilitates interconnection of the many lines to the semiconductor switches used for their selection.

Because of relatively high fabrication costs and limited sources of supply of large printed circuit boards, some electromagnetic digitizers larger than 24 inches to 30 inches use wires cemented to a dimensionally stable base.

Electromagnetic-based digitizers usually exhibit high proximity since the amplitude–phase relationship is not changed as the conductors are separated. Digitizing is totally unaffected by nonmetallic materials, but conductors or magnets will distort the magnetic field to an extent depending upon the material, its size, and its distance from the cursor. Environmental "noise" contributes little interference.

Capacitive (or Electrostatic). The properties of capacitive coupling can be applied to digitizer tablet applications by considering the hand-held cursor or stylus as one plate of a capacitor and the tablet surface as the other. Using an AC signal of given amplitude and frequency, coupling between the digitizer tablet and the cursor or stylus is related to the capacitance they represent. Capacitance is proportional to three factors:

$$C = f\left(\frac{(e)\,(A)}{d}\right) \tag{4.1}$$

where A = relative area of the two plates, d = distance between the two plates, and e = permittivity of the dialectric material between the two plates.

Unlike electromagnetic coupling, there is no orientation effect to give a phase reversal of the signal, therefore, X-Y coordinate determination must be established from analysis of amplitude data alone.

Capacitive digitizers must be designed to tolerate substantial electrostatic noise, especially those that use the relatively large tablet area as the receiver (with the AC signal generated by the much smaller area of the cursor or stylus). Since the capacitor formed by the tablet and the cursor is not electrostatically sealed, with the tablet as one capacitor "plate," the whole environment, including the cursor, represents the other plate. This configuration necessitates extra provisions not only for frequency and spike filtering but also for signal averaging to stabilize jitter.

Changes in dielectric will be caused by moisture (perspiration, humidity), graphite lines, and varying thickness of paper. Their effect on signal amplitude may result in errors in the coordinate position reported.

Digitizer applications of capacitive coupling can be separated into three general categories: 1) scanned X-Y grid, 2) geometry related, and 3) hybrid (combines capacitive coupling with resistance effects). We shall consider hybrid approaches under a separate category.

Scanned X-Y Grid. The scanned X-Y grid approach shares some principles with the electromagnetic technique previously described. Two sets of equispaced, mutually perpendicular conductive lines forming an X-Y grid are imbedded in the digitizer tablet surface with access to each line provided through semiconductor switches. Assuming that the width of each grid line is identical, the voltage amplitude of capacitively coupled signals will maximize as grid lines closest to the cursor are selected. The exact position of the cursor may be interpolated between grid lines through digitizer hardware or software techniques. For comparison, this type of electrostatic approach is shown in Figure 4.2.

In hardware, X and Y grid lines are selected sequentially at a given rate and the resultant capacitively coupled signal is amplified, rectified, and smoothed. This yields a voltage waveform that peaks in amplitude twice, once while the X lines are scanned and again while the Y lines are scanned. To digitize the peak position, a counter, clocked at a multiple of the grid scan rate and initialized at the start of the X scan and the Y scan, is stopped when each peak occurs. The resultant contents represent digital X and Y coordinates.

Alternatively, as grid lines are selected under microprocessor control, an analog to digital converter reads and produces the digital amplitude value of each capacitively coupled signal. The values are read by the microprocessor, which derives the exact cursor position from an algorithm using the amplitude versus grid line relationship.

Practical considerations dictate that the cursor area be circular in shape. This results in decreasing change in the coupled area of any grid line as it approaches the center of the circle, thereby adding to the difficulty of resolving the exact cursor position. Furthermore, the width of the grid lines must be small to minimize interaction between X and Y. However, this also minimizes coupling capacitance, requiring more signal amplification, which tends to increase the noise of the signal.

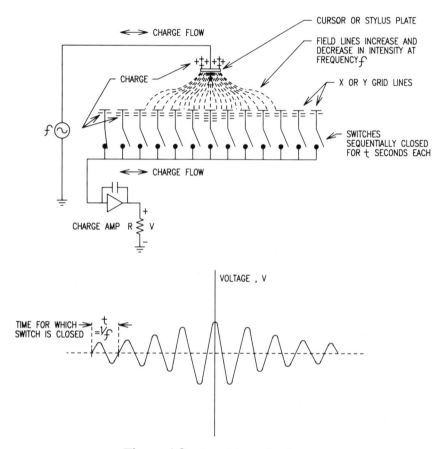

Figure 4.2. Capacitive technology.

Geometry Related. To date, geometry related capacitive digitizing has been limited to one dimension (X or Y) and, therefore, could not rightfully be included as a practical digitizer technique. However, recent developments have brought about a new class of geometry-based capacitive digitizers that overcome the single axis limitation and also minimize the detrimental effects of capacitive coupling.

Geometry related capacitive digitizers use the "area" variable in the capacitance relationship. For example, multiple wedge-shaped conductors extending across the digitizer surface will yield signal amplitudes proportional to the wedge width at the cursor position.

With two complementary sets of wedges, when the cursor is positioned at midlength, coupling between the wedge areas is equal, independent of distance or dielectric. This is a distinct advantage when such a ratio can be derived. However, since there are no repetitive, accurately spaced grid lines to provide periodic references across the length, the total length must be resolved from the signal amplitudes.

Fortunately, due to the larger relative areas, signal amplitudes are significantly larger than signals derived from narrow grid lnes.

Resistive. Resistive technology requires physical contact at an X-Y coordinate point to operate. Construction includes a layer of material of uniform electrical resistance and rectangular size larger than the desired active area. Typically, four contacts are connected to the four sides of the resistive material ($+X$, $-X$, $+Y$, $-Y$) and a known voltage is applied, alternating between one axis pair at a time. The voltage obtained by contacting various points over the resistive surface is determined by the resistance value from that point to each of the four contacts at the sides. The accuracy and resolution of a reading at any point is determined by the resistance uniformity of the resistive material, the characteristics of the analog to digital converter, which reads the voltage, and the proximity to the side contacts where edge-effect distortion can occur.

The fundamental limitation of this technology derives from its construction. It is not practical or desirable to have the resistive layer exposed; therefore, a second "contact" layer is used. Separated from the resistive layer by small spacer dots or a thin layer of foam insulation, the contact layer touches the resistive layer only when and where depressed. However, the insulating dots or foam create discontinuities that become the limiting factor in resolution and accuracy.

Since physical contact is required, resistive technology has limited application. However, it is virtually unaffected by stylus tilt error.

Hybrid.   To overcome one limitation of resistive technology — the need to make physical contact at the point to be digitized — some data tablets combine electrostatic or electromagnetic coupling with resistive technology to determine coordinate positions. There are currently two approaches: one uses a sheet of uniform resistivity, the other uses an X-Y grid. In both approaches, coordinate position related signals must be processed to very high resolution, which requires equally low noise. Consider, for example, the digitizer size and resolution specifications and the corresponding signal conversion requirements shown in Table 4.1.

The number of binary bits required for signal conversion and subsequent processing allows for ±1 least significant bit uncertainty to assure that the tablet output will be stable and jitter-free. Digital averaging techniques could also be used, reducing the conversion requirement by one bit

Table 4.1. Signal Conversion Requirements

Size (inches)	Resolution (lines/inch)	Range (total lines)	Conversion (binary bits ± 1 lsb)
5″	200	1,000	11
8″	1000	8,000	14
12″	300	3,600	13
12″	1000	12,000	15
20″	200	4,000	13
20″	1000	20,000	16
50″	200	10,000	15
50″	1000	50,000	17

but introducing some lag in response. Currently, signal processing electronics and A-D conversion techniques are sufficiently stable, rapid, and economical at conversion resolutions up to 12 to 13 bits to be practical for low cost, reliable digitizer products. Therefore, hybrid techniques are best suited for smaller size, lower resolution units. Furthermore, resistive materials with resistance uniformity of the order of the resolution required are difficult to achieve. In order to extend hybrid techniques to large, higher resolution digitizer tablets, individual tablet surfaces may be compared to a precision reference and corrections for coordinate position errors stored in ROM (read only memory) for use by the tablet's microprocessor to generate accurate coordinate outputs. Substantial filtering techniques must also be used to provide output stability.

Uniform Resistance Sheet. Contacts are made on the four sides of a rectangular sheet of material of highly uniform resistivity (such as vacuum deposited indium-tin oxide on glass). An AC signal, induced by a transducer at some X-Y coordinate, is attenuated in its path toward each of the contacts by an amount related to the distance from each contact. After reading the amplitudes at each of the four contacts, the coordinate location is calculated and corrected for edge effects and, if necessary, for the effects of resistance nonuniformity.

X-Y Grid. Mutually perpendicular, equally spaced grid lines are connected at one end through identical resistance values to the ends of the two adjacent grid lines to make two resistor strings: one for X and one for Y. An AC signal, coupled to the grid lines at the transducer location, is attenuated through the resistance values to each end of the strings of resistors where the two signal values are measured and used to calculate the transducer position. This yields four readings, two for X and two for Y. Both grid spacing and resistance values must be tightly controlled to insure digitizer linearity.

Sonic. Sound travels through still air at approximately 345 meters per second at 20°C. By timing the travel of a sonic pulse from a transducer to a pair of microphones, the location of the transducer can be calculated by triangulation and converted into X-Y Cartesian coordinates. Since X-Y coordinates are determined using only two microphones positioned some distance outside the active area, there is no need for a tablet to contain the active area when using sonic technology. Figure 4.3 shows a sonic digitizer in use.

Accuracy, resolution, and stability of digitizers employing sonic technology are dependent upon three major factors: 1) ambient temperature, humidity, atmospheric pressure, and air movement, which affect the velocity of sound; 2) distance from the microphones; and 3) detection repeatability of sonic pulse versus noise discrimination. These factors limit resolution to 200 to 300 lines per inch. Under stable ambient conditions, accuracy approaches ±0.1 percent of the digitized distance.

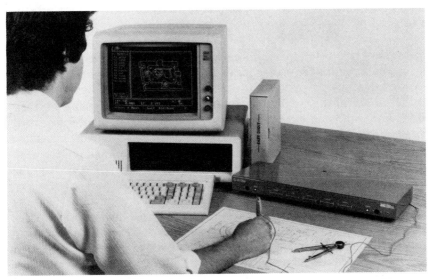

Figure 4.3. Photo of sonic digitizer.

4.2.3 Transducers

The design of digitizer transducers involves a balance between application and user requirements, characteristics of components and materials, ruggedness and reliability, precision, convenience, cost, and human factors. Frequently the most abused component in any computer graphics system, the transducer must withstand repeated falls as well as the habits of the concentrating operator who taps, twirls, or even chews on it. And since, when the transducer fails (or is lost), the whole graphics system becomes inoperative, the most significant properties of a transducer should be ruggedness and reliability.

The cable plays an important role in keeping the transducer captive and in breaking a fall off the work surface. But the cable must present little or no constraint on the free movement of the transducer; it must be highly flexible, as thin and lightweight as possible, yet strong enough to withstand abuse. Cable insulation must withstand the very high voltage of ESD (electrostatic discharge). Strain relief design is important to prevent conductor fatigue from constant cable flexing.

Cursor Design Considerations. The cursor is the transducer of choice for two uses: accurate entry of coordinate data from graphic material and mouselike display cursor control with multipushbutton selection. The cursor also has the advantage of remaining at the position where last used (as opposed to a stylus, which must be put down somewhere when not being held).

Graticule. The distinctive feature of a cursor is its graticule, or cross-hair sight, which enables the user to locate accurately the transducer at a desired coordinate position. To prevent parallax, the graticule is designed as close to the surface of the graphic material being digitized as possible. Furthermore, line width and design of the cross-hairs pattern influences digitizing speed, repeatability, and operator fatigue. For very accurate digitizers, the graticule is etched or bonded to the surface of optical quality glass with 0.003 inch to 0.004 inch line widths. Often a small circle is used at the intersection of the lines.

The functional element (coil or electrode) of the cursor is typically circular or ring-shaped; the intersection of the cross-hairs must be accurately positioned at the center of the element to prevent concentricity errors. Two techniques are employed to achieve concentricity: 1) Design the cross-hair and element components with sufficiently tight tolerances—a reasonable approach for all but the highest accuracy digitizers; 2) Adjust or scribe the cross-hairs in fabrication to coincide with the element centroid as detected by the digitizer systems.

Push Buttons. The number of buttons available on standard digitizer cursors range from one to sixteen, with four buttons being the most common. The button switches must be ESD tolerant and rated for at least three million actuation cycles. Tactile or audible feedback is also important since it is often the operator's only real time confirmation of his choice.

Indicators. LED indicators are available on some digitizer cursors, typically used to indicate power-on, in-proximity, or host programmable functions.

Other Features. Cursors for specialized applications include self-contained *X-Y* coordinate position indicators, graticule magnifier/illumination, optical line tracking, and battery powered cordless operation.

Stylus Design Considerations. A stylus transducer is used by operators desiring the familiar handling characteristics of pen or pencil. The stylus typically accommodates a ball point refill that is provided with or without ink; the choice is determined by whether the application involves marking or not.

Stylus Characteristics. Significant differences between stylus and cursor usage include:

- The stylus can be used to write on or mark graphics materials.
- A stylus cannot be positioned as accurately as a cursor because the tip tends to hide the point to be digitized and because the stylus tilt affects the position indication.
- The stylus cannot be left at a point of interest but must be put down when the user wishes to do something else.
- The stylus cannot conveniently or practically accommodate the number of push buttons of a cursor.
- The stylus is moved with the fingers of the user while a cursor is moved by the wrist. Therefore, the stylus is appropriate for writing and drawing while the cursor is very limiting.
- Although the effects of stylus tilt are a disadvantage for high accuracy digitizing, the characteristic is used to advantage in creating or modifying computer graphics; the stylus acts as a joystick vernier by holding the point stationary while tilting the stylus in the desired direction.

Tip Switch. When the stylus tip is depressed on the digitizer tablet surface, a stylus tip switch is actuated, signaling the digitizer to transmit the condition to the host computer. There are two schools of thought on the characteristics of the tip switch:

- Depression Actuation. The tip switch provides positive tactile feedback; its pressure characteristic is contoured through preactuation and postactuation travel. This actuation characteristic allows a user to generate very positively a tip switch signal as desired while moving the stylus around the digitizer surface.
- Contact Actuation. The tip switch requires a minimum of travel; the tactile feedback is provided by the pressure felt by the operator in contacting the digitizer surface with a predetermined amount of force. This contact actuation characteristic most closely simulates the operation of a ball point pen.

Stylus/Digitizer Surface. For nonmarking writing or creation of graphics, the stylus is moved, with tip switch actuated, over the stylus surface to enter the desired graphics. A smooth, relatively hard digitizer surface is preferred for such applications. Many digitizer systems employ a removable overlay, often printed with "hard" menu functions, to satisfy digitizer surface characteristics.

Push Buttons. Stylus barrel-mounted switches are useful in addition to the tip switch to permit operator choice of additional functions. As with cursor push buttons, they must be very reliable and rugged to withstand use and abuse, and be ESD tolerant. The very tight size constraints of a stylus make these switch requirements a design challenge to achieve economically.

Physical Characteristics. The size, shape, and balance of the stylus affect an operator's effectiveness. The stylus must be comfortable to hold, lightweight, and easily manipulated.

Other Features. Special-purpose styluses provide special application related functions including pressure indication, a pseudo Z axis read from a stylus tip pressure sensing device, LED indicators, and battery powered cordless operation.

4.2.4 Interfaces and Formats

Serial Communications. Currently, communications between a digitizer and a host computer are predominantly accomplished through full duplex, asynchronous serial, RS-232C interfacing.

Serial: signals are sent one bit at a time over a single wire and received one bit at a time over a second wire.

Full duplex: signals may be sent and received simultaneously.

Asynchronous: information is packaged in bytes as a fixed number of data bits between one START bit and one or more STOP bits.

RS-232C: A standard that specifies electrical characteristics, connector types, and pin designations.

In addition to signal ground, shield, transmit and receive pins, the RS-232C connector also specifies pins for "handshaking": data terminal ready—data ready, request to send—clear to send. It has become common practice to achieve handshaking through communication over the serial transmission lines. As a result, the corresponding handshake signal line pairs are typically hard-wired together or left open as required by the host computer.

Output Reports and Rates. The rate at which serial data is sent and received is termed the baud rate. It specifies the number of serial bits communicated per second. Data may be either 8 or 9 bits in length, including a parity bit; adding one start and one stop bit yields bytes of either 10 or 11 bit lengths. Data transmission rates in bytes per second for standard baud rates are shown in Table 4.2.

Serial coordinate position information is sent from the digitizer tablet to the host as either actual ASCII numbers with appropriate delineator and control characters or as "packed binary" characters, which express the coordinate position by using the character bits as binary numbers. As an example of each, consider the Bit Pad One® output formats shown in Table 4.3.

The packed binary format, at five bytes, requires half the transmission time of the ASCII format; this factor becomes significant at lower transmission baud rates as shown in Table 4.4.

Thus, to accommodate the 60 frame per second rate of standard computer monitors requires a 9600 baud rate using ASCII format, while 4800 is acceptable with the packed binary format.

Table 4.2. Data Transmission Rates

Baud rate	10 Bit Bytes/sec.	11 Bit Bytes/sec.
300	30	27
1200	120	109
2400	240	218
4800	480	436
9600	960	872
19200	1920	1745

Table 4.3. Binary Bit Pad One Data Format

Binary Bit Pad One* Data Format (5 Bytes)							
MSB							LSB
Byte	7	6	5	4	3	2	1	0
1	P	1	PB	PB	PB	PB	0	PR
2	P	0	$X5$	$X4$	$X3$	$X2$	$X1$	X0
3	P	0	$X11$	$X10$	$X9$	$X8$	$X7$	X6
4	P	0	$Y5$	$Y4$	$Y3$	$Y2$	$Y1$	Y0
5	P	0	$Y11$	$Y10$	$Y9$	$Y8$	$Y7$	Y6

Where: BIT 7 (MSB) = Parity bit
BIT 6 = Phasing bit; 1 in byte 1 only
PB = Pushbutton identification
PR = Proximity bit; 1 when out of proximity
$X0-X11$ = binary X coordinate; $X0$ = LSB
$Y0-Y11$ = binary Y coordinate; $Y0$ = LSB.

ASCII Bit Pad One Data Format

$X\ X\ X\ X\ Y\ Y\ Y\ Y$ PB CR LF

Where: X = digits of the X coordinate, 0–9
Y = digits of the Y coordinate, 0–9
PB = Pushbutton identification, 0–9
CR = Carriage Return character
LF = Line Feed character.

Mode Considerations. The most common digitizer modes of operation include stream, switched stream, point, and remote request. These establish the manner in which the digitizer tablet communicates with the host computer. De facto industry standards for these modes have been established by Summagraphics Corporation. The modes presented here have been taken from Summagraphics Technical References (Publication 84-DM11-44) for the MM 1201* and MM 961* Data Tablets.

The point mode is used to output a single coordinate pair each time the stylus tip switch is actuated or each time a stylus or cursor button is depressed. In this mode, the operator directly selects the time for output of

Table 4.4. Binary ASCII Transmission Rates

Baud Rate	10 Bit Bytes/Sec.	Packed Binary Reports/Sec.	ASCII Reports/Sec.
300	30	6	2.7
1200	120	24	11
2400	240	48	22
4800	480	96	44
9600	960	192	87
19200	1920	384	175

coordinate pairs. If the transducer is out of proximity, the last valid coordinate is reported once.

In the stream mode, coordinate pairs are updated continuously. The rate can be selected from a range which, depending on the tablet, may vary from under one sample per second to over 100 samples per second. In this mode, the output data will continue at the selected rate whenever the transducer is in proximity. If the transducer is out of proximity with no button pressed, the last valid coordinate data is transmitted three times. If a button is pressed, the last valid coordinate will be transmitted continuously.

The switch stream mode operates in the same manner as stream mode except that coordinate pairs are output only when a button is depressed. This allows the operator to select time intervals for output of data, thus filtering the data that is input to the system. When out of proximity, the last valid coordinate data is transmitted.

Report rates must be set for both the stream and switch stream modes of operation. The maximum is limited by how fast the tablet can calculate coordinates, but is also limited by the communication baud rate and report format used.

The remote request mode is a polled operation allowing the system to request an update from the tablet. When polled, the tablet will provide a coordinate. When out of proximity, the last valid coordinate pair will be reported.

Incremental mode may be used alone or in conjunction with stream, switch stream, or remote request modes. When used alone, it provides a coordinate and status update whenever position has changed by a predetermined or preselectable distance or increment in X or Y. In this mode, a button activation will also trigger an update.

A variation of the incremental mode is the axis update mode. In this mode, the first report after setting the mode or returning to proximity establishes a reference point. From this reference point, an imaginary grid is established with this point at the intersection of two grid lines. Each time the transducer crosses one of the imaginary grid lines, an update report is generated that updates the coordinate pair in the axis that crossed the grid line only. The other axis is held at its last reported value. Thus, all coordinate pairs represent grid intersection points. A switch actuation will cause a report containing the last reported coordinate pair along with the status data.

With the arrival of and acceptance of the mouse as a pointing device, a delta mode of operation has been offered by tablet manufacturers. This allows the tablet to simulate mouse operation by reporting relative coordinate movement between reporting times. Both positive and negative values are used. When out of proximity, the delta coordinate values reported are zero.

Some of the operating modes may be combined; this provides unique operating characteristics. See Table 4.5, which lists the possible combinations along with identification of valid combinations. In this table, the modes are categorized as primary and modifiers. When the primary modes are stream or switch stream and the modifier is increment or axis update, a report will be generated at the next report rate interval time only if the conditions of transducer movement have been met.

This reduces the number of reports when in these primary modes by not transmitting those that do not contain a different coordinate. When in these combined modes and a button is depressed, the last report is reissued once on each occurrence. When the remote request primary mode is combined with either modifier, increment, or axis update, a report with new coordinate data will be generated by a poll only when the conditions of transducer movement have been satisfied. A report containing the last valid coordinate data will be issued if a button has been actuated at the time of the poll. As indicated, the delta mode of reporting can be used with all primary modes except point mode, providing relative transducer movement rather than absolute transducer coordinate position.

Host to Tablet Communications. Upon power-up, the digitizing tablet assumes specific default conditions for certain operating parameters such as location of origin, resolution, report rate, and mode. Many of these may be modified by host transmission of predefined ASCII characters. Other characters will turn off/on data transmission, cause the digitizer to identify or to perform a self-test diagnostic, and to report test results.

Connector Considerations. The RS-232C serial I/O connector is also used in some systems to provide power for the digitizer from the host computer. Typical convention uses pin 9 for $+12$ V and pin 10 or 15 for -12 V.

Serial TTL versus RS-232C Communications. The RS-232C standard specifies bipolar signal transmission voltage levels. The serial line is held

Table 4.5. Combining Operating Modes

Modifiers	Stream	Switch Stream	Point	Remote Request
Increment	Valid	Valid	Invalid	Valid
Axis update	Valid	Valid	Invalid	Valid
Delta	Valid	Valid	Invalid	Valid

normally at a negative voltage defined as a mark level. To initiate transmission of a character, the polarity is reversed to positive, the space level, for one bit length as the START bit. This is then followed by a series of mark (logical one) or space (logical zero) bits, corresponding to the character being transmitted, and terminated by one or more MARK bits acting as STOP bits.

TTL levels originated from the direct use of TTL integrated circuit logic elements as serial transmit and receive devices. These circuits work from a single +5 V power source and therefore define a single voltage polarity transmission system. Furthermore, the signal logical correspondence to voltage polarity may be reversed from the RS-232C standard; that is, while the RS-232C space level or logical zero is positive voltage level, a TTL space level or logical zero could be either positive or ground level.

Parallel Communications. Although the vast majority of digitizer tablets have standardized on serial communications as their sole means of interfacing, parallel interfaces are still available on some large or special-purpose digitizer tablets. As with serial transmission, data is formatted either as ASCII or binary words.

Since parallel interfacing transmits 8 or 16 bits simultaneously, data transmission can be accomplished at significantly higher rates.

Voltage levels for parallel interfacing are typically TTL, with positive voltage corresponding to a logical ONE. However, with the absence of any standards, connector types, electrical characteristics, and data formats vary widely.

4.2.5 Standard Requirements

Standards that apply to computer related user input devices such as the digitizer tablet may be separated into emission, safety, environmental, ergonomic, and other.

Emission Standards. In the United States, it is a regulation of the Federal Communications Commission (FCC) that all electronic devices limit electromagnetic radiation to below specific levels defined as FCC "A" limits. In addition, all such devices designed or marketed for general consumer use in the home must further limit radiation levels to below FCC "B" limits. This is the only standard that is required by law and applies only to products marketed in the United States. A similar emissions standard developed in the Federal Republic of Germany is used by the majority of European countries. Known as Verband Deutscher Elektrotechniker, or VDE, it also specifies "A" and "B" emission limits for industrial/domestic use.

A more stringent emission standard for use exclusively in areas of government or military security is the TEMPEST specification.

Safety Standards. To prevent hazards to users, standards have been established governing methods practice, insulation and grounding of electrical wiring, and flammability of materials. Although safety standards differ throughout the world, most products are designed to meet Underwriters Laboratory (UL) in the United States, Canadian Standards Association (CSA) in Canada, Verband Deutscher Elektrotechniker (VDE) in Europe, or Ministry of International Trade and Industry (MITI) in Japan.

Environmental Standards. Including operating, nonoperating, shipping, and storage categories, these standards specify limits for temperature, humidity, shock, vibration, altitude, and other environmental considerations as appropriate to the application. Environmental standards are frequently expressed as specifications for specific products and manufacturers since no universal set of standards has been accepted in the industry.

Ergonomic Standards. The most inclusive and widely applied ergonomic standards are those established by Verband Deutscher Elektrotechniker. These standards include colors and shades, sizes, shapes, and other factors that have been shown to improve user effectiveness and decrease user strain and fatigue.

Other. Electrostatic discharge (ESD) and electromagnetic induction are two factors that can affect a product's performance or failure rate. ESD describes the discharge of static electricity from a user and its effect on performance. To simulate the discharge for testing purposes, a capacitor is charged to a high voltage and discharged very rapidly through a resistor to the unit being tested. The critical parameters of the test include:

- Capacitor size
- Resistor size
- Discharge rise time
- Voltage magnitude
- Probe shape/diameter
- Grounding of the unit
- Failure type:
  Hard failure—unit must be repaired to operate properly.
  Soft failure—unit must be reset to operate properly.

Electromagnetic induction describes the result of generating a strong electromagnetic field in the local area of the product. Methods of testing have not been widely accepted and standardized for general computer peripheral or digitizer products to date.

4.3 Tablet Classes

We have divided graphic tablets into three classes: digitizer tablets, data tablets, and touch pads. These classes are differentiated by their performance characteristics and operating modes. See Table 4.6 for a chart describing the characteristics of these classes. Typical applications are mentioned briefly to highlight important characteristics of each class.

4.3.1 Digitizer Tablets

Digitizer tablets are high accuracy units used to input precise data from engineering drawings, maps, or other pictorial or graphical hard copy. The accuracy of these units is generally held to ±0.01 inch or ±0.254 mm, and resolution is generally 1000 lpi or 40 lpmm. Figure 4.4 is a picture of a

Table 4.6. Characteristics of Graphics Tablets

	Tablet Classes		
Characteristics	Digitizer	Data	Touch
Accuracy	High	Medium	Low to medium
Best	±0.003 in. (0.076 mm)	±0.01 in. (0.254 mm)	
Typical	±0.01 in. (0.254 mm)	±0.025 in. (0.635 mm)	Unspecified
Resolution			
(Highest)	Medium to high	Medium to high	Low to medium
Best	1000 lpi to 40 lpmm	1000 lpi/40 lpmm	4000 × 4000
Range	200–1000 lpi/	200–1000 lpi/	100 × 100–
	10–40 lpmm	10–40 lpmm	4000 × 4000
Size	Small to large	Small to medium	Small to medium
Predominant	36 × 48 in. (914 × 1219 mm)	11.7 × 11.7 in. (297 × 297 mm)	
Range	11 × 11 in. to 44 × 60 in. (297 × 297 mm to 1118 × 1524 mm)	5 × 5 in. to 20 × 20 in. (127 × 127 mm to 508 × 508 mm)	
Price range	$2,000 to $10,000	$400 to $1,900	$100 to $300
Usage	Accurate digitizing Hard/soft menus	Digitizing Hard/soft menus Cursor steering Drawing	Cursor Steering Soft/hard menus Sketching
Technology			
Predominant	Electromagnetic Magnetostrictive	Electromagnetic Capacitive/Resistive, Charge	Resistive contact

Figure 4.4. Microgrid 36 × 48 digitizer. (Photo courtesy of Summagraphics Corporation, Fairfield, Connecticut.)

typical large digitizer tablet on a stand. It is a Summagraphics Microgrid Series® tablet with an active area of 36″ × 48″ or 914 × 1219 mm.

This is the most popular digitizer tablet size and it will handle English D size drawings or metric A0 size drawings. The technology used in this unit is electromagnetic, the dominant technology for this class tablet.

Digitizer tablets are offered in sizes ranging from 12 inches × 12 inches or 305 × 305 mm up to 42 inches × 60 inches or 1067 × 1524 mm and beyond. Due to the construction and precision testing required in the manufacture of these high accuracy units, digitizer tablets tend to be high in price. A typical, single-unit price for a 36 inch × 48 inch unit is $4,000 to $5,000 dollars.

The introduction of low-cost data tablets in the late 1970s and early 1980s in sizes with dimensions 20 inches and under has limited the use of digitizers under 17 × 24 inches.

4.3.2 Data Tablets

System designs have shifted the burden of input accuracy and precision from the hardware (tablets) to the software by using grid points and other techniques. This allows the use of the much lower cost, lower performance data tablets for most applications. Typical accuracy is ±0.01 inches or less with many units specifying accuracies of ±0.025 inches or ±0.64 mm. The resolution of these units ranges from 200 lpi or 10 lpmm to 1000 lpi or 40 lpmm.

The most popular size data tablet has an active area of 12 inches × 12 inches. Data tablet offerings range from 6 inches × 6 inches (152 mm × 152 mm) to 20 inches × 20 inches (508 mm × 508 mm).

Uses of data tablets include: menu picking and cursor steering on engineering workstations, presentation graphics generation, data entry, and PC-CAD. Figure 4.5 is a picture of a Summagraphics SummaSketch® data tablet being used with AutoCAD® software on an IBM® PC AT®. List pricing for the most popular size data tablets (11.7 inches × 11.7 inches) ranges from slightly under $600 to over $900.

The predominant technology used for data tablets is electromagnetic, but other approaches have been developed in an attempt to lower costs. Capacitance or charge technology holds promise for a low cost, low power unit. However, designs have suffered from operational problems such as limited proximity and high sensitivity to dielectric variations, making the units too sensitive to small changes in moisture on the tablet's surface and inaccuracies introduced from pencil lines.

There have been some hybrid technology units using capacitive coupling combined with resistive ratioing that have had some degree of success. But these units have been limited to the low performance end of the

Figure 4.5. SummaSketch with AutoCAD. (Photo courtesy of Summagraphics Corporation, Fairfield, Connecticut.)

spectrum. An example is the Kurta Series One® data tablets, which offer a maximum resolution of 200 lpi.

Scriptel has also used a hybrid capacitive/resistive approach to develop a clear data tablet aimed at a special segment of the market requiring a transparent work surface. Due to the complexity of hybrid approaches, these units have not realized the full low cost potential of the charge approach.

Touch Pads: These tablets, as the name implies, can be actuated by touch. The touch can be made with a finger or a pointed instrument if more precision is desired. The performance of touch pads is at the low end of the spectrum of graphic tablets, with resolution under 200 lines per inch and unspecified accuracy. Touch tablets are small, generally under 6 inches (152 mm) on a side, and are also low in cost, with end user prices in the $100 range. The predominant technology used in touch tablets is contact resistance. This uses the mechanical displacement of a surface and physical contact between two conductive surfaces at a point or over an area. Various methods are used to maintain the separation between surfaces including: fixed discrete separator elements, gas pressure, and fluid or fluidlike material displacement. Low cost and ergonomic touch characteristics are critical design factors and are important in determining the ultimate acceptance and success of touch tablets.

One well-known example of this class of tablets is the Koala Pad® offered by Koala Technologies, Inc. This unit has found wide usage and acceptance in the home computer market and is used for operating games and sketching. Its interface to the computer is by analog signals input through the game ports common on home computer systems. Due to its operational limitations, the Koala Pad is not suited for professional use.

Higher quality touch pads are offered for use with professional personal computer systems and workstations. An example is the touch pad that Key Tronics has incorporated in some models of their keyboards (Figure 4.6). These units offer somewhat better resolution and, more importantly, a more consistant actuation pressure. The primary uses for these tablets are cursor steering and menu-picking operations, but they can and are being used for limited graphical input. Both absolute and relative modes of operation are offered, with the former being used for graphics input and hard menu selection operations and the latter for cursor steering and soft menu selection operations. Touch tablets hold promise as versatile and cost-effective alternatives to computer mice.

Special Features. Variants of the standard opaque graphic tablets are offered for special applications. These include translucent, rear projection, and water clear tablets. The translucent units are generally backlighted,

Figure 4.6. Key Tronic touch pad.

thus allowing the transmission of light through objects placed on the tablet's surface. A typical usage is the digitization of data from an x-ray. Another use is the digitization of maps or drawings on mylar, which must be digitized with the highest degree of accuracy. Backlighted operation has been found to allow greater operator positioning accuracy.

Rear projection units have special light diffusing surfaces that reduce eye fatigue for applications where maps are projected on the tablet surface. Another application is the digitization of material from photographic slides, such as data to be taken from medical microphotographs. For translucent or rear projection units, it is important that the sensing mechanism not interfere with the image or material to be digitized. Both fine wires, used in electromagnetic based units, and transparent conductive materials, used in charge based tablets, have been successfully utilized to minimize interference.

The water clear tablet requires the construction of the tablet on glass or a glasslike surface with no visible elements within the active surface. These units can be placed over objects from which data is to be taken. An example would be a CRT display covered by a clear tablet used for controlling the display and taking data from the screen. Another would be the taking of positional information from a solid surface, such as a large machined piece. Water clear units must use either transparent sensing mechanisms, as do the Scriptel water clear tablets, or sensing elements outside the active area, such as the sonic units from Science Accessories.

4.3.3 Logical Functions

Foley and VanDam (1982) organize input devices into five logical classes. These classes are: the "locator," a device that indicates position and/or orientation; the "pick," a device used to select a displayed entity; the "valuator," a device used to input a single value in the space of real numbers; the "keyboard," a device to input strings of characters; and the "button," a device used to select from a set of possible alternative actions or choices. Foley and VanDam go on to point out that each logical device has its own corresponding physical device or family of devices. Obvious choices characterizing each logical class are: a tablet as a locator, a potentiometer as the valuator, a light pen as the pick, an alphanumeric keyboard as the keyboard, and a programmed function key as the button.

While many applications have need for all of the five logical devices, it is uncommon to find each device available. Typically, only three physical devices are represented: a tablet or mouse, and a keyboard including several programmable function keys. Through interactive software and menus, these three physical devices can be made to simulate all five logical devices.

For example, picks are often simulated using tablets—where the user moves the screen cursor to the object or area of interest and pushes a button on the tablet's transducer to cause the object or area to be moved, deleted, or copied. This simulation can be powerful if the application takes advantage of the several buttons of the tablet's cursor to cause different actions to occur. In this case, each button is defined differently so the user can select between several actions without returning to the keyboard.

Likewise, tablets can be made to simulate keyboards by displaying a menu of characters and then choosing the desired characters or functions with the stylus pick. These menus can be displayed either as soft screen menus, as on the Apple Macintosh, or as hard menus, which are actually taped or printed on the tablet's active area. An alternative is to program the tablet to recognize handwritten characters. This capability is built into several "intelligent tablets" that recognize block printing and, for specific applications, actually recognize handwritten symbols that cause complex actions otherwise initiated by special function keys.

Valuator simulations are commonly accomplished with tablets in one of three ways. One way is to use a single axis of the tablet to simulate the range of a traditional valuator. Another way is to employ a menu spot as a low resolution valuator by using the spot as an "increment-decrement" button. An interesting way to simulate a valuator is to use the tablet's stylus as a pressure sensor. This implementation is most often used in graphic design applications where the pressure on the stylus controls brush size or color intensity. Similarly, the output of the pressure sensitive stylus can be used directly to create a Z axis for crude three-dimensional design.

Functions and Comparisons within Applications. While logical functions provide a fundamental description of the way input devices are used within application programs, they are not the usual terms used to discuss performance characteristics. Popular discussions of performance characteristics or functional capabilities are more commonly set in terms such as cursor control, menu selection, tracing, text or character input, and digitizing. Several sets of these functional characteristics have been defined (see Foley and VanDam 1984; Phillips et al., 1986), but we have chosen to categorize important input functions as those found in Table 4.7.

Table 4.7 provides a means of comparing the most popular input devices and scoring their performance. Each device listed across the top is rated for its ability to perform the tasks listed down the left, and the overall rating is shown at the bottom. This total represents a nonweighted sum with the highest number representing the highest overall functional capability. Any attempt to assign weights to the performed tasks would need to be associated with specific applications because the importance of each task varies widely within different applications.

As shown, the graphic tablet scores the highest rating, indicating its good overall functional capabilities. While this is certainly an indication that graphics tablets are indeed powerful and flexible, it should not be interpreted to mean that it is the best selection for all input requirements. The best device can only be determined by examining the requirements of the specific applications, as well as by considering other factors, including cost, desk space, etc. For example, applications requiring only character and word input might be better served with a keyboard or CCD scanner.

Graphics Tablets. Tablets receive the highest overall score. They prove to be excellent devices for all cursor control functions and are adequate for text and character applications when used with character recognition firmware or software. For graphics, tablets score higher than any other input device. The only area where tablets are not suitable is in three-dimensional digitizing. For this specialized application, 3D digitizers have been designed. They are discussed in a later section.

Restrained Cursor Devices. Restrained cursor devices are two-dimensional digitizers that use mechanical arms attached to a cursor. They are similar in appearance to common drafting machines, except that they use a cursor for accurate position location instead of a straight edge. Through the mechanical linkage, the position of the cursor is accurately measured. The

Table 4.7. Input Device Functional Comparison

INPUT DEVICE \\ FUNCTIONS	Graphics Tablet	Light Pen	Touch Screen	Scanner/ Digitizer	Mouse	3-D Digitizer	Joystick	Trackball	Voice	Keyboard
Control										
Cursor, Coarse	E	E	E	NA	E	G	E	E	F	F
Cursor, Fine	E	E	G	NA	E	F	F	G	P	G
Menus, Soft	E	E	E	P	E	G	G	E	F	F
Menus, Hard	E	F	F	P	P	G	NA	NA	NA	NA
Data/Text										
Character	G	G	P	G	P	NA	P	P	E	E
Word	G	G	P	G	P	NA	P	P	E	E
Form, Soft	E	G	E	NA	E	G	G	E	F	F
Form, Hard	E	F	F	F	NA	G	NA	NA	NA	NA
Data/Graphics										
Digitizing (2-D)	E	P	NA	E	P	E	NA	NA	NA	NA
Digitizing (3-D)	NA	NA	NA	NA	NA	E	NA	NA	NA	NA
Sketching	E	G	F	NA	P	F	P	P	NA	NA
Tracing	E	P	F	P	F	G	NA	NA	NA	NA
Signature	E	G		F	F	G	NA	NA	G*	NA
Total	46	33	25	17	25	33	15	18	18	17

E - excellent = 4   * voice identification
G - good = 3
F - fair = 2
P - poor = 1
NA - not applicable = 0

accuracy and resolution available on these devices is generally better than that obtained with the more common electronic digitizer tablets. The disadvantage is the mechanical inertia of the mechanical arm, which slows the digitizing operation and reduces productivity.

Restrained cursor devices are used in applications requiring high accuracy but tolerating low throughput. Land survey applications, that require highly accurate data from maps, are an example. For applications requiring high resolution, accuracy, and high throughput, the scanner digitizers offer a more cost-effective solution.

Light Pens. Light pens have been used with CRT displays since the early days of computing. They are penlike devices that are pointed at a CRT display to identify or select an area on the display.

As indicated in the comparison chart, light pens are excellent in performing system control functions but are less well suited for data input requirements. One advantage of light pens is their low cost. They have been used extensively by the military in system control applications, such as the SAGE defense system control consoles. While they have found some acceptance in the low-end personal computer market, light pens have not been widely accepted due to poor human factors such as operator arm fatigue under heavy usage conditions.

Touch Screens. Touch screens are used in conjunction with CRT displays and provide a means for selecting areas on the display by touching or pointing. Some units use a transparent resistive overlay that fits over the display and is actuated by pressure from the user's finger. The position of the user's finger, relative to the screen, is determined by resistance measurements in two orthogonal axes that are converted to screen coordinates. Other touch screens use orthogonal grids of light beams that are placed in front of the display. Detectors sense the presence of each light beam and record when the beam has been interrupted by a finger or other object pointing to the screen. In these units, the finger does not actually need to touch the screen. Figure 4.7 illustrates Hewlett-Packard's Touch Screen offering.

As shown in the comparison chart, touch screens are excellent for coarse cursor positioning and soft menu picking. For these operations, one need only point at the area or item of interest. Since this pointing action is a natural method of identifying items, these units have found wide acceptance in areas where systems are used by unskilled or untrained operators. An example might be a system placed in an area for general public usage such as an information center in a hotel lobby. Desired information is

Figure 4.7. HP touch screen. (Photo courtesy of Hewlett-Packard Company, Palo Alto, California.)

identified by pointing at items in soft menus, causing the requested information to appear on the display.

The resolution and accuracy of the touch screen is quite low compared to other types of tablets, as indicated in the comparison chart shown in Table 4.6. Touch screens are not suitable for fine cursor steering. Also, they are not suited for hard menu usage. In the data text and graphics input areas, the touch screen is most useful with soft forms, where a field is identified along with an entry from a soft menu. Recent product offerings by Elographics have raised touch screen resolution to 4000 × 4000 points across the display face, thus supporting precise calibration and alignment, high quality graphic input, and entries by a finger or stylus.

Scanner/Digitizer.   These are high performance, high accuracy units used to scan hard copy source material (Figure 4.8). Laser beams are used for scanning and can resolve in excess of 100 lpi. Scanners are normally incorporated in specialized systems designed for specific applications. Since these are expensive systems, they are used where high accuracy and resolution are required along with high throughput.

Typical applications include the scanning and subsequent vectorization

Figure 4.8. Scan-Graphics, CF400. (Photo courtesy of Scan-Graphics, Inc., Broomall, Pennsylvania.)

of data from mechanical and electrical drawings. This operation can also be performed by a manual digitizer tablet using an operator to identify elements of the existing drawing. For a small number of drawings, the manual input is more appropriate and cost-effective but, if a large volume of drawings are to be digitized, the scanner is a better choice.

Scanner/digitizers are also used in scanning source material to be used in publications where high resolution and accuracy are needed to conform to the quality standards of the publishing industry.

As indicated in the comparison chart, these units are best suited for the input of graphics data. Text input would normally be handled by optical character recognition software that translates the bit map image of text into ASCII characters for internal storage and manipulation.

Scanner (CCD). A number of lower cost, low resolution scanners aimed at the personal computer market are now offered. These units offer medium resolution of two to four hundred lpi with some offering grey scale and color capability. Three basic types are available: paper feed, flat bed, and camera based. Prices range from under $2,000 for a paper feed unit to $15,000 for camera based units able to scan larger documents. All of these units are based on CCD array technology that limits the resolution in the electronically scanned axis to the array resolution, typically from 1728 elements to 4096 elements. By optical scaling, a wide range of resolution densities can be supported, but the total resolution elements in any axis are generally limited to the array elements. Using an array of 4096 elements, one could realize a 200 lpi resolution (considered adequate for most text) over a 20 inch working distance. This gives an indication of the practical limits in input document size with the currently available technology.

These scanners are used for both graphic and standard font text input. Generally, the data from the input documents is scanned by the device and a bit map image is fed into the microcomputer. Software is then used to process the image. For text, OCR (optical character recognition) software converts the input text into ASCII characters and stores the data in a standard word processing record format. This software is presently able to handle standard fonts in a few sizes, and the technology is continually being improved to handle more variations in style and size. The technology for recognition of handwritten characters is also improving and should soon be available for use with these systems.

Software is also available to transform line drawings input by these scanners in bit map form into vector form. This is the internal storage form used by CAD systems to represent line drawings mathematically. The resulting file sizes are much smaller than bit map representations, and they also allow for easy presentation and modification of the drawings. This conversion technology requires operator intervention and fairly extensive cleanup, but it is still much faster than manual input.

Pictorial images are left in bit map form, but compression software can be used to reduce the storage requirement of these files. A common technique is based on CCITT Group 3 facsimile standards and leads to compression ratios of several times.

These low cost scanners are finding acceptance in desktop publishing systems. These systems are used to input both text and graphical data, and their resolution is matched to laser printers. The most popular resolution of the laser output devices is 300 lpi.

In looking at the comparison chart, note that the CCD type scanner is listed as an excellent input device for text input applications and good for graphical input. It would be rated higher for graphical input if it were not limited by the size of the documents that can be handled. These units are designed for page sizes most popular in word processing and desktop publishing, rather than large drawings used in CAD applications.

3D Digitizer. Several digitizers are now offered that can take measurements in three dimensions. Several technologies are used in the commercially available devices. One device, offered by Micro Control Systems,

Inc., is called the Perceptor® and uses a mechanical armlike structure. Potentiometers are used on precision rotary joints to measure the location of the pointer tip in three dimensions. It works within a limited volume of 40 inches in length (101.6 cm), 31 inches in height (78.7 cm), and 38 inches in depth (96.5 cm). Its accuracy ranges from 0.007 to 0.020 inches (0.018 to 0.050 cm) and resolution ranges from 0.007 to 0.010 inches (0.018 to 0.025 cm). (See Figure 4.9.)

Another approach has been taken by Polhemus Navigation Sciences who offer a unit called 3 Space® Three Dimensional Digitizer. This unit uses low frequency magnetic fields and a cable connected stylus with tip switch that can be moved freely in the working volume. This volume is specified as 20 inches $\times$ 20 inches $\times$ 10 inches (50.8 $\times$ 50.8 $\times$ 25.4 cm) and up to 40 inches $\times$ 40 inches (101.6 $\times$ 101.6 $\times$ 50.8 cm) at reduced accuracy. The specified accuracy within the smaller working volume is 0.032 inches (0.081 cm) RMS in X, Y, and Z for stylus position and 0.5 degrees RMS for stylus angular orientation. The resolution is specified as 0.016 inches (0.041 cm) for position and 0.1 degrees for stylus orientation. A lower accuracy model is also offered called the 3 Space Tracker®, which will operate at up to ±60 inches from the sensors, thus allowing a very large volume to be covered. Units based on sonic technology are offered by

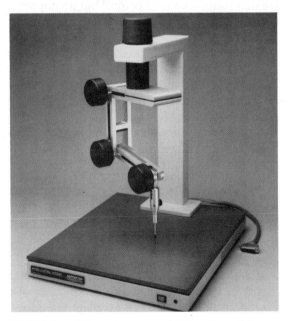

Figure 4.9. 3D digitizer. (Photo courtesy of Micro Control Systems, Inc., Vernon, Connecticut.)

Science Accessories Coporation. The Model GP-8-3D® unit is specified to cover a volume of 120 inches × 120 inches × 120 inches (304.8 × 304.8 × 304.8 cm) with a resolution of 0.01 inches (0.0254 cm) selectable by the user. A typical application for 3D digitizers is the building of three-dimensional data bases from a model or part for use in CAD systems.

As shown in the comparison chart, these units are the only input device suited for digitizing solid objects.

Mouse, Joystick, Trackball, and Voice. These input devices are covered in depth in other chapters of this book so their characteristics and applications will not be discussed here. They are included here only for a comparison of their functions with the graphics tablets.

As shown in the comparison chart, the mouse is an excellent device for most control functions except for hard menus, where it cannot be used. For text or graphics, it falls short of the graphics tablet in its functional capability. Some mice are used for sketching applications, particularly in conjunction with PC Paint programs, but this requires the operator to use unnatural hand/arm movements rather than the more natural and precise hand/finger movements normally used for sketching. Mice are also very poorly suited for tracing and digitizing functions.

Joysticks are well suited to coarse control but do not perform well when fine control is needed. They have no real strengths in the text or graphics input area.

Trackballs, like mice, are well suited for control functions with the exception of hard menu selection. However, they do not exhibit a natural coupling to the user's hand-eye coordination as do mice. Although they have been used extensively in aircraft control and game applications, they have not received general user acceptance.

Voice input, in comparison with other input technologies, requires a great deal of computational power and memory, and is just beginning to be economically feasible. Because it is natural, voice input is expected to be well accepted by users. However, in looking at its functional characteristics, it is seen to have a fairly narrow range of capabilities. Its strengths lie in the area of text input and applications where voice commands can be used for control functions. Voice input is presently not suitable for graphic inputs, but can be used for identification purposes, as is indicated under the signature function.

The keyboard is the most widely used input peripheral. It is furnished with most systems in use and is dominant in the area of text input. As shown in the comparison chart, it is an excellent text input device. It has also been adopted for control functions with the inclusion of special cursor control keys. However, for cursor steering functions, it is not as well suited as many of the other devices. In the graphics input area, it is of little, if any value, and for systems requiring these functions the keyboard is always supplemented with another input device.

4.4. Application Areas

For convenience, we have grouped graphics tablet and digitizer applications within seven application areas. These application areas are: 1) graphical desktops, 2) data entry, 3) handwritten character recognition, 4) computer aided publishing, 5) graphic arts, 6) CAE/CAD, and 7) scientific analysis. Each heading is meant to be descriptive, but most application areas include several related applications and are, therefore, broader than they might at first appear.

4.4.1 Graphical Desktops

Graphical desktops include graphical operating systems, like those found on Apple's Macintosh, as well as operating system shells like Microsoft's Windows®, IBM's Top View®, and DRI's GEM Desktop®. While some of the software companies claim that a pointing device is not a requirement with their graphical desktops, there is little question that the applications are more intuitive and much easier to use with a pointing device. The pointing device of choice in each of the examples cited is a computer mouse rather than a graphics tablet or digitizer. The reasons for this choice are clear. The computer mouse is a low cost device, thereby making the mouse well suited to "bundling" along with the computer or software as a standard or a standard option. Also, the logical functions that need to be performed within a desktop application are just the combination of functions best suited to mice: locating menus and controlling menu selections with a button or pick. And, despite the name graphical desktops, these applications do not actually require the user to input graphical information. Therefore, these applications can tolerate the low resolution afforded by mice and the drawback of their relative pointing system that makes drawing difficult and tracing impossible. These disadvantages are offset by the mouse's high performance to price ratio within these special applications.

4.4.2 Data Entry

Another nongraphical application, but one sometimes requiring a tablet or digitizer because of the absolute pointing system of these devices, is data entry. Data entry is a broad classification area that includes specific applications like order entry, construction cost estimation, and other systems where items from a hard menu are chosen and entered into the computer. A light pen could also be used to perform the logical pick function if the items were displayed as a screen menu, but the majority of these applications use paper forms that are placed directly on the tablet's surface, thereby allowing a hard copy to be produced by the tablet's marking stylus at the same time the information is entered into the computer system.

Construction cost estimation is an interesting example of data entry. In this application, information about the cost of building materials, quantity discounts, and the amounts and percentages of various materials used are all stored in a data base. When contractors need to produce cost estimates for a job, they simply place the blueprint on the tablet's active area and outline walls, floors, rooms, etc., using the stylus or cursor, and then type in codes for various materials and specifications. The computer looks up the material costs and calculates the amount of bricks, lumber, pipes, etc., needed to build the structure from the dimensions input from the digitizer. This procedure replaces the laborious checking of cost data and hand calculation.

For most data entry applications, high resolution and high accuracy are not needed. The exception is where there are many menu items and the menu boxes are very small. Two hundred lines per inch resolution is usually more than adequate for hard menu applications where the menu boxes are typically 0.5 inch squares. The requirements that make the tablet the device of choice for many data entry applications are: the absolute pointing system, so that paper forms can be used as templates, and large size. Large size is particularly important in construction cost estimation where large blueprints (up to E size drawings) must be fixed to the tablet's active area.

4.4.3 Handwritten Character Recognition

Handwritten character recognition is an application where the term "character" is used, but where the information is essentially graphical. This is, perhaps, the most exciting application for graphics tablets and digitizers since no other input device can be substituted. But despite the exciting possibilities, relatively few applications exist today. Pencept and CIC have developed tablet systems for form filling and for use with several traditional applications, but as yet, no clear advantage for handwritten entry over typing has emerged for applications that are keyboard oriented.

The most promising area for handwriting recognition is for Chinese and Japanese word processors. CIC and other software developers are working on applications where Kanji characters are sketched in a defined area on the tablet's surface and are automatically entered into the computer for word processing or translation. These applications are much superior to the keyboard systems that require the user to learn complicated combinations of keys to make single Kanji characters.

Another use for handwriting recognition is signature verification for banks and security systems. One of the advantages of using a graphics tablet for signature recognition is that the recognition system can be dynamic. Dynamic signature verification takes into account the speed, direction, and special dynamics of the way people sign their names. While it is relatively simple for a forger to copy the signature, it is nearly impossible to copy the dynamics of the signature.

The special requirements of tablets used for handwritten character recognition include special sizes and increased report rate. (See Ward & Phillips, 1987.) Unlike many of the other application areas, many signature verification applications require small tablets with active areas as small as 2 inches × 5 inches. But the most difficult requirement is the increased report rate needed for real time cursive style recognition. The report rate needed has been specified as high as 400 coordinates per second. The difficulty in meeting this requirement is one of the reasons that most present day recognition systems require the user to print block, capital letters.

4.4.4 Computer Aided Publishing

Computer aided publishing is one of the traditional applications for graphics tablets and digitizers, but also one of the fastest growing. Because of the advent of powerful graphical desktop publishing systems based on the latest generation of powerful microcomputers and sophisticated applications where text and graphics are easily merged and edited, we have included presentation/business graphics under the heading of computer aided publishing. These applications place broad demands on input devices; computer mice, graphics tablets, and OCR scanning devices are all used in electronic publishing.

Some of the uses of tablets in computer aided publishing are in font generation, page layout, and illustration. For these applications, moderate to high resolution is often needed. Particularly when illustrations are being transferred directly to typesetting, the full 1000 lines per inch resolution of electromagnetic tablets can be an advantage. High resolution can also be important in font generation, although many systems use cameras to enter fonts and use tablets only for editing.

4.4.5 Graphic Arts

The applications area termed graphics arts contains some of the most spectacular applications for graphics tablets and digitizers. This application area ranges from paintbrush programs, image processing, and slide generation to animation and simulation. Special tablet requirements range from large size and high resolution to backlighted and rear-projection digitizers. There are even applications that require the use of multiple cursors for generation of 3D images from orthogonal views.

Image processing is different than other graphic arts applications because tablets are typically used to edit images entered into the computer by cameras. In these applications, the tablet does not need to be high resolution since it is used primarily for locator and pick functions, as well as moving and copying images under control of the software.

For some of the graphics arts applications, like paintbrush programs, special pressure sensitive styluses are used as valuators. In these applications, the artist can control the intensity of color or the width of the brush stroke by pressing the pen more firmly on the tablet's surface, giving the artist the "feel" of a real paint brush.

4.4.6 Computer Aided Engineering and Computer Aided Design and Drafting

(CAE/CAD) are probably the most familiar of the applications using graphics tablets and digitizers. Many exciting new CAD and CAE programs have recently been developed for microcomputers, and these new PC CAD programs certainly represent fresh opportunities for graphics tablets.

CAE/CAD applications required a broad range of tablet features, and digitizer manufacturers have long concentrated on this market. Small graphics tablets, from 6 inches $\times$ 9 inches active area to 12 inches $\times$ 18 inches active area, are the mainstream products for architectural and design applications, including the new PC CAD products. Larger sizes are used for circuit board layout, schematic design, and general drafting. While the small tablets used for PC CAD and architectural applications need only moderate resolution and accuracy, the large tablets used for circuit board and logic design applications are high resolution models with accuracy as fine as .003 inch.

4.4.7 Scientific Analysis

The last application area is termed scientific analysis and is the broadest application area, including applications like strip chart analysis, x-ray analysis, survey and aerial photo analysis, photomicroscopy, cartography, and geological analysis—all applications requiring high resolution, high accuracy graphics tablets and digitizers. In addition to the resolution and accuracy needs, rear projection and backlighting are common requirements, and some applications even require transparent tablets for use over the CRT. Special interfaces and specialized accessories are also sometimes needed for this application area, resulting in high prices for specialized custom designs.

References

Dunn, Kathy. "Choose Digitizer Technology and Features to Suit Applications." *Computer Technology Review* (Fall/Winter 1981).

Dunn, Kathy. "Plotters and Digitizers." *Dataguide* (Spring 1981) 7-1–7-3.

Dunn, Kathy. "Understanding Digitizer Resolution and Accuracy." *Mini-Micro Systems* (December 1981).

Foley, James D., Wallace, Victor L., and Chan, Peggy. "The Human Factors of Computer Graphics Interaction Techniques." *"IEEE Computer Graphics and Applications"* (November 1984), 13–48.

Foley, James D., and Van Dam, A. *"Fundamentals of Interactive Computer Graphics,"* Addison-Wesley Publishing Co., 1982.

Ohlson, Mark. "System Design Considerations for Graphics Input Devices." *IEEE* (November 1978), 9–18.

Tappert, Charles C., Fox, Shawhan, Kim, Joonki, Levy, Stephen E., and Zimmerman, Luther L. "Handwriting Recognition on Transparent Tablet Over Flat Display." *SID Conference Proceedings 1986* (May 1986).

Ward, Jean Renard, and Phillips, Mark J. "Digitizer Technology: Performance Characteristics and the Effects on the User Interface." *IEEE Computer Graphics and Applications* (April 1987), 31–44.

5   Mice

CARL GOY

MSC Technologies, Inc.
Santa Clara, California

5.1 Introduction

5.1.1 What They Are

Mice are small, hand-held pointing and selecting devices that are used to control the motion of a cursor on a computer's screen. The motion of the cursor corresponds to the movement of the mouse across a surface. Mice contain a motion-sensing mechanism and one or more switches that can be actuated by an operator's fingers. Switch actuations can cause menus to appear or can select certain commands or options from existing menus. The size and shape of mice are dictated by the size of the human hand, and they are usually about 2.5″ wide × 4″ long × 1.25″ high. A typical mouse and computer system are shown in Figure 5.1.

5.1.2 What They Do

The motion-sensing mechanism of the mouse converts motion across the work surface into electrical signals that can be easily interpreted by the computer. These signals include switch status information and may be in the form of either parallel or serial data.

The computer uses the motion signals to move a cursor on its screen and uses the switch closure signals to select items from a menu or to perform an action on the screen, for example, drawing or editing.

5.1.3 How They Do It

Mechanical or optical means are usually used to convert the motion of the mouse into electrical signals. Rotating wheels or a rolling ball are used to

Input Devices

219

Figure 5.1. Work Station with Mouse.(Courtesy Sun.)

rotate commutators or potentiometers in mechanical mice; printed grid lines or dots are sensed by photodetectors in optical mice. The outputs from the potentiometers, commutators, or detectors are then transmitted electrically to the host computer.

5.2 History

The mouse was invented in 1965 at Stanford Research Institute by Douglas Engelbart (US Patent 3,541,541; English et al., 1967). The original mouse used a pair of wheels turning potentiometer shafts to encode X and Y motion into analog signals.

The mouse was redesigned at the Xerox Palo Alto Research Center to use ball bearings as wheels, and optical shaft encoders to generate digital quadrature signals. The mouse was again redesigned to use a single large ball driving mechanical digital shaft encoders (US Patent 3,987,685), thus eliminating the drag of side-slipping wheels.

Early mechanical mice were unreliable: the balls or wheels would get dirty and slip rather than roll or the commutators would get dirty and skip. All of the mechanical parts made the mice very expensive.

The problems with mechanical mice led to the development of optical mice, which track motion without moving parts by optically imaging a special surface onto an optical detector within the mouse. This concept was first demonstrated in December 1980 by two researchers: Steven Kirsch at MIT in Cambridge (US Patents 4,364,035 and 4,390,873) and Richard Lyon at Xerox in Palo Alto (US Patents 4,521,772 and 4,521,773). They independently built completely different optical designs within days of each other some fifteen years after the original invention of the mouse.

Subsequent to the invention of the optical mouse, other innovative mechanical mouse designs have emerged from Alps, Logitech, and Torrington. An acoustic mouse (US Patents 4,514,726 and 4,550,316) was invented after the optical mouse, but it was not a market success. The acoustic mouse was invented by Albert L. Whetstone, former chairman and founder of Summagraphics. Whetstone had resigned from Summagraphics to start a company, Display Interface Corp., to manufacture an optical mouse but ended up manufacturing his acoustic mouse instead.

Mice are supplied on computers and workstations from Apollo, Apple, DEC, IBM, SUN Microsystems, Symbolics, Xerox, and many others. The largest mouse vendors are Alps Electric, Logitech, and Mouse Systems.

5.3 Human Factors

5.3.1 Discussion of the Literature

Summary. A number of papers have been published that compare mice with other pointing and positioning devices. These studies invariably conclude that the mouse is faster, more error free, and less fatiguing than the other devices that were tested, and that its advantages are apparent to experienced as well as first-time users.

English et al., 1967. A study by English et al. (1967) compared the mouse with a number of input devices, including a light pen, absolute and rate mode joysticks, and a knee control. The experiments were designed to test for the time required for a subject to locate the pointing device and to move the device (and the cursor) to select a word or individual character on the screen.

Inexperienced users generally located individual characters within 2.5 to 3.5 seconds with any of the devices, excluding the rate-mode joystick, which required about 5.5 seconds. The mouse's selection times were marginally slower than those of the light pen and knee control by a tenth of a second, but its error rate was one-half to one-third that of the other devices.

Experienced users were able to select characters faster with the mouse and, again, its error rate was about half that of the other devices. When selecting words, the error rates for most of the devices were similar, except that the light pen's error rate was approximately double that of the mouse.

Card, et al., 1978. Another study by Card et al. (1978) evaluated the performance of mice, rate-controlled joysticks, step keys, and text keys in the selection of text on a screen.

The step keys would move the cursor one line vertically or one character horizontally at a time and would repeat automatically if depressed for more than one tenth of a second. A "HOME" key would move the cursor to the upper left of the screen. The text keys would move the cursor one character, word, line, or paragraph at a time and could also be used in a repeating mode.

The experiments were designed to test for the learning curve, overall speed, effects of distance and target size, and error rate. The authors concluded that the mouse was superior on all counts for the selection of text on a CRT screen.

Embley and Nagy, 1981. In a study of the behavioral aspects of text editors, Embley and Nagy (1981) concluded that the mouse appeared to have an edge over the light pen, joystick, and trackball. Human pointing performance using any of these pointing devices approaches psychophysical limits, so the greater performance of the mouse may not be significant.

5.3.2 Relative and Absolute Pointing

Types of Motion. The computer's response to the mouse's pointing function can be visualized in relative or absolute terms; that is, the cursor will move with respect to the mouse's relative movement over the work surface or it will be placed on the screen in a direct correspondence with the mouse's position on the work surface.

The type of motion, relative or absolute, is generally a function of the design of the mouse and cannot be arbitrarily determined by the computer's applications software.

Relative Motion of a Cursor on the Screen. Most mice sense motion relative to their own coordinates. Motion in the direction of their X and Y axes is translated directly into X and Y motion data and is transmitted to the host computer. Any tilt or rotation relative to the coordinates of the work surface will be ignored because mice can only sense motion relative to themselves.

Absolute Position on a Work Surface. Mice that sense absolute position are used in conjunction with a special work surface, such as a digitizing pad. The pad will contain a position sensing mechanism that can sense the exact location of the mouse with respect to the pad's X and Y axes. The position and switch information is interpreted and transmitted to the host, usually as serial data.

5.3.3 Shape/Form Factor

The shape of the mouse as shown in Figure 5.2, has evolved through necessity to a size and form factor that is comfortably grasped by the human hand. The size is usually 2.5″ wide × 3.5″ long × 1.0″ to 1.5″ high.

The front of the mouse (the end pointing away from the user) is usually lower than the back (or near end). This downward slope from back to front approximates the slope of the user's fingers when the hand is at rest, palm down, on a flat surface.

When the mouse has two or more switches, they are usually spaced $\frac{3}{4}$ inch apart (the average distance between the fingers of the hand).

The edges of the case are usually rounded so that the mouse is as unobtrusive to the hand as possible.

The connecting cable is pointed away from the user's hand so that it does not interfere with the mouse's motion.

5.3.4 Buttons/Switches

Mice will have from one to three buttons or key switches; the number is usually determined by the end user's application. A single button mouse is the easiest to use and is usually paired with applications software that is intensively menu driven. Items can be selected from a menu by moving the mouse, hence the cursor, and clicking the switch button.

Two and three button mice give the user the option of selecting multiple

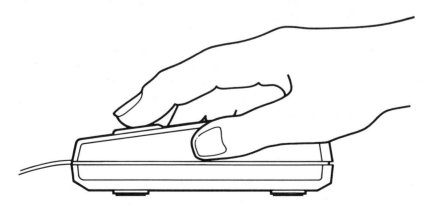

Figure 5.2. Hand and Wrist on Mouse (to show slope of case).

activities by actuating one or more switches with the index, middle, and ring fingers. Clicking two or more switches simultaneously is called chording and is commonly used to cancel a previous mouse command or to bring hidden menus or commands to the fore.

5.4 Analysis of Various Types of Mice

5.4.1 Methods of Analysis

Mice can take many forms and can generate motion information in many ways. Some of the more common mice will be analyzed in the following pages. Their methods of converting motion into electrical signals will be described first, then their electrical signals and protocols will be investigated.

5.4.2 Motion Sensing

Types of Motion. As stated previously, mice sense their displacement and direction of motion across a work surface. This motion can be sensed in one of two ways: relative to the work surface or relative to the mouse.

Motion Relative to the Work Surface. When a mouse senses motion relative to a work surface, its output corresponds to its motion relative to the X and Y axes of the surface. The surface is usually printed with a regular pattern of lines or dots; sensing means within the mouse detect its motion over the patterned surface. The output is independent of the orientation or rotation of the mouse, within limits, and is related only to its motion over the work surface.

Motion Relative to the Mouse. When the mouse senses motion relative to itself, it does so independently of its orientation on the work surface. It can be moved in any direction, or rotated, and its output will correspond only to the motion relative to its own X and Y axes. Its orientation with respect to the work surface is unimportant.

5.4.3 Mechanical Mice

Motion Tracking Methods. Mechanical mice use wheels or balls to convert their linear motion across a surface into the rotary motion of commutators or shaft encoders.

Analog Motion Sensors. *Wheels.* Mice that use wheels and shafts to drive the motion sensing element can be represented by the mechanical system shown in Figure 5.3b.

As the mouse moves across a surface with velocity V in the direction of the wheel, the velocity of the circumference of the wheel, Vr, equals V, the velocity of the mouse. The angular velocity, ω, of the wheel and its shaft is determined by

$$\omega = Vr/R \text{ radians per second}$$

Where R equals the wheel's radius. The shaft's rotation angle, θ, is also directly related to the distance the mouse moves across the surface:

$$\theta = X/R \text{ radians}$$

where X is the distance moved and R is the wheel's radius.

If the motion is not exactly in the direction of the wheel, as shown in Figure 5.3a, the wheel will slip, and the resultant rotation will be less than expected.

$$\omega = Vr \times \cos \alpha/R \text{ radians per second, and}$$
$$\theta = X \times \cos \alpha/R \text{ radians}$$

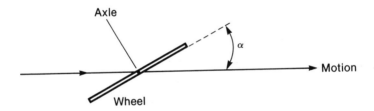

A

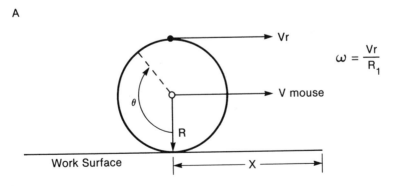

B

Figure 5.3. Wheel Showing Velocities and Slip Angle.

where α is the angle between the wheel and the direction of motion.
A wheeled mouse will have two sets of wheels and shafts: one oriented to detect horizontal motion, the other for vertical motion.

Balls. Mice that use a ball for motion sensing can be represented by the system shown in Figures 5.4 and 5.7a.

The velocity of the circumference of the ball, Vr, is equal to the velocity of the mouse, V. This is the same relationship shown earlier for the mouse with wheels. The angular rotation is also the same as above, but in this case the shaft is not directly attached to the axis of the ball but is resting against its circumference. Assuming no slippage, the velocity of the circumference of the shaft is equal to the velocity of the circumference of the ball.

The shaft's angular velocity and rotation are now related to the motion of the mouse with the equations above, but the radius, R, is now much smaller and the shaft rotates much faster.

$$\omega = V/R1 \text{ radians per second}$$

where V = the velocity of the mouse and $R1$ = the radius of the shaft. As the shaft is made smaller, it rotates faster for a given mouse velocity.

How the Motion is Transmitted to the Sensors. The shafts that are rotated directly or indirectly by a wheel or ball are connected directly to motion sensors. These sensors can take a variety of forms and can be classified as one of two types: resistive sensing elements or optical interrupters.

Resistive Sensing Elements (Commutators). *Outputs.* Resistive sensing elements produce an electrical output that is related to their rotation: a voltage is applied to the sensor and its output varies as it is rotated. The output may be in the form of an analog voltage, as from a potentiometer, or as a series of On/Off voltage transitions from a commutator or optical interrupter.

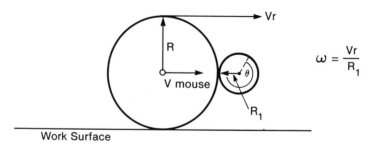

Figure 5.4. Ball and Shaft.

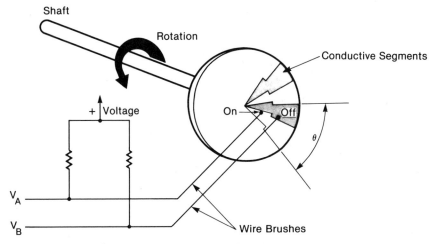

Figure 5.5. Commutator and Brushes.

Multiturn Potentiometers. Early mice used multiple turn potentiometers connected directly to wheels as sensing devices. The output voltage would vary in direct proportion to the movement of the mouse over the work surface: the voltage would increase as the mouse moved in the positive direction and decrease as it moved in the negative direction. An analog to digital converter was used to convert the analog voltage to a digital word that the computer could recognize.

This approach is fairly straightforward, but the useful travel of the mouse is limited by the potentiometer's rotation. As the wheels slip across the surface, eventually the potentiometers reach the limits of their rotation; the wheels must be rotated manually to put the pots in the center of their rotation.

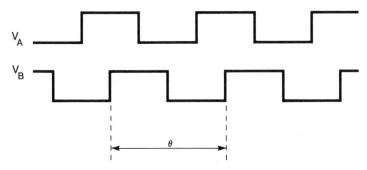

Figure 5.6. Quadrature Signals.

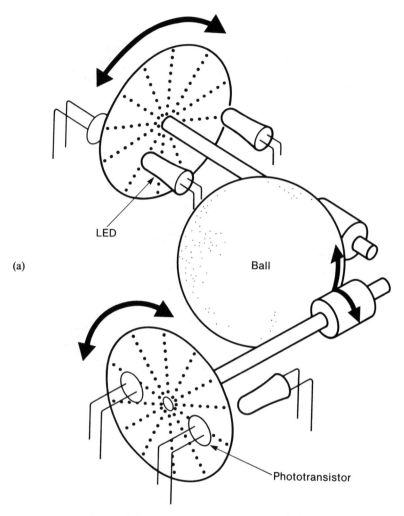

Figure 5.7a. Ball and Shafts with Optical Interrupter.

Commutators with Brushes.   Commutators use brushes and conductive segments on a rotating disk to generate voltage pulses that correspond to rotation.

Figure 5.5 represents a simple commutator and brush system attached to a rotating shaft. As the shaft rotates, the conductive segments of the commutator make contact with the brush and short the pullup resistor to ground. A negative-going voltage pulse will be generated for each segment that passes beneath the brush.

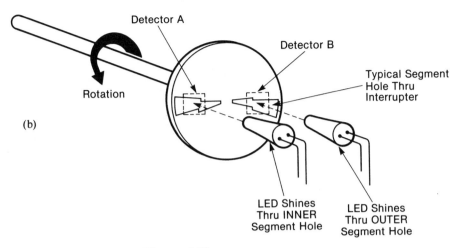

Figure 5.7b. Optical Interrupter.

There are two sets of segments on the commutator. One set is offset from the other by one-quarter of their angular arcs. The brushes contact the commutator on the same radial line, so the output voltage pulses will be offset from each other in the same proportion as the commutator's offset. The output waveforms from brushes A and B will appear as shown in Figure 5.6. When the commutator rotates counterclockwise, waveform A will lead waveform B, that is, a positive-going transition of A will precede a positive-going transition of B. If the commutator is rotated clockwise, the positive-going transitions of B will lead those of A. These signals are said to be in quadrature because their phases are shifted by one-quarter of their period.

The phase relationship of A and B indicates the direction of rotation of the commutator; the number of transitions indicate how far it has rotated. These A and B quadrature signals are the most common form of output from mouse sensing mechanisms, whether they are optical, mechanical, or optomechanical.

Optical Interrupters. Optomechanical mice use a device called an opto-interrupter to generate the A and B quadrature signals. As shown in Figure 5.7b, the optomechanical system consists of a light source, usually a light emitting diode (LED), a photodetector, and the opto-interrupter, which is connected to the rotating shaft of the mouse.

The interrupter has a series of slots that allow light from the LED to shine onto the detector. As the interrupter rotates past the light beam, the

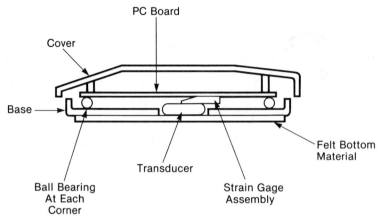

Figure 5.8. Acoustic Mouse.

solid segments between the slots will interrupt the beam and a series of voltage pulses will appear at the output of the detector.

A second quadrature output is obtained by using a second LED and detector that are offset from the first LED and detector by one-quarter of the angle of the radial slots or by using slots that are offset by one-quarter of their period, similar to a commutator's offset conductive segments. A mask with two holes through it may be used with the commutator to insure that the light beams are in quadrature with respect to the rotation of the interrupter. The mask can be pierced or molded so that the holes are precisely 90 degrees out of phase.

5.4.4 Acoustic Mice

Like mechanical mice, acoustic mice generate output signals that are proportional to their speed and direction across a work surface, but the signals are derived from a microphone and strain gauges.

Figure 5.8 depicts a simplified acoustic mouse. The base of the mouse is covered with a suedelike material; a piezoelectric transducer and diaphragm rest against the material at the bottom of the mouse. As the mouse is pushed across the work surface, the suede material generates sounds whose amplitudes are proportional to velocity. The transducer amplifies these sounds and an analog to digital (A-D) converter, in turn, generates digital outputs proportional to the velocity.

The direction of the mouse across the surface is sensed by a strain gauge assembly. An A-D converter generates digital signals that are proportional to the direction of the mouse. A microprocessor in the mouse converts these motion and direction signals into serial data bytes that are transmitted to the host computer.

5.4.5 Optical Mice

Work Surface. Optical mice generally use a special work surface in conjunction with an optical system and photodetectors to generate motion signals. The special work surface, or mouse pad, is usually printed with a grid of lines, dots, or other geometric shapes that can be illuminated and focused onto a detector that generates signals proportional to the movement of the mouse.

Three Types of Optical Systems. *Orthogonal Printed Lines.* The most common form of optical mouse pad has a reflective surface and is printed with a grid of closely spaced orthogonal lines as shown in Figure 5.9. The vertical lines are printed in one color; the horizontal lines in another. The colors are chosen to absorb light at different frequencies, so that the

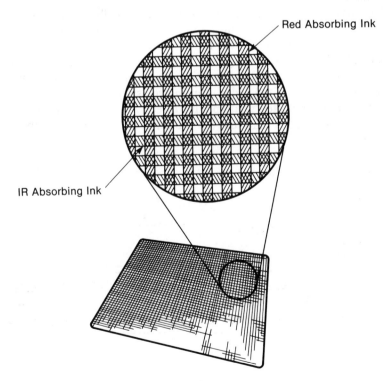

Figure 5.9. Mouse Pad Showing Ink Lines.

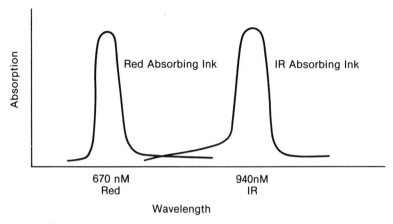

Figure 5.10. Red/IR Spectral Response of Ink.

mouse's optical detectors can differentiate between horizontal and vertical movement.

The absorption spectra of the two inks would ideally appear as shown in Figure 5.10. Each ink would have a narrow peak of maximum absorption at its own wavelength and a very low level of absorption at the other ink's wavelength. The two wavelengths commonly used coincide with those of standard red and infrared light emitting diodes: 670 and 940 nanometers.

When the surface of the pad is illuminated as shown in Figure 5.11, light from the LED is reflected unattenuated directly from the mirror surface of the mouse pad, and is reflected, but attenuated, from the light absorbent ink lines.

This light and dark object can be focused with a lens and mirror system to form an image on a photodetector. The magnification is adjusted to

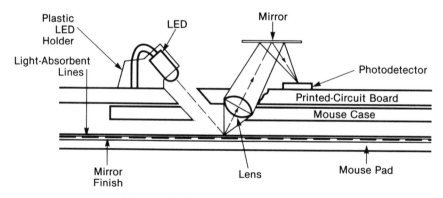

Figure 5.11. Optical Mouse System.

focus one complete line/space period exactly to the length of the four element photodetector.

As the mouse is moved across the pad, the light and dark image will move across the elements of the detector, and each will generate a current that is proportional to the amount of light striking it. These currents are usually very low, on the order of 50 to 100 nanoamperes, and must be amplified and converted to voltages before they can be easily interpreted. Operational amplifiers can be used to convert the photodiode currents to large voltages as shown in Figure 5.12b.

If a simple magnitude comparison is made of the voltages generated by detector elements 1, 3, 2, and 4, the resultant waveforms will appear as two square waves in quadrature; the direction of motion determines which wave is leading the other.

The voltages generated by elements 1, 2, 3, and 4 and the results of their comparisons are plotted in Figure 5.12a.

A second LED, lens, mirror, and detector can be oriented orthogonally to the first system to detect motion in the direction orthogonal to the first. The first LED would radiate energy at 670 nanometers, which would be absorbed by the 670 nM ink; the second would radiate at 940 nanometers and would be absorbed by the 940 nM ink. The energy from each LED would be absorbed by the appropriate ink; the other ink would be transparent to light of the wrong wavelength and there would be no absorption.

The outputs from the comparators can be transmitted directly to a host computer's parallel input port or they can be sensed by an internal microprocessor and transmitted as serial data to a standard RS-232 serial port.

Reflective Lines at Different Focal Lengths. Another type of optical mouse uses a transparent pad that contains an orthogonal grid of reflective lines, where the lines in the X direction are placed at a depth below the surface of the pad that differs from the depth of the lines in the Y direction.

Figure 5.13 shows that the upper set of lines is focused correctly on a photodector, while the lower set of lines would be imaged out of focus, hence as a common mode signal that affects all the elements of the detector uniformly.

A second optical system focuses the image of the lower set of lines correctly at its own photodetector, and the upper set of lines appears out of focus as a common mode signal.

The outputs from the detectors can be used directly or converted to serial data.

Hexagonal Array of Dots. An optical mouse that senses the image of an hexagonal array of dots was developed at Xerox Palo Alto Research

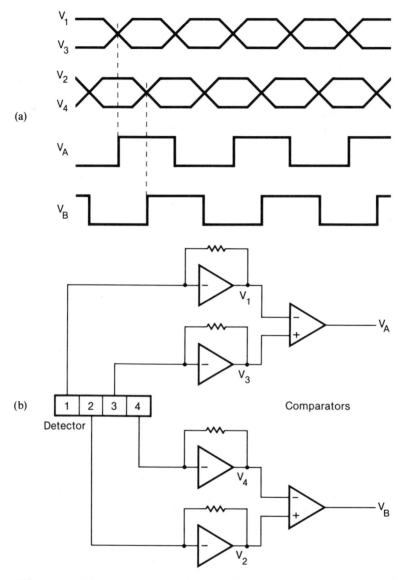

Figure 5.12. Detectors, Op-Amps, and Comparators with Quadrature Signals.

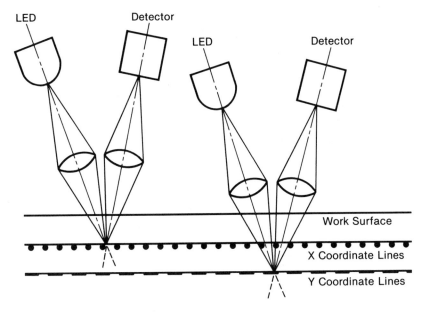

Figure 5.13. Lines at Different Focal Lengths.

Center. The dots are imaged onto a 4 × 4 array of photodetectors; Figure 5.14 shows the array of dots and some of the stable images they can produce on the array.

The outputs of the detectors are amplified and fed to logic arrays that convert the detector signals to digital data that represents the movement of the mouse.

5.5 Electrical Outputs from Mice

5.5.1 Types of Data

The electrical outputs from mice usually take one of two forms: parallel or serial data.

A mouse with parallel outputs presents its motion and switch information to the host computer over an interface that consists of one wire or data bit for each bit, or piece, of information. A three button mouse would have four wires for the X and Y motion information and three wires for the switch closure information, and additional wires for its supply voltage and ground.

A serial mouse presents its motion and switch data to the host over a single wire by using a specific serial communications protocol.

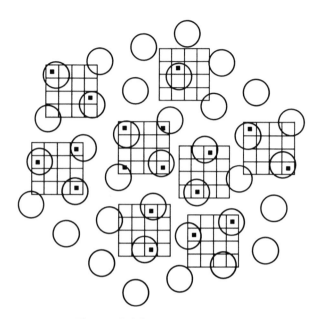

Figure 5.14. Xerox Dot Pattern.

5.5.2 Parallel Outputs

Electrical Characteristics. The output signals generated by parallel mice are usually TTL compatible voltage levels. A logic "0" will be .4V DC or less; a logic "1" will be 2.4V DC or greater.

The vertical and horizontal motion signals (Va, Vb, Ha, and Hb) will have phase relationships as described earlier.

The switch closure signals are usually negative logic. that is, a logic "0" indicates that the user has pressed the switch. The switch signals may or may not be debounced, so the host software should include a debounce routine to let the switch settle to a valid state after it is first closed. Ten milliseconds is usually a sufficient debounce period for even the noisiest of switches.

Standard Pinouts/Connectors. *Standard Connector.* The most common form of connector for parallel mice has been a 9-pin D-subminiature male plug. There is a limited number of connector pinouts and they are tabulated in Table 5.1.

Microsoft Connector. MicroSoft uses a 9-pin mini-DIN connector; details are shown in Table 5.2.

Table 5.1. Quad Pinouts

Pin Number	Mouse Systems	Logitech	Apple
1	+5V	+5V	Ground
2	Xa	Ya	+5V
3	Xb	Yb	Ground
4	Ya	Xb	Xa
5	Yb	Xa	Xb
6	L switch	Ground	Ground
7	M switch	M switch	Switch
8	R switch	R switch	Yb
9	Ground	L switch	Ya

5.5.3 Serial Output

Electrical Characteristics. Serial mice will usually have an internal microcontroller or state machine that can interpret the motion and switch information and convert it to a simple serial output.

Serial mice generate outputs that are in one of two forms: RS-232 or TTL voltage levels.

RS-232 signals from mice conform to the EIA standard: a MARK is represented by a voltage of −5V or less; a SPACE is +5V or greater.

TTL outputs can be either true or inverted logic, and the manufacturer's data sheet must be consulted for the mouse's logic convention. True logic implies that a MARK is 2.4V or greater and that a SPACE is .4V or less.

Table 5.2. MicroSoft Mini-DIN Pinouts

Pin Number	Function
1	+5V
2	Xa
3	Xb
4	Ya
5	Yb
6	Switch 1
7	Switch 2
8	Switch 3
9	Ground

The inverted logic convention is the one most often used, and it implies that a MARK is .4V or less and that a SPACE is 2.4V or greater.

A common pinout is shown in Table 5.3.

Communications Protocols. *Common Protocols.* Serial mice transmit data in a variety of packet sizes and protocols. The most common packet sizes include either three or five bytes of data; the data is transmitted in a sequence that first sends sync and switch information, then X and Y motion information. The most common mouse protocols are listed below.

8-Bit, 5 Byte Binary Data Protocol (Mouse Systems). Protocol: In the Mouse Systems Five Byte Packed Binary format, five byte data blocks are transmitted by the mouse when, and only when, there is a change of mouse state. The start of a data block is indicated by a sync byte whose upper five bits are 10000. The next three bits are the debounced state of the switches (0 means depressed). The next four bytes contain two updates of the mouse movement counters, X, Y, X', Y', where X is the horizontal distance moved relative to the coordinate system of the pad since the last transmission of X and Y is the corresponding vertical distance. X' and Y' are not the same as X and Y, but represent the distances moved since X and Y were transmitted. Bytes two through five are two's complement eight bit binary numbers. The contents of the five bytes are tabulated in Table 5.4.

Direction of Motion: Positive motion is defined as being to the right in the X direction and upward, or toward the cord, in the Y direction. Bit 7 (MSB) of the X and Y bytes will be 0 for positive motion and 1 for negative motion.

Bit Pad One Protocol (Summagraphics). Absolute Motion Protocol: The Summagraphics Bit Pad One data format consists of five eight bit data bytes. The same format is used for both absolute and relative position data.

Table 5.3. DB-25 Serial Pinout

25-Pin D-Connector	
Pin Number	Function
1	Protective ground
2	Data from host to mouse
3	Data from mouse to host
7	Signal ground

Table 5.4. MSC Protocol

Bit Number	MSB 7	6	5	4	3	2	1	LSB 0
Byte 1	1	0	0	0	0	L	M	R
Byte 2	X7	X6	X5	X4	X3	X2	X1	X0
Byte 3	Y7	Y6	Y5	Y4	Y3	Y2	Y1	Y0
Byte 4	X7	X6	X5	X4	X3	X2	X1	X0
Byte 5	Y7	Y6	Y5	Y4	Y3	Y2	Y1	Y0

Parity: None
L, M, R: Left, middle, right switches; 0 = switch pressed
X0–X7: X distance
Y0–Y7: Y distance

In the Absolute Bit Pad One format, the X and Y position information consists of 12 bit positive binary numbers that represent absolute position on the work surface. The first data transmission assumes that the mouse started at the origin (0,0). Negative coordinates are never transmitted. If the mouse moves in a negative direction, the coordinate and origin are reset. The contents of the five bytes are tabulated in Table 5.5.

Relative Motion Protocol: In the Relative Bit Pad One format, the X and Y position information consists of 12 bit signed two's complement data. They report the distance the mouse has moved since the last report.

MM Series Delta Data Protocol (Summagraphics). Protocol: The MM series data format transmits relative movement information in the form of

Table 5.5. Bit Pad One Protocol

Bit Number	P	MSB 6	5	4	3	2	1	LSB 0
Byte 1	PE	1	0	L	M	R	0	0
Byte 2	PE	0	X5	X4	X3	X2	X1	X0
Byte 3	PE	0	X11	X10	X9	X8	X7	X6
Byte 4	PE	0	Y5	Y4	Y3	Y2	Y1	Y0
Byte 5	PE	0	Y11	Y10	Y9	Y8	Y7	Y6

Parity: Even
L, M, R: Left, middle, right switches; 1 = switch pressed
X0–X11: X position
Y0–Y11: Y position

Table 5.6. MM Delta Data Protocol

Bit Number	P	MSB 7	6	5	4	3	2	1	LSB 0
Byte 1	PO	1	0	0	Dx	Dy	L	M	R
Byte 2	PO	0	X6	X5	X4	X3	X2	X1	X0
Byte 3	PO	0	Y6	Y5	Y4	Y3	Y2	Y1	Y0

Parity: Odd
Dx, Dy: X and Y direction bits. 1 = positive; 0 = negative
L, M, R: Left, middle, right switches; 1 = switch pressed
X0–X6: X distance
Y0–Y6: Y distance

three nine-bit bytes. The first byte contains key switch data and two bits that report the direction of motion in the X and Y axes. Bytes two and three are positive seven bit binary numbers that represent the distance traveled in the X and Y directions since the last report. The contents of the three bytes are shown in Table 5.6.

Microsoft Compatible Data Format. Protocol: The Microsoft Compatible data format transmits relative motion information in the form of three seven-bit bytes. The X and Y motion information consists of eight bit two's complement binary numbers. The first byte contains the switch information and the two most significant bits of the X and Y data. The next two bytes contain the lower six bits of the X and Y data. The contents of the three bytes are shown in Table 5.7.

Identification Character. Upon power-up, The Microsoft protocol transmits one character: an ASCII "M" (4DH).

Table 5.7. Microsoft Protocol

Bit Number	MSB 6	5	4	3	2	1	LSB 0
Byte 1	1	L	R	Y7	Y6	X7	X6
Byte 2	0	X5	X4	X3	X2	X1	X0
Byte 3	0	Y5	Y4	Y3	Y2	Y1	Y0

Parity: None
L, R: Left, right switches; 1 = switch pressed
X0–X7: X distance
Y0–Y7: Y distance

Table 5.8. Three Byte Packed Binary Protocol

Bit	MSB							LSB
Number	7	6	5	4	3	2	1	0
Byte 1	0	0	0	0	0	L	M	R
Byte 2	X7	X6	X5	X4	X3	X2	X1	X0
Byte 3	Y7	Y6	Y5	Y4	Y3	Y2	Y1	Y0

Parity: None
  L, M, R: Left, middle, right switches; 1 = switch pressed
  X0–X7: X distance
  Y0–Y7: Y distance

3-byte Packed Binary Format. Protocol: In the three byte packed binary format, relative motion information is transmitted in the form of eight bit data bytes. The first byte contains five bits of zeroes, and the lower three bits contain switch information. Bytes two and three contain X and Y motion information and are signed two's complement binary numbers. The contents of the three bytes are shown in Table 5.8.

5.6 Interpreting the Outputs

5.6.1 Methods

The outputs from mice, whether quadrature parallel data or serial data, can be interpreted easily in either hardware or software. By interpreting as much data as possible in hardware, the load on the host computer will be minimized, and its throughput will be maximized.

5.6.2 In Hardware (Quadrature Mice)

Interpretation. Quadrature mice generate X and Y motion and switch signals simultaneously and present them to the host computer without any conditioning or interpretation. The host must determine what the mouse is doing by comparing its current state with its previous state. If the mouse is moving rapidly, the interpretation of its signals could absorb a significant fraction of the host's computing power. Fortunately, many techniques are available for rapidly interpreting motion signals from mice in hardware. One such circuit is shown in Figure 5.15.

Random Logic. U1 stores the current and previous states of the A and B inputs; U2 interprets those states and determines whether counter U3

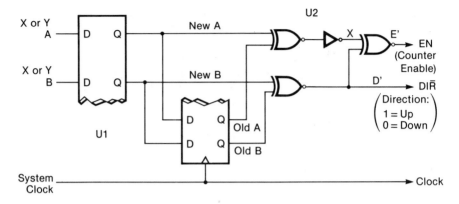

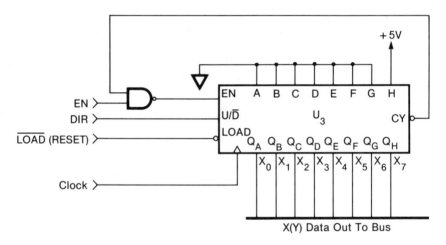

Figure 5.15. Schematic Diagram of Quadrature Up/Down Decoder and Up/Down Counter.

should count up or down. The outputs of the counter can be presented to the host's data bus through a standard buffer.

The outputs of the counter represent two's complement binary information. Data bit X7 (Y7) will be 0 for positive movement and 1 for negative movement. Each time the host reads the data from the counter, it must reset the counter to zero if it expects to see only incremental movement, that is, data that represents how far the mouse has moved since its motion was last reported. If the counter is not reset, the data will represent total accumulated mouse movement and the counter may overflow for large movements.

The timing diagram of Figure 5.16 illustrates how U1 and U2 generate the direction and enable signals for the counter. The system clock should be greater than or equal to ten times the fastest A or B input frequency.

Switch debouncing can be accomplished easily by any one of the techniques shown in Figure 5.17.

Specialized IC. Specialized quadrature decoder ICs have been developed by Texas Instruments, Inc., and Alps Electric Co., Ltd. The TI THCT2000 and the Alps 64H101 condition and decode the four quadrature input signals and count their transitions to produce parallel output data.

Figure 5.18 illustrates a simple mouse to host interface using the Alps decoder chip. U1 is the decoder chip; U2 is a standard bus buffer or parallel I/O interface chip. The quadrature inputs are interpreted and counted by U1. The outputs of the counters are presented to the bus buffer as four four-bit nibbles. The X/Y and select lines select the X and Y counter; the enable line gates the data to the buffer and then clears the counters.

Microcontroller within the Mouse. An inexpensive microcontroller is commonly used inside the mouse itself to interpret the quadrature and switch information. Figure 5.19 shows a simple circuit that generates serial data for a host computer. IC U1 is a common four bit microcontroller.

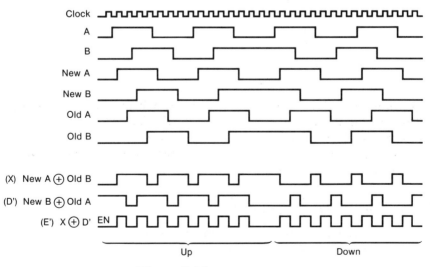

Figure 5.16. Timing Diagram.

SWITCH DE-BOUNCERS

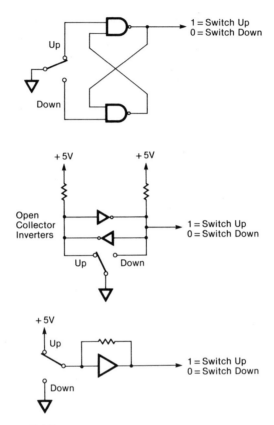

Figure 5.17. Schematic Diagram of Switch Debouncers.

Decoding and debouncing are done in firmware that is masked in the chip. The data out can be formatted as standard serial data with a start bit, seven or eight data bits, an optional parity bit, and one or two stop bits.

The host can read the data from the mouse through a standard serial port at TTL or RS-232 levels.

5.6.3 In Software (Serial Mice)

Though mice may transmit data in any one of several protocols, a simple software tracking algorithm can be used.

1. Read a byte.

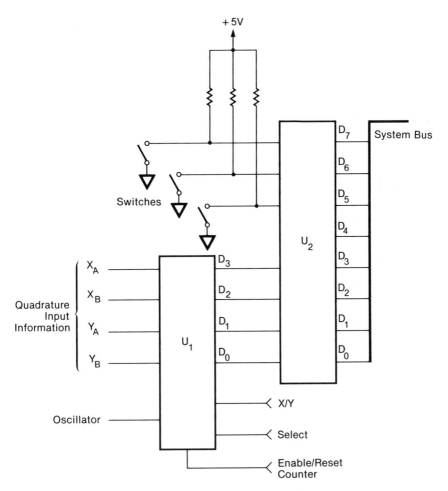

Figure 5.18. Schematic Diagram of Specialized IC Decoder.

2. If the upper bits match the sync byte information, then save the byte in a switch/status register. Otherwise go back to step 1.
3. Process the switch information bits if necessary.
4. Get the next byte and add its value to the variable that is accumulating horizontal movement. If the data represents absolute rather than relative motion, compare its value with the previous data and add its resulting signed value to the horizontal movement accumulator.
5. Get the next byte and add its value to the vertical movement accumulator. If the data represents absolute rather than relative motion, compare

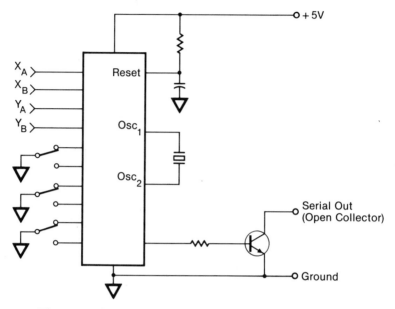

Figure 5.19. Schematic Diagram of Microcontroller Decoder.

its value with the previous data and add its resulting signed value to the vertical movement accumulator.

6. If the data format has more than three bytes, read and process the next two bytes. If not, go back to step 1.

After the proper number of bytes is transmitted, additional bytes may be sent before a sync byte appears. The tracking software should ignore spurious bytes until the reception of a valid sync byte.

Each data byte should be read using interrupts. Read a byte in the interrupt service routine, process it as appropriate, and set a counter to indicate which byte has been read, then return from interrupt. This will minimize the time that the host will be running with interrupts disabled. Other parts of the applications program or operating system that run for extended periods with interrupts disabled may cause mouse bytes to be lost.

5.7 Putting the Information to Work

5.7.1 The Software Interface

After the movement of a mouse has been transmitted to the host and represented as motion across a work surface, yet another interpretation is required: that of motion or position on a display screen.

The cursor's position on a screen is a specific case of a more general representation. An image of the application will be maintained in the memory of the host computer and will represent, within the constraints of the applications program, an arbitrary graphics image. This image will usually be larger than the screen is capable of displaying, so some means of viewing the image one screen size at a time must be available to the operator.

Viewing one screen at a time may be considered as looking at the larger image through a small window. Only a small portion of the image may be viewed at one time, but the window can be moved arbitrarily so that any portion of the image may be viewed at will.

Usually, the cursor's motion is kept centered within the window of interest, and the window will be moved across the image as necessary to follow the cursor's motion. The motion of the window can be controlled by maintaining pointers that define the beginning and ending addresses of the window.

Moving the window can be accomplished by changing its starting and ending addresses, or pointers.

5.7.2 Cursor/Pointer Motion on the Screen

The cursor's motion within the window will, of course, be related to the motion of the mouse across the work surface, but its position and velocity within the window can be made a function of the mouse's velocity and position as well as a function of its relative position within the window.

If the cursor is located in the central area of the window, its motion may be directly related to the mouse's motion. If it is near an edge of the window, it may move more slowly, while the background image moves past the window's aperture.

5.7.3 Scaling Factors

The scaling factor or sensitivity of the mouse can be adjusted by filtering or modifying its data input before it is translated into motion on the screen. Sensitivity is changed by multiplying or dividing the delta motion values by a constant before moving the cursor on the screen. Multiplying causes the cursor to move further relative to mouse motion; dividing causes the cursor to move less and gives the user finer control over its motion. Sensitivity can also be made nonlinear. For instance, rapid mouse motion could move the cursor a greater distance than slower motion.

A common algorithm for sensitivity doubles the cursor's motion relative to the mouse's motion if the mouse travels at a velocity that generates more than 64 transitions per second. In general, the appropriate scaling factor depends upon the application and the user's preference.

5.8 Applications

The pointing characteristics of mice can be applied to any number of applications, especially those where rapid and precise movement of a cursor across the screen image is required. Traditionally, cursor motion and menu selection have been accomplished through the use of cursor keys and the "RETURN" key. Repeated actuation of cursor or special function keys has been demonstrated by Card (1981) to be less accurate and more time-consuming than using a mouse for the same function.

The inherent human hand to eye coordination makes it possible to move a cursor and select menu items with a mouse very quickly, even though the hand must be moved from the keyboard to the mouse. A smooth intuitive hand motion with immediate feedback from the eye can move a cursor across the face of a screen faster and more accurately than repeated key strikes on cursor or special function keys.

5.9 The Next Generation

5.9.1 Human Factor Enhancements

The shape of the mouse will most likely change in order to fit a wider variety of hand shapes and sizes. None of the current rounded, squared, blended shapes fit all hands comfortably, so the next generation of mice will have a shape that will be developed from extensive human factor studies. The size may be slightly smaller than that of present mice, and the shape may be radically different.

Mice are most conveniently grasped between the thumb and little finger. The thumb provides force when moving the mouse toward the right (directions are reversed for the left-hander); the little finger when moving it toward the left. The little finger is not normally used to exert lateral pressure in either direction, so it quickly becomes fatigued when it is called upon to use a mouse for any length of time.

A mouse that uses the thumb and forefinger or middle finger for its lateral motion may be less fatiguing for the operator. The user's hand will most likely rest upon the mouse at an angle, with the thumb and forefinger providing the motion and with the ring, middle, and little fingers providing switch actuation.

The three lesser fingers are not as agile as the thumb and forefinger, but they could be very effective if the shape of the mouse placed them in a stress-free position where their only activity would be to press a button in the direction of their natural motion.

5.9.2 Mechanical Improvements

Mechanical improvements in mice will be most apparent in the area of usability. The shape of the mouse and its work surface requirements will change dramatically as its design and form factor are developed.

The shape will evolve into a less fatiguing design, as mentioned earlier. Left- and right-handed shapes may be necessary in order to improve the efficiency of the mouse for as many users as possible.

Optical mice will not require special pads or surfaces, but will be able to sense their motion from an arbitrary work surface. Mechanical mice will be able to respond to rapid movements and complex angular accelerations more accurately through the development of materials that have high friction coefficients and very low masses.

5.9.3 Electrical Improvements

As the development of the mouse progresses, its power requirements will diminish and its intelligence will be enhanced.

Reductions in power consumption will follow the development of low power CMOS ICs. Even though CMOS technology has produced ICs with very low power dissipation, the reduction of integrated circuit geometries through process improvements will further reduce power requirements so that a mouse could conceivably operate from the output of a solar cell mounted on its housing. Even though the operator's hand could obstruct the illumination of the photocell from time to time, the net amount of solar or ambient (incandescent or fluorescent) energy would be sufficient to power the mouse.

As the efficiency of solar cells and CMOS integrated circuits improves, the effectiveness of infrared and acoustic transducers will increase so that wires between the host computer and the mouse will not be required. Eliminating the cable that is required to power the mouse and receive its data will provide greater freedom (or lack of constraint) to the user.

ICs will become smaller and more efficient, as stated earlier. More importantly, ICs will be able to process greater amounts of information at much higher speeds than they are capable of today. The microprocessor within the mouse will be able to anticipate its motion and more accurately report not only where it is going but also where and when it is most likely to move or select an action or menu item.

5.10 The Future

Future mice and hand-held pointing devices will inevitably have three-dimensional pointing capability. The third axis of motion information will be extremely useful for CAD and CAE applications that present data in three-dimensional images. An operator will be able to draw and select quickly action items anywhere in the three-dimensional image space without having to return to the keyboard for special commands or multiple keystrokes.

Motion and distance sensing for a three-dimensional mouse could be accomplished with acoustic, optical, or electromagnetic means. The mouse would be lightweight to avoid fatigue and wireless so that it could be oriented in any position without interference from a cable.

References

Andrews, E. W. Trackball-Interfacing Techniques for Microprocessors. *Byte,* December 1983.

Card, S. K., English, W. K., and Burr, B. J. Evaluation of mouse, rate-controlled isometric joystick, step keys, and text keys for text selection of a CRT. Xerox Palo Alto Research Center, SSL-77-1, April 1977.

Embly, D. W., and Nagy, G. Behavioral aspects of text editors. *ACM Computing Surveys,* Volume 13, No. 1, March 1981.

English, W. K., Engelbart, D. C., and Berman, M. L. Display-selection techniques for text manipulation. *IEEE Transactions on Human Factors in Electronics,* Vol. HFE-8, Number 1, March 1967.

Goy, C. A. Mice. *Electronic Engineering Times,* April 1, 1985.

Kirsch, S. T. Six types of mice offer range of options for easy cursor control. *High Technology.* January 1984.

Lyon, R. F. The optical mouse, and an architectural methodology for smart digital sensors. Xerox Palo Alto Research Center, VLSI-81-1, August 1981.

Lyon, R. F., and Haeberli, M. P. Designing and Testing the Optical Mouse. *VLSI Design,* January/February 1982.

Mehr, M. H. Prediction of human operator performance in two dimensional tracking and positioning systems, 3rd International Conference on Ergonomics, Birmingham, England.

Mouse Systems Corporation. PC Mouse Reference Manual, 1985.

Teschler, L. Interfacing Mice to Computers. *Machine Design,* January 12, 1984.

6   Trackballs and Joysticks

DAVID DORAN

Weston Controls
Archbald, Pennsylvania

6.1 Introduction

This chapter describes three groups of controls that are very effective
devices for enabling human manipulation of graphic displays with a computer. From the human factors point of view, there is considerable difference in the performance of the various controls described here, especially
relating to physical and mental operating fatigue, accuracy, and speed of
operating performance. For a specific application, the optimum control
depends upon the task to be performed. Other controls mentioned here are
described in detail elsewhere in this book.

The controls discussed here are used to provide a very effective human
interface between the computer and the brain, through the use of the hands
and fingers, with the eyes providing the necessary feedback. The incredible
dexterity of a concert pianist establishes clearly how highly these faculties
can be developed in human beings. The typewriter keyboard is still used to
talk to the computer, but it is inept for cursor positioning or CAD/CAE
use. For example, in text computer applications, the up/down and left/
right arrows may be adequate for cursor positioning in word processing use
but in graphics applications, where many curves and lines must be drawn,
the keyboard needs to be supplemented by a joystick, mouse, touch pad,
touch screen, light pen, trackball, or other input device.

From an ergonomics point of view, these controls differ widely from one
another at the interface between the fingers and the control. For example,
there are almost as many different kinds of handles used as there are tasks
to be performed. Each individual handle design is made to enable the most
critical tasks to be performed quickly and accurately with minimum men-

tal and physical fatigue. Other differences include handle displacement, handle force, electronic curve shaping, scale factors, and, in the case of the trackball, the ball size and ball inertia.

The block diagram shown in Figure 6.1 points out the four basic sections of an ergonomically designed joystock or trackball. They are:

- Mechanical design in relation to the human hand
- Mechanical to electrical transducer
- "Ergonomic" circuits
- Output "interface" circuits

The internal "ergonomic" circuits and/or software have, by design, a marked human factors effect. The effects of these circuits are covered at the end of this chapter.

The "interface" circuits between the control and the computer make little ergonomic difference, unless the output signal is serialized. The electrical output circuits are only used to match the control to the computer. The circuit output and the software protocol must both match the system into which the control is working. When a serial output such as the RS-232 specification is required, the design technique will usually require temporary accumulation of data followed by batch transmission of this data periodically, at the accommodation of the computer. These transmissions cause computer interrupts each time they are received, and most computers have limited patience or time for too many interrupts. Data accumulation by the control greatly reduces these interrupts to a manageable level. When this technique is used, however, it can alter the human factors qualities adversely if design care does not take this into account. (This is also covered later in this chapter.) So, while the keyboard is the most commonly and frequently used device for computer entry, it needs to be supplemented by an ergonomically designed hand operated control with appropriate circuitry when serious computer graphics work is involved. Some very effective devices for doing this are discussed here. They are:

- Displacement joysticks
- Force joysticks

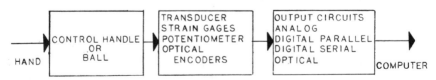

Figure 6.1 Typical data translations within a trackball or joystick from hand motion to computer signal.

- Combination force/displacement joysticks
- Trackballs

Some devices covered in other chapters are:

- Mice
- Light pens
- Page digitizers
- Touch screens
- Voice control
- Touch pads

6.2 Displacement Joysticks

Displacement joysticks most commonly have two degrees of freedom in a horizontal plane, which is referred to as an X and Y axis. The joystick handle may vary in size from a pencil-size handle operated with two or three fingertips, as shown in Figure 6.2, to a full-size grip, molded to fit the contours of a typical hand, as shown in Figure 6.3. Some fingertip handle designs are shown in Figure 6.4. The handle may be held in a rest position with springs (spring return) or held where positioned by friction. In the spring return case, it is important to insure that the spring design holds the joystick firmly and repeatably at null without backlash. Figure 6.5 shows a scissor and spring arrangement that accomplishes this. In some cases, it is

Figure 6.2 Finger tip X & Y force joystick.

Figure 6.3 Three axis grip type displacement joystick with trigger, bar and thumb switches.

desirable to provide an additional restraining force at null, such as a spring loaded ball and detent to cause the handle to be positioned and held at null more precisely.

The amount of spring return force, if used, is important. It depends mostly on the type of handle used. For the fingertip handle more commonly used for graphics work, two to three pounds is just about right. For

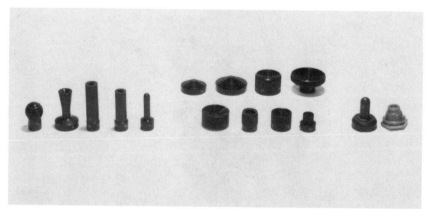

Figure 6.4 Some of the many different types of finger tip handles used to enhance ergonomic properties.

Figure 6.5 Illustration of the scissor and spring arrangement used to eliminate mechanical backlash at the null position.

hand-held grips, as illustrated in Figure 6.6, five to ten pounds is more common. The displacement is typically 6 to 30 degrees in either case, however. The mechanical motion in a displacement joystick is usually converted into an electrical signal by using potentiometers. This is because the ergonomically effective handle displacements couple mechanically to a rotary shaft very easily. Potentiometers are very reliable when properly selected and specified to meet the application. In addition, they are readily available in many types and sizes at reasonable cost. For joystick use, plastic film potentiometers are usually specified because:

- They have infinite resolution.
- Their specifications are well defined for:
  Dead band at null
  Full-scale symmetery on either side of null
  Linearity
  Torque
  Predictable life expectancy.

Figure 6.6 Three axis displacement grip with removable handle.

Almost any resistive value can be specified. If the joystick output is to be an analog voltage, this resistive value should be low enough to reduce noise and create low source impedances but not so low as to cause self heating in the potentiometer or require unnecessarily large power supply currents. One 1 K to 5 K ohms, powered by a commonly available five volt supply, is most often used for voltage outputs. When the joystick potentiometers are used as variable resistors in RC timing circuits, as in many computer games, the need for this value to be high is great enough to sacrifice noise immunity; about 100 K ohms is typical.

- Models are available commercially using:
  Switches
  Optical encoders
  LVDTs
  Photocell potentiometers
  Fiber optic techniques with no electronics in the control. (Electronics are, of course, required elsewhere before interfacing with a computer.)

Figure 6.7 shows a joystick that uses only four switches, mounted 0, 90, 180, and 270 degrees. The handle operates one or two switches at a time to indicate one of eight positions. This type of control is very often used with video games but not for graphic control because it does not have the

Figure 6.7 Finger tip X, Y joystick using switches.

resolution that graphics tasks require. Optical encoders and LVDTs can be used in place of potentiometers where the calculated life expectancy of the potentiometer would cause unacceptable life expectancy predictions. This is rare, however. Optical encoders have an extremely long mechanical life but the increase cost, additional circuitry, and reduced resolution make them difficult to justify. LVDTs have infinite resolution and long life but require additional mechanical parts, space, and circuitry. Fiber optic controls have been developed for critical environments such as military and critical industrial use, where immunity from all kinds of radiation is necessary.

An inherent design advantage that displacement joysticks have over force joysticks shows up when the joystick handle is pushed into the full upper right-hand corner position. The X and Y signals are not only equal to each other but are also equal to the individual full scale values that each axis would give if positioned to full scale separately. With force joysticks, however, the locus of all full force positions generates a circle, not a square, as with the displacement stick. Therefore, while force joysticks do generate equal full scale X and Y signals when positioned in the full northeast position, this signal will only be 0.707 times the individual full scale values. When necessary, a mechanical mask can be provided to give the same square full scale force pattern as the displacement joystick. With this mask, all full scale values are mechanically limited to 0.707 times their unmasked values.

Every graphics controller requires at least one pushbutton switch that can be assigned to such functions as cursor reset, target hook, window selection, execute, etc. These can be mounted on a panel near the joystick but may require the use of a second hand to operate. When only one switch is needed, a pushbutton switch is put on top of a displacement joystick.

A third axis is easily added to a displacement joystick by allowing the handle to rotate and causing this rotation to turn a third potentiometer as shown in Figure 6.8. A rotational twist clockwise or counterclockwise rotates the potentiometer off null, producing a Z axis signal. Here again, the handle on top of the joystick could either be spring loaded to rest at a 0/360 degree location with hands off or held where set by friction. This is very convenient, for example for "zoom" control on a television camera control or CAD/CAE display.

Grip controls with four axes are available for helicopter and aircraft use, where the grip is moved vertically up and down to provide the fourth axis. This is rarely found in graphic use. When grip handles are used, over five switches are frequently employed, as shown in Figure 6.3.

Figure 6.8 Third displacement axis added by placing a third potentiometer under the knob.

6.3 Force Operated Joysticks

The typical two axis force joystick responds to pressure on the joystick handle in the X and/or Y coordinates to generate two output signals. For proper tactile feel, the force joystick is designed to yield slightly to pressure. Like the displacement joystick, the force joystick has many different handles available for best ergonomic performance for a specific task. Anything from a small rod to a full-size grip is made. For graphics use, a smaller joystick such as the one shown in Figure 6.2, is more common. With this joystick, a $\frac{3}{8}$ inch diameter elastimer-covered handle is used. This gives just the right ergonomic feel for two finger control with a pleasantly soft feel that is not hard on the fingertips. Such a joystick is ideal for graphics use. With this size handle, a full scale force of two to three pounds is best for most graphics applications. Full scale grip handles are available with 5 to 20 pounds of force, but these are used for machine control or aircraft use.

Force joysticks, as described earlier, are also available with a third, or Z, axis. One way to implement this is to twist the handle clockwise or counterclockwise as with the displacement joystick. Performance measurements show that it is difficult for the fingers to twist a force joystick without also applying some unwanted force in the X or Y axis at the same time. This is commonly called *interaxis cross talk*. The amount of this interaxis cross talk can be objectionable in some applications. In these cases, it is better to have the third axis controlled separately with the thumb and middle finger on a lever that rotates a collar placed around the base of the joystick as shown in Figure 6.9.

Force is detected on the rod by means of piezoelectric semiconductor sensors bonded to the lower part of the rod. These are very cleverly bonded to the rod and wired in such a way that common mode effects, particularly from temperature and aging, are negligible, especially at null when no force is applied. A voltage source (5 to 12 volts or plus or minus 5 volts) is applied across this network as shown in Figure 6.10. With this arrangement, each axis is taken off the junction of two elements. This makes the signal voltage almost half the power supply voltage when no fingers are touching the control. There is a manufacturing skill required to maintain the resistance values equal at null, regardless of temperature and age. When force is applied to the joystick handle, it is translated to each of the two elements in an axis pair oppositely such that one element is under compression while the other is under tension, changing the voltage at the junction linearly with the applied force. The voltage repeatability for a given force is better than plus or minus 1 percent, which is much better than the plus or minus 10 percent noticeable ergonomically. Perhaps more important, however, is that the null drift is less than plus or minus 6

Figure 6.9 Third force type axis added with collar and thumb action.

percent over the life and ambient conditions around the joystick. This is well within the optimum dead zone (applied force changes around null that should be neglected), which is usually plus or minus 8 percent. This dead zone is easily established by subsequent circuitry or software and also masks any null drift. The net result of the joystick and the dead band portion of the circuitry must be such that no output is ever produced when no fingers are touching the joystick.

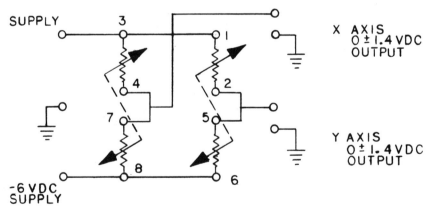

Figure 6.10 Typical schematic of strain gage connections in a force joystick.

The electrical output can be taken directly from the strain elements. In this case, the output signal will be two linear analog voltages, one for X and one for Y, proportional to the applied axial forces. A typical joystick, with 5 volts applied across it, will give full force outputs of 2.5 volts plus or minus 0.5 volts from a 200 ohm source impedance with linearity better than 1 percent. In this case, ergonomic circuits would have to be written into the computer and the host computer would have to accept analog inputs. As with the displacement joystick, it is more common for the joystick to include the ergonomic and interface circuitry suitable for RS-232c computer inputs. While this circuitry will fit into the joystick shown previously in Figure 6.3, a larger package is desirable from a human factors point of view, as illustrated in Figure 6.11. This console package firmly holds the joystick on the table and provides the right sloping surface on which to rest the heel of the hand.

An important part of the overall human factors behavior of a control is the ergonomic circuitry and/or software that is added. This may be located within the control housing or in the computer. If these circuits and/or software are located in the computer, then the output from a joystick can be taken directly from the potentiometers or other sensors providing, of course, that the computer is equipped to accept analog circuits. Most computers prefer to receive serial RS-232c signals. For reasons covered later in this chapter, it is better to have the ergonomic circuitry precede a serial communications link, which means that the joystick would have to contain both the ergonomic circuits and the RS-232c circuits. Fortunately,

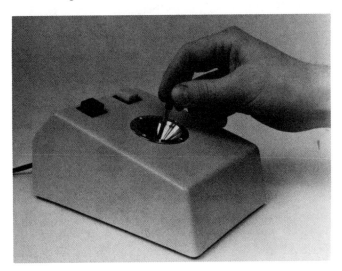

Figure 6.11 Table top mounting for displacement joystick.

with the advent of microprocessors, it is easily possible to get all the circuitry needed into a joystick with little, if any, extra space requirement. This makes the joystick ergonomically independent of the computer.

6.4 Trackballs

Trackballs are very effective for rapidly moving a cursor from one point to another on a large display such as a radar or graphics screen. Trackballs vary in size from a thumb operated marble-size trackball up to a 3.5 inch diameter billiard ball. A three inch trackball mounted in its own housing is shown in Figure 6.12. Trackballs are mounted either into a horizontal surface such as a desk or keyboard, or built into their own module. They can also be mounted into a hand-held paddle for thumb operation. A combination trackball and mouse has been made where a trackball is turned upside down and used as a mouse.

The trackball has an advantage over a mouse in that it takes a fixed amount of space and can be slewed or spun very fast to move the cursor large distances. The mouse, on the other hand, can be moved continuously without stopping the cursor. In most applications, both devices work better if the ergonomic circuitry is nonlinear. This is because, at low ball or mouse speeds, a low pulse count per ball revolution allows very precise cursor control, and at faster ball speeds, a higher pulse count per ball

Figure 6.12 Three inch trackball.

revolution will move the cursor faster over large screens. This calls for a low pulse count at low ball speeds and a high pulse count at high ball speeds. A curve approaching an exponential works best. It can be generated by using several straight lines positioned to simulate an exponential curve, which may be easier to do if the circuitry is analog. The results are dramatic, especially when the trackball is used for cursor positioning over large screens such as air traffic control radar screens. In this application, fine resolution is needed when the cursor is near the target and must be positioned right on top of it for target "hooking." However, a high count rate is then needed to move the cursor near the next target. Here the nonlinear or variable rate trackball is well applied. Note, however, that the variable rate ergonomic circuitry and/or software is much more easily accomplished if it is applied before any serial data encoding. This means that it should be provided before an RS-232c or RS-422 serial data communications link is used. With the mouse, the main advantage of a nonlinear curve is that the mouse takes much less table space to do a good job. With variable rate, only two to three inches of table space is needed. The mouse has been rejected for many applications where it really belongs because it did not have variable rate and therefore took too much table space.

6.5 Ergonomic Circuitry and/or Software

The ergonomic behavior of a control is not only determined by its mechanical or physical properties but also by its circuitry and, if a microprocessor is used, software. If the ergonomic circuitry is to be included with the control, as is usually the best arrangement, then minimizing the amount of space taken up by these circuits is a top design priority.

Force and displacement joysticks are unique because they can be designed to generate either position data or rate data. With positional data output, the output signal is proportional to the force or displacement of the joystick handle. For example, in cursor positioning, a full scale handle deflection to the right would position the cursor to the full easterly part of the CRT as fast as the fingers can move the joystick. This works well where the target is moving very slowly or is stationary and finger positioning resolution of the joystick handle is accurate enough to match the cursor positioning task requirements. Usually, this is not the case. Most positioning tasks require a CRT screen resolution of 0.01 inches or better, which means a CRT precision of 1 part per 1000. A practical joystick handle operates over a plus or minus 30 degree arc. While the resolution of the sensors in the joystick may even be infinite, finger positioning to one part in 1000 is tedious if not impossible. Another disadvantage is that all of the subsequent circuitry must have a 1000 to 1 resolution. For parallel digital outputs, this would require ten bits or better for analog to digital converters, counters, adders, digital to analog converters, and, in the current world of 8, 16, and 32 bits, would be a misfit. With eight bit microprocessors, the extra two bits would spill over into a second port or require multiplexing. Higher bit micros would require more space. Also, if the data must be serialized with RS-232c eight bit words, then more words and host computer interupts are needed.

On the other hand, with rate data output the cursor velocity is controlled by the hand operation of the joystick, which is similar to driving a car. The foot pedal controls the velocity of the vehicle, not its position. While it would be nice to set the accelerator to where you want to go instead of how fast, the idea brings in too many unsolved problems. The eye now becomes a vital part of the control system to provide the needed feedback and this method of positioning the cursor becomes a closed loop servo system with the brain at the center. Since the control is now only providing second-order corrections, the control resolution is not as critical. Speed and accuracy are greatly improved and fatigue is reduced substantially.

An advantage that joysticks share with trackballs and mice is that the curve of output signal versus hand action can be made to be any shape that best suits the application. Fortunately, nature having its propensity for linear, sinusoidal, or logarithmic relationships, the variety of choices that must be considered and evaluated is manageable. In this case, it boils down to linear or exponential (logarithmic).

Since most sensors used in joysticks are linear, the linear output is the easiest to generate and sometimes the best. A criteria for deciding this is to see or estimate how often the control must be pushed to the stops in order to perform the task at hand. If rarely, then a linear control will be the easier to adjust to and the least fatiguing. On the other hand, if it turns out that a linear control, properly scaled to get the proper resolution at the low end, would be pushing the full scale limits much of time, then an exponential response will solve this dichotomy very nicely. As mentioned earlier, the exponential response also overcomes the major objection to the mouse, which is that the mouse, without it, always seems to require more table space than is allowed for it. With an exponential control the mouse is fully effective using only three to four inches of table space. The joysticks described previously in this chapter also use exponential response curves when generating pulse rates.

In practice, a curve made up of two to four straight lines that simulate an exponential curve can be used and may be easier to design with available hardware and/or software. The first or lowest slope, which may not start exactly at the origin, should be scaled for optimum performance when moving a cursor at slow speed where accurate positioning is required. The sharper slopes should not be noticeable in this region. At higher cursor speeds used to move the cursor to a distant location, the sharper slopes should come into play. The user acclimates surprisingly quickly to a particular curve to the extent that, in a few minutes, he can jump very close to a remote target with one motion of the control.

With a joystick that generates pulse rates, an exponential curve that starts at the origin should not be used, from a human factors point of view, because the point at which pulses begin would not be defined well enough. The curve coming off the origin would be too flat to be useful. For example, a very slight force or displacement could produce a pulse rate of one pulse per minute, which would be too slow for any application. The exponential curve should be modified at the low end to create a dead zone threshold with a predetermined initial pulse rate when this threshold is exceeded. Further, the first pulse must start immediately when the threshold is exceeded with no pulse rate time delay. In almost every application, the most comfortable dead zone is around plus or minus 8 percent of the full force for displacement pulse rate with an initial pulse rate of two to five pulses per second.

6.6 Output Circuitry

The output circuitry of a control should be designed to match the computer it feeds without altering the ergonomics that have been designed into the control. This is not a problem except possibly with serially encoded output signals such as RS-232c. Typical of these are:

- Analog primary signals directly off the sensor
  Displacement joystick potentiometer output
  Force joystick piezoelectric output
  LVDT or magnetic sensor output
  Optical output

- Incremental encoder quadrature output
- Pulse output
  Up pulse/down pulse (two wire)
  Pulse and direction level (two wire)
  Pulse plus up level plus down level (three wire)

Serial outputs are frequently called RS-232c whether or not they really are. Among other things, the RS-232 standard specifies:

- Connector type (25 pin dp)

- Connector pin functional assignments for each of the twenty five pins
- Mark and space voltage output levels (plus or minus 5 to 12 volts)
- Pulse rise and fall times
- Load and source impedance
- Synchronizing parameters (start and stop pulses)
- Word length (eight bits)
- Bit pulse repetition rate (baud rate)

When this specification is fully complied with, it does not mean that any RS-232 device will work properly when plugged into any RS-232 computer terminal socket. It does at least mean, however, that neither device will damage the other when connected and powered up. Be aware that the hand controls used for computer graphics that claim RS-232 compliance may require that power supply voltages from the host computer be provided through reassigned connector pins that do not meet the RS-232 pin assignments. Permanent damage can occur if, for example, the plus 12 volt supply from the computer is connected to a connector pin that the control was expecting to get five volts on. Even if the control has its own power supplies, an RS-232 control may work in one computer and not another. This is because the protocol of the control must match the protocol of the computer both in basic setup and in word encoding. The basic setup of a computer can usually be easily changed with the computer's keyboard. This pertains to such things as baud rate, number of stop pulses, and parity. The word encoding requires that a program be written for the computer that will decode the controller's code and direct the computers cursor movements according to commands required by the computer used. (The computer would require a software "driver" for this control.) This means that, if a control is to be added to an existing computer, a software installation disk will probably be provided as part of the purchased package and will have to be used at least once to modify the computer's initiation. There are many different combinations of word encoding or protocol. A particular protocol may be developed to transfer the required data with a minimum number of computer interrupts. Another protocol may be required to transfer larger numbers than can be handled by an eight bit binary word; the design of that protocol is based on a different criteria or priority. As an example, a trackball that is used for X, Y cursor positioning will be required to transfer X and Y ball rotation values as the ball is rotated. A typical trackball has an X and Y optical incremental encoder that generates a pulse for every 0.030 inch ball movement in the given axis. For slow ball motions, the resulting encoder pulse rate of under ten pulses per second would not cause too many interrupts on the computer to matter, even if a word was sent for every encoder pulse. For fast ball rotations, however, the encoder pulse rate could easily be over

2400 counts per second. Interrupts coming at that rate will upset most computers. This rate is much faster than the computer needs to adequately update the position of the cursor on the CRT. With the persistence of CRT phosphors and the response of the human eye, it is not necessary to update a CRT more than one hundred times a second. Furthermore, most computers are much too busy to handle that high an interrupt rate. The RS-232 word encoding that transfers the required data with the fewest computer interrupts would be one that sends data no more often than one hundred times a second. To handle these higher pulse rates, the control can accumulate the pulses in a counter or microprocessor register and then send the accumulated value at one hundred times per second. In this case, a counter or register would have to handle numbers up to plus or minus 30. A six bit binary word in complimentary two's compliment can handle plus or minus 32. Fortunately, this fits well within the eight bits per word limitation of RS-232. It means that only one word is required per trackball axis and, since the two most significant bits are not needed for data, either one or both can be used to identify the axis that each number represents, providing the most significant bit is not used as a parity bit. Parity, in this case, is either not used or is added in a ninth bit.

Typical word encoding for this case would be as follows:

> One start bit: required for RS-232 synchronization
> Word bits one through seven: data number
> Word bit eight (identification bit): $0 = X$, $1 = Y$
> One stop bit: required for RS-232 synchronization

This requires only two computer interrupts per 32 pulses, one for the X word and one for the Y word. A driver must then be software installed to tell the computer how it is to process this data.

If a third word for a Z axis and a fourth word for switch information is to be added, the encoding might be as follows:

> One start bit:
> Word bits one through 6: data number
> Word bits seven and eightW: word identification
> $$0,0 = X$$
> $$0,1 = Y$$
> $$1,0 = Z$$
> $$1,1 = \text{Switches}$$

When more than 8 bits are required for data the formate might look as follows:

First word: Device identification

Second and third words: X data
Fourth and fifth words: Y data
Sometimes switch data is included in the first word along with device identification. There could even be an extra word at the end as a sign-off statement.

Devices with bidirectional information are also available but they are not as common. In this case, the host computer might set up the baud rate, parity, stop bits, and even the format it wants from the control. All of the above formats require the same hardware. Only the software is changed.

6.7 Advances in Trackballs

Recent advances in trackballs have concentrated on cost reduction and volume production. This has been brought on by the demand created for them by computer CAD/CAM systems and games. As a result, performance, size reduction, and circuit output options have been neglected. However, major advances have been made in the optical and electrical components that have become available for trackball use. Encoders, using these components, can now be made smaller, better, longer lasting and less expensive. This is due primarily to the development of photoelectric devices with advanced circuitry built right into the photocell. These can be made in sealed servo mount military housings or in open construction where the code wheel is visible. The space saved by packing the encoder circuitry into the photocell will be taken up by microcontroller circuits with the variable rate software described earlier and serial RS-232 output signal format. Included with the RS-232 software will be more "handshake" conversation between the trackball and the computer that it serves. This feature will allow the computer to tell the trackball what baud rate and serial protocol it wants. The advent of low current electronics now makes battery operated trackballs with radio links to the computer practical.

Advancements in displacement joysticks for computer and game use will be primarily in cost reduction such that they can be incorporated in every keyboard and control panel. More and more, these products will have standard RS-232 connectors and serial data outputs. On the other hand, the highly human factored, fingertip force joysticks will still be the first choice where precise or fatiguing work is required, such as laser beam positioning or air traffic control work. With both joysticks there will be more attention paid to the ergonomic coordination of the joystick and the related pushbutton functions used with them.

The most significant technical advances in joysticks and trackballs are now being brought about by new military requirements for controls that will be immune from nuclear blast and other electromagnetic countermeasures that can nullify electronic circuits. To meet this requirement, optics will replace electronics, at least in the controls themselves. This means that optical motion transducers will replace electronic rotary and linear encoders, and fiber optic light pipes will replace interface wire cables. In addition, techniques are being refined for digitally multiplexing the light data so that one fiber cable can handle all data transfers. Optical encoders are already available where LEDs and photocells are replaced by input and output light pipes. One technique for optically multiplexing that has already been tried uses an optical delay line method. With this method, monochromatic laser beam light is beamed down a fiber optic cable from a computer to a control. The control takes some of the initial light received for the most significant bit in the encoder. The rest of the light is passed through a coil of fiber cable, which time delays it by a precise amount; some of this light is used for the next most significant encoder bit. Unfortunately, each delay also reduces the light intensity each time it delays the light. This is repeated until the required number of bits is obtained. A disadvantage of this method for joystick use is the size of the optical delay coils. It takes a lot of fiber to slow light down far enough to reliably detect. Practical delays require large coils with a lot of light attenuation. Another technique that shows promise uses wavelength or color multiplexing. Here, white light is passed down a fiber light pipe to the control. At the control, the light is split up into different color bands — as many as there are bits of resolution required by the encoder. This can be done by band pass filters or a prism, for example. The encoded light color bits are returned back through the same fiber cable that the white light used. Back at the computer, the data light bits must be separated again for detection. This method could be less costly and even better than the current electronic approach when a multiwavelength laser diode light source is available at reasonable cost and size.

References

Comerford, R. (1984). "Pointing Device Innovations Enhance User/Machine Interfaces," *EDN,* July 26, 54–66.

Cook, M, (1985). *Micro User* 2 118–121.

Cornwell, P. J., (1984). *Electron. Prod. Des.* 5 71–73.

Foley, J. D., and van Dam, A. (1982). *Fundamentals of Interactive Computer Graphics.* Reading, MA: Addison-Wesley Publishing Co.

Hutzel, I., and Peters, C. (1985). "The current state of the art in users interfaces," *Systems and Software,* March, 131–140.

Martindale, D., (1984). *Proceedings of Graphics Interface 1984.*

Mehr, M. H., (1982). "Manual Control Design for Automated Systems," *Proceedings 1st Annual Control Engineering Conference.*

Mehr, M. H., (1983), "Manual Control of the Line of Sight in Optical Systems," *Proc. SPIE,* **389,** Jan.

Mehr, M. H., and Mehr, E. (1972). "Manual Digital Positioning in Two Axes: A Comparison of Joy Stick and Trackball Controls," *Proceedings of the Human Factors Society 16th Annual Meeting* (pp. 110–116). Santa Monica, CA: Human Factors Society.

Mims, F. M., III. (1984). "A Few Quick Pointers." *Computers and Electronics,* May, 64–117.

Rubinstein, R., and Hersh, H. M. (1984). *The Human Factor: Designing Computer Systems for People.* Burlington, MA: Digital Press.

Ritchi, G. J., and Turner, J. A. (1975). "Input Devices for Interactive Graphics," *International Journal of Man-Machine Studies,* 7 639–660.

Scott, J. E., (1982) *Introduction to Interactive Computer Graphics.* New York: Wiley.

Sherr, S., (1979) *Electronic Displays.* New York: Wiley.

7 Voice Input Systems

S. S. VIGLIONE

Interstate Voice Products
Orange, California

7.1 Introduction

Although technology has produced some spectacular aids to human communication, nothing can replace or equal speech. It is the most familiar
and most convenient way for humans to communicate. In the past, man
has been required to interact with machines in the language of those
machines. With speech recognition and speech response systems, man can
communicate with machines using natural-language human terminology.
The use of voice processing systems for voice input and output provides a
degree of freedom for mobility, alternate modalities for command and data
communication, and the possibility of substantial reduction in training
time to learn to interface with complex systems. These salient characteristics of speech, when incorporated into an effective voice control or voice
data entry system, yield positive advantages to complement and supple-
ment other methods of man–machine interaction. A major goal of automated speech recognition is to use this natural means of communication to
achieve direct human interaction with computers.

The commercial applications of automated speech recognition began in
the early 1970s. Since that time, many advances have been made in the
development of more powerful algorithms for speech analysis and classification, the extraction of word features to permit improved performance in
discrete and connected utterance recognition, and in the reduction of the
cost of the hardware required to implement these speech processing
methods. The latter has been most notable and has permitted board-level
solutions to larger sizes of recognition vocabularies with an order of magnitude reduction in costs. Projections lead us to still further reduction in

costs of the implementation function, with improving performance and expanded capabilities as the speech recognition products evolve into their second generation. This chapter analyzes the requirements and describes implementations by means of a few representative systems.

7.2 The Characteristics of Speech

Speech is communicated by creating rapid fluctuation in air pressure. When we speak, we create acoustic waves that are transmited by the air medium as longitudinal waves alternately compressed and expanded as a function of the modulation imposed by the vocal generation apparatus. The vocal organs include the lungs, the larynx, and the vocal tract. The larynx contains the vocal cords. The vocal tract is terminated at one end by the vocal cords and at the other by the lips. It includes the throat (pharynx) and oral and nasal cavities. The shape of the vocal tract can be changed by movement of the articulators (lips, teeth, and tongue) in the oral cavity. It can also be modified by the position of the soft palate (vellum) as it cuts off or adds the nasal cavity.

Sound is generated in the vocal system by modifying the stream of air that is emitted from the lungs as we exhale air through the larynx. The vocal cords act like a vibrating reed at the top of the larynx. The built-up air pressure either forces the vocal cords apart, causing them to vibrate, or passes through the opening (glottis) and is acted upon directly by the vocal tract. The frequency of vibrations in the vocal tract can be varied during the speech generation process and is known as the pitch period. Voiced sounds (vowels) are produced when these vocal cords vibrate, setting up quasiperiodic pulses that excite the vocal tract, causing it to be resonate. These resonances are called formants, or the formant frequencies. Fricative sounds (for example, s, h) are generated by forming constrictions along the vocal tract. Air passing over these constrictions becomes turbulent, causing the hissing sound, or frication. Plosive sounds (for example, p, t) are produced by making a complete closure of the vocal tract, building up pressure behind it, then abruptly releasing the built-up air supply. These three methods of sound production are modulated and combined in various ways by the vocal system to produce the acoustic speech waveform. The task of the speech processing system is to capture this acoustic wave; analyze its spectral, time, and amplitude characteristics; and relate these to words and speech features for speech recognition.

7.2.1 Speech Recognition System Design Considerations

Most information for word recognition is contained in the first three to four formant frequencies. This information lies in the spectral band between 250 and 3600 KHz, with variation caused by the shape of the vocal tract, sex and age of the speaker. The plosive sounds can be detected by analyzing the energy levels in the acoustic wave, while the fricative sounds are most discernible by noting the low energy but primarily high frequency (above 3 to 4 KHz) spectral activity.

Numerous methods are available for analyzing or modeling this speech information. Most often, spectrum analyzers constitute the front end processors.

Figure 7.1 shows a basic block diagram for a speech recognition system. The microphone is the key to capturing the acoustic wave and converting it to electrical energy for subsequent processing. Microphone response characteristics should include the ability to reproduce, with fidelity, the frequency and amplitude characteristics of the low energy speech waveform. Sound pressure variations of a factor of 100 or more occur in a single word containing both vowel and fricative sounds. Similarly, a factor of 100 or more can occur between whispered speech and normal conversation. Mi-

FUNCTIONAL BLOCK DIAGRAM

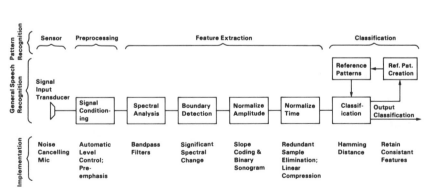

Figure 7.1. Speech Recognition System Functional Block Diagram.

crophone designs must accommodate this range of variability. The spectral response characteristics of the microphone again need to be considered to respond with fidelity to the frequency characteristic of the speech sound. A flat frequency response from 100 Hz to 6–8 KHz is minimal for capturing all the subleties of the speech signal. Noise rejection and directionality are also desirable microphone design features to improve the speech signal to noise ratio.

The preamplifier at the input stage of the speech recognizer is a broad band, high gain amplifier that boosts the microphone output to a signal level more suitable for the subsequent spectrum analysis. The pre-emphasis filter compensates for the signal level variability between the higher energy, low formant frequencies (first and second) and the lower energy, high formant frequencies. There can be as much as 40 to 50 decibels difference in intensity, but the information content in the higher frequencies is mandatory for good recognition accuracy. The spectrum analyzer provides a sampled spectrum of the amplified speech sounds. The sampling period is made pitch synchronous or sampled frequently enough to detect the modulation caused by the variations of the vocal tract. Sampling periods of 5 to 20 ms are used to adequately sample the signal. A line spectrum of 16 to 24 spectral lines, logarithmically spaced between 200 and 4000 Hz, provides adequate spectral representation, with two or three broad band filters to capture the energy levels in the bands from 3000 Hz to 7–10 KHz. This sampled spectra forms the input to the speech recognition algorithm. A variety of methods are used to code, compress, and classify this spectral information and relate it to the word or speech to be recognized.

7.3 Speech Recognizers

The basic operational modes of a speech recognizer are either speaker dependent or speaker independent. A speaker dependent system requires that an individual user adapt or train the system to his or her way of speaking. This provides a high degree of accuracy for an individual user. In a speaker independent system, the device must recognize any user with little or no prior knowledge of their speaking characteristics—a noteworthy but difficult task.

A second categorization of the recognizer is whether it is a discrete or continuous word recognition system. Discrete word recognition refers to the identification of words or phrases uttered as isolated entities with a perceptible pause between successive words. Dealing with discrete utterances provides the distinct advantage of well-delineated word boundaries for performing analysis and comparison with word pattern prototypes. Continuous speech recognition must deal with ill-defined word onset and cessations as well as coarticulation effects, which change the characteristics of the word features.

Most speech input devices currently available are trainable (i.e., speaker dependent) discrete word recognizers. They are offered in a variety of forms ranging from plug-in cards for various personal computers, to standalone peripheral devices with communication protocols including serial ASCII and parallel binary, to chip sets for custom design. These systems are characterized by vocabularies of 100 to 500 words. They come with on-board editors or software programs running with the PC or host computer operating system to permit generation of the vocabulary to be recognized, training and establishing the user vocabulary reference file, and performing the recognition and output command generation when in the operational mode.[1]

A limited number of systems are available to do speaker dependent continuous speech recognition. They are characterized by 50 to 100 word vocabularies and firmware or software for the supporting functions noted earlier. In addition, a few devices are available for speaker independent discrete word recognition. Their vocabulary size is 10 to 20 words, and performance is degraded from the speaker dependent systems.[2]

To characterize these different categories of speech recognizers, typical products will be presented. These include: 1) a standalone peripheral with on-board editor and a 200 word vocabulary of user specific discrete utterances; 2) a plug-in board for the IBM PC with on-board RAM and processor to permit up to 240 word input and emulating the keyboard without using the PC processor or memory; 3) speech peripheral capable of continuous speaker dependent speech recognition; and 4) a chip set capable of 200 word discrete utterance recognition for custom design applications.

A number of human factors issues are alluded to in the specifications of these speech input devices. The vocabulary size, the need for training, and the ease of system integration into an application are frequently a function of the task to be accomplished by end-users, their training, and their motivation. Proper microphone and microphone use may mean the difference between acceptable recognition performance and complete dissatisfaction with the speech recognizer. Providing an interactive scenario, with measurable end results related to the task to be accomplished, can readily overcome minor recognition system performance limitations.[3] In using the speech input devices in specific applications, these issues are addressed in the system integration phase. Applications can illustrate not only how the system can ease the data entry task, but also provide cost beneficial solu-

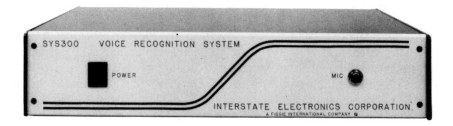

Figure 7.2a. SYS300 Front View.

tions to end-user problems. This chapter is not meant to address the host of potential applications for voice recognition, nor to demonstrate their utility in actual operation. For that information, the "Proceedings of the Annual Voice I/O System Application Conference" and the "Proceedings of Speech Technology Conference" are recommended.

7.3.1 A Standalone Speech Input Peripheral (SYS300)

The System 300 speech recognizer shown in Figures 7.2 and 7.3 is a speaker dependent discrete word recognizer, one that requires each speaker to provide it with a sample of how that speaker says each item in the vocabulary. This sample is saved by the recognizer as a reference pattern. The task of generating this sample is referred to as training the system, or enrollment. When training the system, the speaker is required to repeat the vocabulary one or more times. Each time that the vocabulary is repeated, it

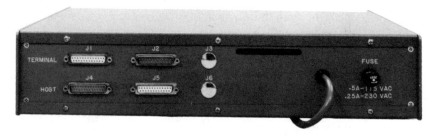

Figure 7.2b. SYS300 Rear View.

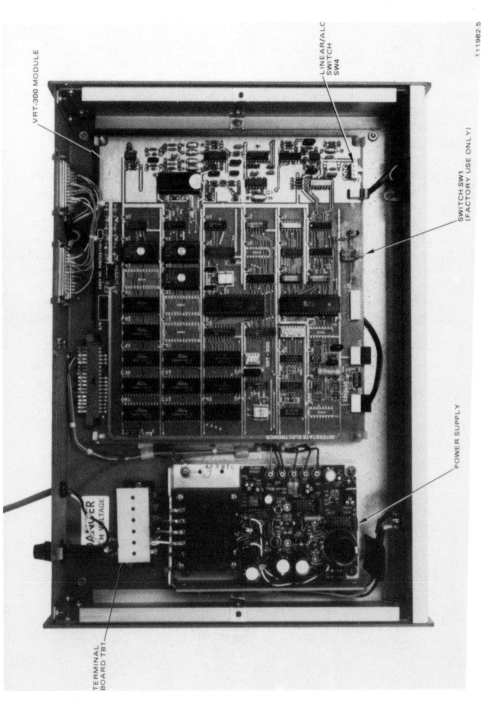

VRT-300 MODULE

LINEAR/ALC
SWITCH
SW4

SWITCH SW1
(FACTORY USE ONLY)

POWER SUPPLY

TERMINAL
BOARD TB1

111982-5

Figure 7.3. SYS300 Internal View.

is referred to as one training pass. Typically, three to five training passes are required to produce an optimum set of reference patterns. Ideally, once a reference pattern set has been generated, it is stored in a host computer, thus allowing the operator to download the information each time a different operator signs on the system.

Discrete word recognition systems, as mentioned, are those that require a pause between each vocabulary item. This does not mean that each vocabulary item or utterance must be a single word. An utterance may consist of several words such as "voice actuated terminal," as long as the words are spoken with little or no pause between each word and the total time for the utterance is 1.25 seconds or less.

A functional block diagram of the SYS300 is shown in Figure 7.4. Speech input from the microphone is amplified, then spectrum equalization is performed to compensate for the high frequency speech signal roll-off. This signal is then coupled through a 16-channel spectrum analyzer and converted to a digital representation of the spoken input. This digitized data is converted to a fixed size pattern that preserves the information-carrying content of the spoken inputs while discarding redundant features.

During the training process, these patterns are used to define templates for each utterance. The templates are used in the recognition process for

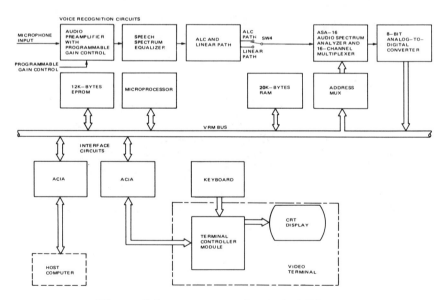

Figure 7.4. SYS300 Functional Block Diagram.

comparison with the digitized representation of incoming spoken words. The vocabulary template is stored in the voice board's on-board random access memory (RAM), while the processing algorithms are contained in the on-board read only memory (ROM), operating in conjunction with the on-board microprocessor.

When an utterance is recognized, a user-defined ASCII string is routed to either the terminal, host computer, or both. The SYS300 receives all keyboard inputs and examines them. Those inputs that are to be passed to the host are sent unchanged to the host computer. Those signals intended for the SYS300 speech module are processed by the on-board microprocessor. Likewise, all characters from the host computers are examined and those that are intended for the SYS300 module are processed; the other signals are passed on to the video terminal. All data transferred to and from the SYS300 module are ASCII coded.

The SYS300 operates in two modes: 1) a terminal mode and 2) a maintenance mode. The terminal (or host) mode is the standard operational mode. Alternately, the terminal mode can be entered from the maintenance mode by typing an (ESCAPE) sequence on the video terminal keyboard. In the terminal mode, the SYS300 module acts as a standard terminal, routing character data to and from the host computer. The host computer can also command the speech system to perform tasks such as reference pattern upload and download, vocabulary partitioning, and parameter modification. All recognized utterances result in user-programmable ASCII strings being routed to the host computer. If an utterance is not recognized, an audible alarm will sound and nothing will be routed to the host computer. The maintenance mode is used for setup and training of vocabularies, testing of reference patterns and vocabularies, and stand-alone demonstrations.

Voice Recognition Circuits.   The recognition circuits consist of analog circuitry for speech spectrum analysis and recognition processor circuitry for reference pattern storage and comparison. The incoming utterance is converted to a digital form and compared to a reference pattern initially obtained by training the SYS300. If an acceptable comparison is made, an appropriate ASCII coded output is sent to the host computer.

The utterance captured by the input microphone is first fed to a preamplifier. The preamplifier output is then fed to the speech spectrum equalizer, whose gain increases with input frequency. The equalizer compensates for the roll-off in speech frequencies above 750 Hz. The equalized signal is then fed to the automatic level control (ALC) and linear path circuitry, which provides a means for controlling signal variations due to microphone location and speaking effort, and allows the use of micro-phones of varying sensitivities.

The input speech path, either linear or ALC, is switch selectable and is then applied to the common inputs of 16 bandpass filters that make up a 16 channel spectrum analyzer. This custom VLSI spectrum analyzer chip separates the speech spectrum (200 Hz to 7 KHz) into 16 adjacent fre-quency bands, and rectifies and low-pass filters each band. This chip is connected to an 8 bit analog to digital (A-D) converter. Each of the 16 channel spectrum analyzer outputs is scanned in sequence and digitized by the A-D converter to eight bits. The resultant samples of spectral data are output to the microprocessor bus. Sampling and analog to digital conver-sions are accomplished for all 16 channels every five milliseconds under microprocessor and real time clock control. The recognition processor circuitry consists of a microprocessor, 20K byte RAM and 12K byte erasable programmable read only memory (EPROM). The microprocessor processes the digitized spectral data from the bus and compares it with utterance templates stored in the RAM. The processing algorithms are stored in the EPROM. If the digitized spectral data agrees with a stored template, an appropriate output is obtained from the microprocessor and placed on the bus for use by the interface circuits.

The interface circuits consist of two asymchronous communication interface adaptors (ACIAs). One ACIA interfaces through a communica-tion cable to the video terminal controller module. The other ACIA inter-faces to the host computer. The signals processed by each ACIA are identified in Figure 7.5. The system is activated by ensuring that the terminal and SYS300 are interconnected and properly powered. The ter-minal will perform exactly as a standard terminal that has not been modi-fied. A download can now be executed to load the SYS300 RAM with the vocabulary and reference patterns stored at the host, or the maintenance mode can be entered to build and train a new vocabulary.

The maintenance mode is used to build, test, and modify vocabularies, and to train reference patterns. It includes commands for editing vocabu-laries, reference pattern training and update, vocabulary and reference pattern testing, system demonstration, and diagnostics. In this mode, var-ious checks are made on the validity of data and commands, and appropri-ate error messages are displayed when necessary. The vocabularies contain the words to be used by the operator in entering data or executing com-mands. A second string is appended to the vocabulary words, which are the equivalent ASCII characters to be sent to the host computer as a result of recognition of that vocabulary utterance.

The SYS300 also supports a sophisticated host mode command proto-col, which allows the user to take advantage of many features not available

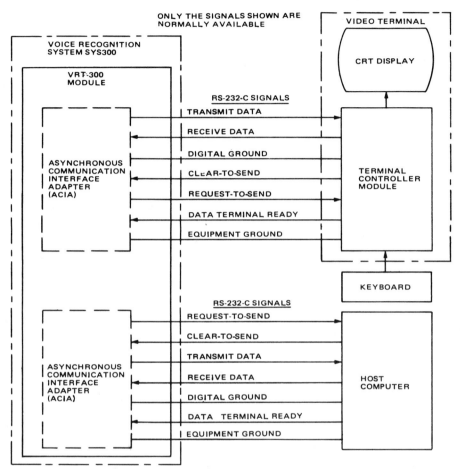

Figure 7.5. SYS300 Interface Diagram.

through the use of the standard maintenance mode operation. However, in order to make use of these features, it is necessary to generate appropriate software to execute on the host computer.

All information flow between the host processor and the SYS300, regardless of direction, is in the form of ASCII characters. These commands adhere to the following general format:

FRAMING CHARACTER, n, CHARACTER STRING, TERMINATOR

where:

FRAMING CHARACTER = ASCII control character, either a default character (STX) or one specified by the user.

n = command identifier, "1, 2, 3, 4, 6, 7, 9, A, B through H, J through N, and P through W," indicating host command or a SYS300 response to the command

CHARACTER STRING = control parameters or text

TERMINATOR = message/command terminator in the form of a carriage return (CR) or a carriage return/line feed.

The host mode commands include training and update commands to establish and modify the user voice template; parameter control commands, reference pattern upload and download commands; several recognition commands to execute self-test; and commands to modify the communication protocol.

Once the vocabulary and the reference patterns are generated and stored in the on-board RAM, the system can be used with the user-supplied application program. Commands and data can be entered either by keyboard or by voice to operate the program.

7.3.2 A Plug-in Voice Recognition Board for the IBM PC (CSRB)

The personal computer (PC) is an intelligent device. It usually includes a readily available I/O port, programmable microprocessor, memory, and software operating system. Taking advantage of these permits speech system suppliers considerable flexibility in designing their products. Perhaps a preferred implementation is one that utilizes the PC intelligence to initiate the operation of the speech recognizer, then fades into the background and becomes transparent to the PC and users, as they run their application programs. To permit this, the speech system must be able to emulate the keyboard and contain at least some of its own processing power and memory to do the speech function on a noninterference basis.

The PC-oriented speech recognition boards developed by Interstate Voice Products (VocaLink® Model CSRB, Figure 7.6) permit this by providing multiple character strings for each word in the recognition vocabulary. These strings are the equivalent ASCII characters of the messages that would have been sent to the display or the PC processor from the keyboard. By placing the voice recognition board in the keyboard controller path, all voice inputs are keyboard encoded by the recognizer prior to being passed on to the processor bus. Keyboard entries are transmitted directly through the voice board. Hence, the PC reacts to both voice and keystrokes, and is oblivious to the source of the input. In this fashion, having prespecified a vocabulary and provided the equivalent command or data ASCII character set required for this function, voiced inputs are readily appended to existing or newly generated software application pro-

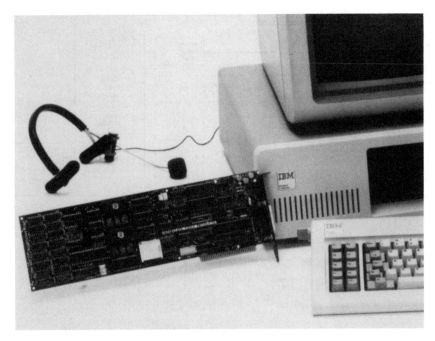

Figure 7.6. VocaLink® CSRB.

grams. One word can be made equivalent to many keystroke entries and used concurrent with the keyboard.

The CSRB implementation shown in Figure 7.7, incorporates a 16 bit INTEL 80186 microprocessor, as well as 128K byte of dynamic RAM and 32K byte of EPROM. The algorithm incorporates the dynamic programming technique for connected word recognition. The CSRB also incorporates Interstate's proprietary ASA-16 spectrum analysis chip. The CSRB is inserted between the keyboard and the PC's processor bus, where it intercepts all inputs. If inputs come from the keyboard, it passes them on. If input is by voice, it processes them and transmits them as equivalent keyboard commands. Note that the board contains the keyboard controller interface to monitor all keyboard functions as well as handle all voice functions. A parallel port, directly accessing the PC micro's bus, permits high speed access and writing of new programs using the command list available. The CSRB is supplied with a menu-based utility program, including a set of subroutines written in BASIC and supplied in source code. This greatly simplifies the utilization of voice input for the user. The program prompts the user with questions and instructions via the PC's display. A HELP display is available at each menu level. Combined with a

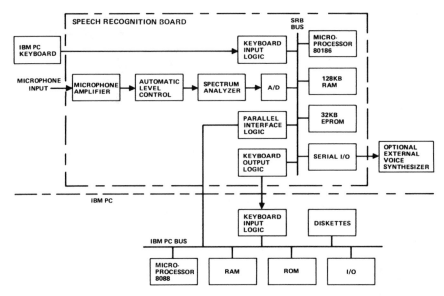

Figure 7.7. VocaLink® CSRB Block Diagram.

system of simplified keystrokes, the menu allows the uninitiated user to become familiar quickly with the speech input method of data entry and permits a user to add voice to any existing software package.

For adding voice input to existing programs, the menu-driven utility software package is supplied with the CSRB on diskette to allow users to operate in the keystroke emulation mode. Building a vocabulary of up to 240 words/phrases to be "recognized" by the CSRB, assigning the ASCII character commands to be associated with each spoken word, and "training" the device to recognize a user's voice are simplified by responding to the utility program's prompts.

The following steps are required to add voice input to an off-the-shelf program such as WordStar® or Lotus 1-2-3®:

1. On paper, the user makes a list of the spoken commands to be used instead of keystrokes to operate the program. For menu-driven programs that repeatedly use the same commands or words to initiate operations or indicate selections, the user may partition the vocabulary into syntax nodes or blocks. For each block, a syntax node name is assigned. For example, a block comprised of vocabulary entries "Worksheet," "Graph," "Utilities," and "Exit" might be assigned the syntax node name of "Menus."

2. After planning the vocabulary, the CSRB's utility program is brought into action. By responding to the utility program's menu prompts, the

user builds a table listing the vocabulary of words for operating a program in the keystroke simulation mode. For each vocabulary word, an ASCII character string is assigned or "associated."

For example, if the user is defining voice commands to operate WordStar on the IBM PC in the keystroke simulation mode, the phrase "delete line" might be selected to send the ASCII character string/command (CRTL-Y) required by the program to initiate this operation.

3. As each spoken command and its associated ASCII character string is entered into the vocabulary table, the CSRB utility also allows the user to assign an echo/response word to be output by the optional voice synthesizer. The user simply skips this field entry if no voice output word is needed.

4. A special next node field may also be specified for each spoken command to hold the syntax node name defined at the time the vocabulary is planned. Entering a syntax node name in the next node field indicates to the CSRB that the next command will be one of the entries in the requested partition. As a result, instead of comparing an incoming command's template against several hundred vocabulary templates, the CSRB can be directed instead to examine small subvocabularies. Reducing the number of template matches required to identify a spoken command speeds program execution and ensures recognition accuracy.

For example, in an airline reservation program, the operator might begin by saying the command phrase "flight to." When setting up the vocabulary entry for the command "flight to," the user could indicate a predefined list of "destination cities" as the next node. As a result, when the command "flight to" is spoken, the CSRB checks the table entry, identifies the next node requested, and immediately changes the program's active vocabulary to the "destination cities" partition. Since each of the words in the next node field may also have a next node field defined for it, changing to other predefined vocabulary blocks is easily facilitated.

If no "next node" field is required, the user simply skips this field.

5. A user-definable recognition threshold is the last table entry the CSRB utility associates with any given vocabulary word. This field is used to specify an acceptable recognition threshold rating. The threshold rating is used by the CSRB to determine if an incoming spoken command's spectral pattern/template adequately matches one of the vocabulary templates. If the incoming pattern matches a vocabulary entry template by the user-defined minimum or better, the data assigned to the word will be processed. If not, the input is ignored.

After completing steps 1 through 5, the vocabulary table information is stored on disk. Later, before the standard software program is operating, the vocabulary table will be downloaded from disk into the CSRB's on-board memory ready for use.

6. Training the CSRB to recognize the words or phrases spoken by a specific individual is the last step in the initial setup process. As the utility program displays each entry in the vocabulary, the user speaks the word into the microphone and the CSRB's speech processing logic creates a digital code template. Each word's unique template is stored in the memory contained on the CSRB board to build a file of vocabulary patterns.

To avoid recognition errors, which result when the user selects words that sound too much alike, the utility program permits a "separability" test. Each template in a given vocabulary is compared to detect any close similarities. If a close spectral pattern similarity match is found, a screen display message requests the user to either select an alternate word or say the word again to generate a new reference pattern for testing.

The CSRB module offers a number of firmware resident convenience programs, including a "software microphone switch," which allows the operator to activate or deactivate the CSRB through spoken commands; a correction capability to immediately cancel a spoken command by speaking a word defined by the user for this purpose; and a message prompt asking the user to repeat a word or phrase when the CSRB does not find an acceptable voice recognition match in the vocabulary (referred to as a "soft reject").

The software microphone switch will deactivate the CSRB when the user says the word "relax." To reactivate the module, the user first says "ready," followed immediately by the word "attention." Requiring the user to say the word "attention" within a few seconds eliminates unwanted reactivation of the board if either word is spoken while on the phone or talking to a fellow worker. The words used to activate or deactivate the CSRB are user-definable, with "relax," "ready," and "attention" being the defaults.

Following this procedure provides the user and system integrator the benefits to be derived by at least a partial utilization of his most natural means of communication — spoken inputs and vocalized responses.

7.3.3 VocaLink® S4000 — Continuous Speech Recognizer

Continuous speech recognition poses some difficult tasks for the design of a speech recognition system, the end points between words are ill-defined and the word pronunciation, hence its frequency and time features, vary considerably depending on the word string context. To perform continuous speech recognition, the S4000 uses a grammar structure to specify all utterances that are permitted in any phase of the application vocabulary. This grammar permits multiple words at any node in the speech input string. The input data is continuously compared against the grammar-defined set of legal utterances. Those that are not matched are discarded, and a final decision is deferred until a complete grammar sequence is spoken and recognized. The search strategy includes a forward and backward comparison so that each word provides clues about the words to its left and right. During the enrollment process, when the templates for the word are being established, the user speaks each word in isolation initially to build up a reference template as a baseline. Subsequent enrollment puts the word in context of the grammar. This refines the word templates to accommodate the variations caused by coarticulation and context.

There are two primary parts of the recognition algorithm: 1) the creation of acoustic parameters characterizing the speech input signal, and 2) calculation of the most probable word sequence by comparing the acoustic parameters to a set of templates under constraints imposed by the grammar.

A basic block diagram of the S4000 is shown in Figure 7.8. The acoustic pattern generation is performed by the analog input system and the signal processing portion of the TMS320 code. The input signal from the microphone is band limited to 4000 KHz. The input signal is differentiated to compress the dynamic range of the speech input and pre-emphasize the high frequencies. The spectrum of this signal is computed using a DFT algorithm in the TMS320 and 15 spectral samples computed for each sample (sampling period of 10 ms). The amplitude of the spectrum is also computed. Each sample frame then consists of 15 spectral values and an amplitude value.

The classification of the utterance is performed using the gate array and the dynamic programming algorithm implemented in the TMS320. Each spectral sample in the incoming signal is compared, using the gate array logic, against corresponding frames in each reference pattern under the constraint of the grammar-defined active words and the search limits imposed by the search strategy. A distance score is generated and held in a file for the subsequent dynamic programming classification. The dynamic programming search finds the accumulated minimum distance score for each word and for each word sequence.

Again, the end of utterance detection is conditioned by ensuring that word sequences abide by the constraints of the grammar. The system generates models (templates) for the words during the training sequence. In addition, templates for different types of noise patterns are also stored as

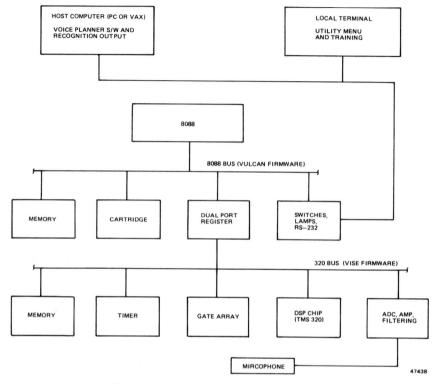

Figure 7.8. S4000 System Block Diagram.

reference patterns for the recognition process. These noise samples are upgraded during system operation to provide the system its high noise immunity.

The S4000 has a serial ASCII communication port, which permits it to act as a peripheral to most terminals and computers. In addition, it is provided with voice planner software (compatible with either the IBM PC or the DEC VAX computers) to permit users to generate their vocabulary and grammar structure, and to perform the training, editing, storing of reference files, and system and performance tests. The system has a RAM cartridge interface for users to retain a personal copy of the vocabulary and grammar (master cartridge) and a second RAM cartridge to store their voice templates (user cartridge) for each application. These cartridges, when plugged into the S4000, act as an extension of memory. They have a battery backup and permit users to store their reference pattern and permit quick exchange of operators, negating the requirements for file upload when a new user signs on.

The S4000 is a very accurate continuous word recognizer suitable for many industrial applications with its inherent noise immunity and high data rate input.

7.3.4 Speech Recognition Chips — VocaLink SRC-200

Speech Recognition Chip Set Model SRC-200, Figure 7.9, consists of three chips and is used as a building block for speech recognition systems capable of recognizing as many as 100 words or short phrases. This capability may be expanded to 200 words by use of additional random access memory (RAM). The chip set permits a flexible system design to meet user requirements. Figure 7.10 shows a simplified block diagram using the chip set. Two of the chips are the integrated front end (IFE-8) system spectrum analyzers. The other is an erasable programmed read only memory (EP ROM) chip.

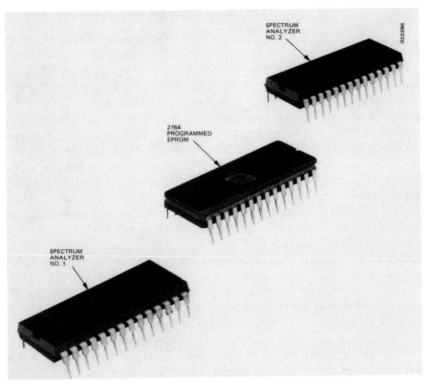

Figure 7.9. Speech Recognition Chip Set SRC-200.

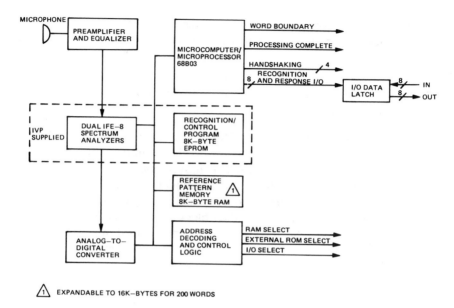

Figure 7.10. SRC-200 Simplified Block Diagram.

Speech input is analyzed by the dual eight channel spectrum analyzers and converted to a digital representation of the characteristics of the spoken input. This digital data is then converted to a fixed-size pattern that preserves the information content of the spoken inputs while discarding redundant features. During word training, these patterns are used to derive reference templates for each vocabulary item. The templates are then used in the recognition process for comparison with incoming spoken words. Vocabulary templates are stored in external RAM, while the processing algorithms are contained in the recognition/control program (EPROM).

The EPROM firmware accommodates several user commands, including two training commands. The normal training command is issued when all or part of the specified vocabulary is cleared and then trained a selectable number of times. For best performance, three to five training passes are recommended. The training update command is used when the stored reference patterns of the specified vocabulary are to be augmented by additional training. For changes in speaking characteristics or environmental conditions, a single update pass may be all that is required.

The training algorithm automatically rejects utterances during training that do not sufficiently agree with the same utterance from previous training samples of the word. This prevents significant alteration of a vocabulary reference pattern caused by spurious noise (bumping the microphone, door closure, coughing), speaking inconsistencies, or simply failing to utter the prompted vocabulary item. In such an event, it may be necessary to repeat an utterance before being prompted to the next sequential utterance. User prompting is accomplished via the host processor and display. Verification is provided during training.

The major operational command is the recognize command. This command allows recognition of any specified vocabulary up to 200 words. The command allows recognition of both contiguous and/or random syntax with one or more common subvocabularies. Additional commands include those for train and update, upload and download of reference vocabularies, read and set parameters, and test.

The IFE-8 chip, shown in block diagram form in Figure 7.11, is a 28-pin integrated circuit. It provides audio spectrum analysis over the range of intelligibility for speech. The IFE-8 is an advanced CMOS device incorporating switched capacitor technology designed to provide eight channels of audio spectrum information. The center frequency of the eight channels can be linearly shifted by changing the clock frequency. The device interfaces to a number of popular processors able to accommodate both R/W and RD, and WR control signals. Bus compatibility is accomplished by tristate output buffers. The clock signal can be from an external source or

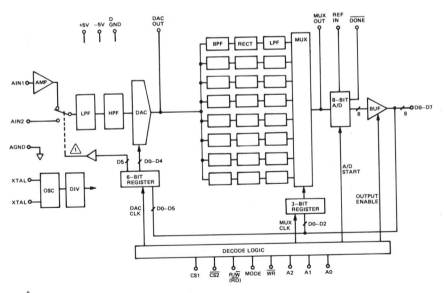

Figure 7.11. IFE Spectrum Analyzer Block Diagram.

generated by the chip using a crystal or ceramic resonator. All other required clocking signals are generated on the chip. Both TTL and CMOS signal levels are accommodated.

Each IFE-8 spectrum analyzer allows for program control of one of two analog inputs. Each has a 30-step 12 decibel range programmable digital to analog (D-A) converter. The eight channels of information resulting from bandpass filters are output coupled through full-wave rectifiers and smoothed by 25 Hz low pass filters. Each channel feeds one of eight multiplexers, which provides an input to the 8 bit analog to digital (A-D) converter, which is made bus compatible with tristate buffers.

The program is contained in a programmed 2764 EPROM for the specific processor shown in the logic diagram of Figure 7.10. This chip contains the entire algorithm for recognition of isolated speech utterances, including 1) word boundary detection, 2) word feature encoding, 3) end point time compression, 4) template comparison with an input utterance, 5) final decision algorithm, and 6) system control function. The word features include coding to preserve the frequency versus time characteristics and the energy versus time characteristics.

The sequence of commands provided within the EPROM permit designers to write their own programs to control the function of the speech recognition chip set. A host to SRC-200 instruction consists of a binary data input with command numbers, a parameter to establish the command function, and a terminator. In response, the SRC-200 will echo the command number and command status message (also in binary). As an example, for the train command, the host to SRC command is (in binary) 1,FW,LW, TP, where:

$$1 = \text{Train command number}$$
$$FW = \text{Number of first word to be trained}$$
$$LW = \text{Number of last word to be trained}$$
$$TP = \text{Number of training passes}$$

The SRC-200 will issue the following to the host as a result of that command: 1,WD#,ΔS,NBA,NP, where:

$$1 = \text{Train command}$$
$$WD\# = \text{Number of word to be trained}$$
$$\Delta S = \text{Difference between winner and runnerup score}$$
$$NBA = \text{Number of bits in agreement—a measure of correlation score}$$
$$NP = \text{Current number of training passes for that word}$$

This command structure permits designers to control completely the SRC-200 recognition system to serve their application needs. Once the system has been designed, programming completed, and system trained, the SRC-200 recognition system will process incoming speech and output recognition results over the serial or parallel communication port. This chip set permits an inexpensive custom integration of speech recognition for a variety of applications, including low cost consumer product usage, and a custom data entry peripheral for terminals and personal computers.

7.4 Future Projections

Future products that will emerge from the speech community will address the continued need for larger vocabularies and more natural discourse with the user.[4] With the advances in knowledge-based systems (artificial intelligence), word and sentence structure can be addressed, leading to more natural conversational systems. These systems require extensive computational and memory requirements and, for the immediate future, will be limited in application and scope. The rules for implementing the grammar and language structure are available; this implementation will not be long in coming. These advances, along with the utilization of signal processing and statistical signal communication methods for signal to noise enhancement, should permit the user friendliness that has been long sought and usher in a new area of input systems for man–machine communication.

In considering the projection and direction of speech recognition systems in the future, one must first take a quick glance at the past. What we have seen emerge in the last decade is not a wealth of new knowledge about speech analysis or insight into the key features that permit recognition of speech — or even words. Rather, what has occurred is that the computational tools were made available that permitted implementation of techniques developed in the 1960s and 1970s in a cost-effective fashion and encouraged the development of low-cost speech products and the integration of these products into useful applications. With the cost reduction and the spread of voice recognition products into the user arena, limitations of the technology have become apparent. Now in the mid 1980s, we find ourselves at the threshold of a challenge — to advance further our understanding of the basic structure of the speech signal that conveys the meaning and linguistic information necessary for recognition — even in the presence of noise, talker variability, and changing environmental conditions.

Introduced during 1984 and 1985 were products capable of connected word recognition on vocabularies of 50 to 100 words. The implication is that the effects of coarticulation and word length variability are not insurmountable with restricted vocabularies. Even with larger vocabularies, recognition performance is not the major concern as much as implementation cost to provide real time performance. The dynamic programming algorithm, used so successfully to permit connected speech recognition, requires large memory arrays for pattern storage and ultrafast processors for sample frame correlation with stored templates. As vocabulary size increases, we find ourselves in nonreal time operation — or costly implementation solutions.

These obstacles will be partially overcome as the semiconductor industry continues its assault on submicron VLSI integration. Larger memory chips at lower prices are inevitable, as are faster microcomputers and digital signal processors with extensive built-in hardware computational capabilities such as array processing. These semiconductor devices will permit larger vocabulary connected word recognition systems to emerge, such as the 1000 to 5000 word dictation machine currently in the research labs and early prototyping stages. They also have permitted the development of speaker independent systems capable of 10 to 20 word recognition, in a discrete utterance mode, which have found utility in telephone applications such as voice messaging and call processing.

These hardware advances do not by themselves, however, permit the extension of speech recognition out of the realm of a forced learning, template matching machine, with its inherent limitations, into the speech recognizer that will allow true man–machine communication. Speech recognition is an ongoing interaction between the talker and the listener, and involves language structure, semantic, syntactic, and pragmatic information exchange. Many cues are provided to listeners to permit their successful interpretation of the discourse, even in the presence of noise, stress, and other distractions. Current research into the basic elements of the speech waveform, invariant under the changing environmental, physiological, and psychological conditions, will lead to the specification of word or language primitives that can form a lexicon for word recognition. Digital signal processing devices will permit reliable extraction of these word features and background noise rejection. The rules for combining these features into meaningful words and phrases, followed by higher level rule-based systems to permit sentences to be constructed, will make possible the true man–machine discourse system.

That evolution is what is projected within this technology. In the near-term, larger vocabulary connected word recognizers will be offered to the user community. As techniques for extracting word features are developed and expert systems are constructed with their rule-based knowledge structure to combine the features into word units, more extensive, speaker independent systems will be implemented. Advances in microcomputer and digital signal processor speed, instruction sets, and built-in functions, combined with further reduction in cost of memory and peripheral chips, will permit cost-effective integration of larger primitive libraries, large resident knowledge bases, and more detailed search strategies. They will foster speech recognizers with still larger vocabularies and speaker independent, connected speech capability.

However, I would concur with J. S. Bridle in his comment made at the September 1984 European Speech Technology Conference in Brighton, England.

> . . . machines are likely to fall far short of human performance with large vocabularies and unknown speakers until it is possible to acquire and use far more knowledge of speech structure than seems possible with current recognition approaches.

Perhaps 'real' automatic speech rcognition will elude us until the pattern processing in our machines is equivalent to the perceptual processing performed by the brain.

Notes

[1] For specific information, see the articles "TI Speech Command Systems," "IBM Voices Its Options," "AT&T Conversant System," "Kurzweil Voice Terminal in Debut," "ITT Voice Communication System," and "Plug-In Card for IBM PC Delivers Ultimate Man/Machine Communication" in the references.

[2] See the articles "Voice Control Systems" and "Votan's Speaker Independent Digit Recognition" in the references.

[3] Information on the human and human engineering considerations can be found in Nisbaum and Pisoni (1986), Mangione (1986), Dintruff et al. (1985), Swan (1985), and Taylor (1986).

[4] See Meisel (1986), and the article by the Speech Recognition Group at IBM Watson Research Center, "A Real-time, Isolated Word, Speech Recognition System for Dictation Transcription."

References

"AT&T Conversant System," *Voice News.* September 1985.

Dintruff, D. L., Grice, D. G., and Wang, T. G. (1985). "User Acceptance of Speech Technologies," *Speech Technology.* march 1985.

"IBM Voices Its Options," *P.C. Products.* April 1986.

"ITT Voice Communication System," *MIS Weekly.* June 1986.

"Kurzweil Voice Terminal in Debut," *MIS Weekly.* June 1986; also "Freedom of Speech," *P.C. Products.* March 1986.

Mangione, P. A. (1986). "What about the User," *Proceedings of Speech Tech '86.* April 1986.

Meisel, W. (1986). "Talk Writers: Fact or Function?" *Proceedings of the Voice Processing Conference.* Wembley, England, July 1986.

Nisbaum, H. C., and Pisoni, D. B. (1986). "Human Factors Issue for the Next Generation of Speech Recognition System," *Proceedings of Speech Tech '86.* April 1986.

"Plug-in Card for IBM PC Delivers Ultimate Man/Machine Communication," VPC 2000 Product Brochure, Votan, Hayward, CA.

Speech Recognition Group, IBM Watson Research Center. "A Real-Time, Isolated Word, Speech Recognition System for Dictation Transcription," *Proceedings of ICASSP '85.* Vol. **2,** March 1985.

Swan, K. E. (1985). "Pragmatics of Programming Voice Recognition Applications," *Proceedings of the Voice I/O Systems Applications Conference '85.* September 1985.

"TI Speech Command System," *Voice Processing Newsletter.* March 1985; also Haas, M. (1984). "The Texas Instruments Speech Command System," *Byte.* June 1984.

Taylor, M. M. (1986). "Issues in the Evaluation of Speech Recognition Systems," *Journal of the American Voice I/O Society.* Vol. **3,** June 1986.

"Voice Control Systems (VCS)," *Voice Processing Newsletter,* April 1985; also Helms, G. E. (1986). "Voice Control of Mobil Telephones," *Proceedings of Speech Tech '86.* April 1986.

"Votan's Speaker Independent Digit Recognition," *Voice Processing Newsletter.* April 1985.

Index